A HUMAN NECKLACE

A HUMAN NECKLACE

The African Diaspora
and Paule Marshall's Fiction

MOIRA FERGUSON

Cover: "A new map of the world : with all the new discoveries by Capt. Cook and other navigators : ornamented with the Solar System, the eclipses of the sun, moon & planets &c. / by T. Kitchen, geographer." London: I. Evans, 1799. Library of Congress Geography and Map Division Washington, D.C. 20540-4650.

Published by
State University of New York Press, Albany

© 2013 State University of New York

All rights reserved

Printed in the United States of America

No part of this book may be used or reproduced in any manner whatsoever without written permission. No part of this book may be stored in a retrieval system or transmitted in any form or by any means including electronic, electrostatic, magnetic tape, mechanical, photocopying, recording, or otherwise without the prior permission in writing of the publisher.

For information, address State University of New York Press, Albany, NY
www.sunypress.edu

Production by Diane Ganeles
Marketing by Anne M. Valentine

Library of Congress Cataloging-in-Publication Data

Ferguson, Moira.
  A human necklace : the African diaspora and Paule Marshall's fiction / Moira Ferguson.
      pages cm
  Includes bibliographical references and index.
  ISBN 978-1-4384-4419-2 (hardcover) ISBN 978-1-4384-4418-5 (paperback)

  1. Marshall, Paule, 1929– —Criticism and interpretation. 2. African Americans in literature. 3. African American women in literature.
  4. Blacks in literature. 5. Identity (Psychology) in literature.
  6. African diaspora in literature. 7. Postcolonialism in literature.
  8. Caribbean Area—In literature. I. Title.
    PS3563.A7223Z67 2012
    813'.54—dc23
                                    2011051055

10 9 8 7 6 5 4 3 2 1

For Martha Jane Starr and Mary Kay McPhee

Contents

Acknowledgments	ix
Chapter 1. Introduction: Paule Marshall's Fiction	1
Chapter 2. Wanting Brownstones, Departing Brownstones	7
Chapter 3. *Soul Clap Hands and Sing*: Sadness, Resistance, Redemption	23
Chapter 4. A "Nation of Diabetics" Meets Empire	37
Chapter 5. Water and Nomenclature: *Praisesong for the Widow*	55
Chapter 6. Paule Marshall's *Daughters*: Wars of Independence	75
Chapter 7. *The Fisher King*: A Culmination and New Beginnings	93
Epitaph: *Triangular Road: A Memoir*	103
Notes	107
Bibliography	127
Index	163

Acknowledgments

This book has taken rather a long time as I gradually finalized my transatlantic journey back home. So I have incurred many debts that I am very happy (and relieved) to acknowledge.

First off, I read parts of the book to academic audiences who responded very constructively: at the California Institute of Technology, the University of Oregon, the Massachusetts Institute of Technology, Carnegie Mellon, Oregon State University, George Mason University, and particularly at the University of Hawaii at Manoa.

I thank friends and colleagues in the United States and the United Kingdom for invaluable support, friendship, and scholarly camaraderie.

Kimberley Banks, Grace Bauer, Duncan Campbell, Anne Cvetkovic, Mantia Diawara, Stephen Dilkes, Alex Djkovic, Paul Gilroy, Avery Gordon, Emiliano Huet-Vaughn, Cora Kaplan, Daniel Mahala, Orna Neumann, Edward Said, Sabby Segal, Ahmed Sheikh, Joseph T. Skerrett, Jr., Paul Smith, Gayatri Chakravorty Spivak, Vron Ware, and members of book clubs at Harlesden Public Library and Portobello Road. Sherry Harris, Grace Bauer, and Ingrid Johanson deserve a special mention for their cheery and supportive friendship.

David Huet-Vaughn provided venues where several aforementioned individuals discussed cultural/political issues with relish and good humor. At Modern Language Association meetings in New York, Toronto, Chicago, New Orleans, and San Diego, Cheryl Wall, Nellie McKay, Mary Helen Washington, and Debby McDowell created spaces of peace and friendship, where Hortense Spillers, my dear friend, always shone a steady light.

ACKNOWLEDGMENTS

In Kansas City, Maude and Jimi Wahlman welcomed me with a home from home, while in London, Stuart and Catherine Hall helped my re-adjustment, answering worrywart questions with great good humour. Over the long haul, Bobby Watson's music and bonhomie were always an inspiration at the Blue Room and other venues in Kansas City and, most recently, in London.

Additionally, it gives me great pleasure to thank Paule Marshall herself, who graciously granted my request for an interview. During her tenure as the Frances and Floyd Horowitz lecturer for 2003–2003 at the Hall Center for the Humanities at Kansas University, Marshall gave a keynote address on the "Triangular Quest for Self and Community: Brooklyn-Barbados-Benin." This talk helped me clarify my ideas about the powerful influence of the African diaspora on her fiction.

As luck would have it, generous funding made research in Barbados possible; thus the landscape that pervades Marshall's fiction opened up for me. I send a warm thank you to the University of Nebraska-Lincoln for a Faculty Development Fellowship and the Research Council for a Maude Hammond Fling Fellowship that enabled that research in Barbados. Bookshops in Barbados, moreover, rank high on the list of venues where staffs were constantly friendly and helpful. Many landmarks, especially those huge Boulders on the West coast, both overwhelmed and inspired me; they are a sight to behold, of beauty drenched in tragedy.

At the State University of New York Press at Albany, I thank my editor, Diane Ganeles, for her unintrusive fine work. I extend inestimable gratitude to my publisher, James Peltz, for his generous understanding and attentiveness over many years. He is, in the best possible sense, one of a kind.

As always, I thank students at various institutions for smart perceptions and engaged discussions, research assistants, Margie Kine and Randy Kreifel, and research typists Kristen James and Nancy White for all their invaluable collective work. Rachel Bateman, my research assistant from Kansas University, was unfailingly diligent as well as intuitive about alternate sources. Our discussions enhanced the project. I thank Lisa Cooper for her careful attentiveness to the final draft.

Lastly, I thank my son, Christopher, for steadfast assistance, technical and otherwise. He is a joy to work with.

CHAPTER 1

Introduction
Paule Marshall's Fiction

Each of Paule Marshall's major works of fiction—*Brown Girl, Brownstones, Soul Clap Hands and Sing, The Chosen Place, the Timeless People, Praisesong for the Widow, Daughters,* and *The Fisher King*—features originally displaced communities of the African diaspora. The protagonists in this sextet, all women excepting the last, travel to geographical and spiritual continents as they face down their complex histories of home and exile. Collectively, these novels and novellas recite a saga of forced migration, of diasporic experience. Marshall herself tellingly suggests the dynamics of these intricate tales in two statements, the first addressing the influence of voyages on her writings, the shorter affirming her own intersecting ethnicities:

> I think it is absolutely necessary for black people to effect [a] spiritual return [to origins in Africa]. As the history of people of African descent in the United States and the diaspora is fragmented and interrupted, I consider it my task as a writer to initiate readers to the challenges this journey entails.[1]

> I am Afro-Caribbean and Afro-American. . . . I am embracing both these cultures and I hope that my work reflects what I see as a common bond.[2]

Bearing Marshall's statements in mind, I argue that these fictions constitute a long, discontinuous, imaginative saga of African diasporic communities, perhaps the first of its kind. They address a range of topics from colonizers and colonized people in Africa, Britain, the Caribbean, France, and the United States; tradition and the role of elders and ancestors; colonial dehumanization; black female agency; black male leadership; collective insurgency; and urgent quests for identity.

Brown Girl, Brownstones (1959) explores the palpable frustrations that abound in the home of Caribbean migrants in a Brooklyn brownstone.[3] A second-generation Barbadian daughter who grows up there, adolescent Selina Boyce slowly embraces a political and sexual awakening in her ambivalent struggle with traditional values. Her reactions to a host of both positive and adversarial mentors ground the narrative. In Carole Boyce Davies's phrase, Selina is traveling between identities as she ends up voluntarily migrating to the Caribbean diaspora, as her father tried to do.[4] Among the participants in *Brown Girl, Brownstones* are Silla Boyce, Selina's tough, first-generation, Barbadian mother; her devil-may-care yet sensitive father, Deighton Boyce; the brownstone denizens; easy-going Suggie Sweet, one of the recurring outcast figures who populate Marshall's novels; and Miss Thompson, the wise, battle-scarred ancestor-warrior, also a recurring figure, whose love prompts Selina's maturation; Father Peace, the black community evangelist who transforms Deighton Boyce's life; Beryl, Selina's close friend from childhood from whom she gradually drifts apart; and Rachel and Clyde, close friend and lover respectively. After a community tragedy, Selina Boyce recapitulates her father's return to the Caribbean, but unlike her father Selina survives.

Soul Clap Hands and Sings (1961) stages very old men searching for a loss that underpins their lives and a love to replace it that will comfort them. In the first novella in *Soul Clap Hands and Sings*, "Barbados" features Mr. Watford returning to his natal island from the U.S. diaspora, where he remains detached from the community despite formidable interventions by a young, unnamed, black servant woman. In an ultimate, too-late effort to connect—one human being to another—he is poignantly thwarted. In the second story, "Brooklyn," professor of French Max Berman, the only caucasian protagonist, unilaterally decides that a black female student in his class will empower him to reclaim his life, a somewhat ironically correct assumption. Miss Williams exposes

Berman to an eye-opening encounter that in turn exposes his threadbare existence in contrast to her own emotional tenacity. He returns home defeated, while she moves proudly forward. "British Guiana," the third fiction, dramatizes Gerald Motley immured in a colonial past that prevents him from embracing the stance of cultural icon/spokesman. Too late like Mr. Watford, he extends himself to Sidney with a selfless, anti-colonial gesture, yet that tiny altruistic moment has not gone unnoticed by Sidney, for whom Gerald appears to have an emotional attachment. In the last novella entitled "Brazil," protagonist and popular entertainer Caliban is bent on recapturing Hector Guittirez, his born name, and abandoning his synonymous and interchangeable roles as the butt of tourist jokes and scapegoat for colonial voyeurism. Comprehending regretfully that an ersatz identity has been thrust upon him by a demeaning colonial culture, Caliban decides to plunge into his former community life. Echoing Shakespeare's *The Tempest*, he recognizes the erasure of his identity, and, as the "son" of mother Sycorax who has the power to reconstruct events, he reclaims himself. More perceptive and open than Berman, Watford, and Motley—perhaps the product of more fluid circumstances—Caliban feels so connected to others that he feels the possibility of an unknown freedom within himself. Unlike the other old men, he cherishes a hope that he will live a forward-looking life from now on.

In its dramatic metaphorical opening, *The Chosen Place, the Timeless People* (1969), Marshall's second novel stages another significant journey from the mythical Bourne Island in the Caribbean, to Africa. At the start, Merle Kimbona rages when her car gets stuck in the mud of the symbolically named Westminster Low Road. Now she will be late in meeting U.S. (imperial) visitors at the airport. Her equally symbolic, religion-tinged jewelry, the anti-colonial history of the Caribbean that she teaches her students, and the eclectic mix of furniture, books, and art in her bedroom collectively enhance the profile of a magnificent rebel. "Striving to be both European and black," Merle is attuned to her doubled location in Black Atlantic culture.[5]

Soon Merle finds herself interacting with the visitors: Saul, the well-meaning Jewish consultant, and his wife Harriet, an ultimately treacherous U.S. "philanthropist." In addition, she spars equally with a conflicted Caribbean elite, while she fights on behalf of poverty-stricken yet ultimately independent community members. In the end, she declines any further complicity in colonial mystification and heads for her diasporic origins in Africa to seek out her daughter and estranged husband.

Published fourteen years later, *Praisesong for the Widow* similarly opens on an ocean—specifically on a cruise ship from which Avey Johnson means to disembark, without alerting her two cruise companions. Emboldened by still blurred but emotionally overwhelming memories of a recent experience, Avey navigates a winding course in search of her history, ultimately rejecting "home" in the urban Northern White Plains. With historical memory and ancestor Lebert Joseph assisting her, she throws herself joyfully into a pan-African celebration on Carriacou in the Grenadines. Gentle elder Joseph intuits how to introduce Avey Johnson to cultural practices that survived the Middle Passage.[6] A numbed Avatara, formerly Avey, finally feels rooted. She knows who she is and where she came from and why. Following that epiphany, Avatara Johnson leaves White Plains behind for good—along with white values—and returns to her father's Gullah/Barbadian roots in the South Carolinas where she spent summers as a child living with her extraordinary great-aunt Cuney. Like Selina Boyce and Merle Kimbona, Avatara Johnson starts piecing her past, present, and future together, venturing to the Caribbean home of her descendants and site of slaves' arrival from Africa.

Daughters (1991) continues the intercontinental journey that features Africa as a point of reference and of origin. Protagonist Ursa Mackenzie's mother hails from a U.S. civil rights family, and her Caribbean father leads the opposition on Triunion Island, his political principles embattled by colonial blandishments. Following in the footsteps of Selina Boyce, Merle Kimbona, and Avey Johnson, Ursa integrates her complex identities by undertaking a spiritual and physical journey in contrasting diasporic communities, the United States and the Caribbean. Ursa's father exemplifies the strangling force of U.S. interference in the Caribbean, while her friends in the States—Viney Daniels, Lowell Carruthers, and May Ryland—successfully endure daily battles with institutionalized corruption over issues of race and class. Ursa has suffered twin abortions, a recent physical one and a professional one years earlier when her doctoral supervisor denied her the right to pursue her heritage via a PhD thesis on slave insurgency. A resistant Ursa, about to start a new job, caves in to her mother's pressing request that she return to Triunion for her father, Primus Mackenzie's election.

With two fathers (her academic supervisor and Primus) subsuming her personal and collective identity, Ursa retaliates. Resembling Selina, Ursa claims female mentors, even more widely dispersed. During her childhood, moreover, her radical mother always pointed the daughter in a sound, astronomical direction by acclaiming two ancestor-slaves, Congo Jane and Will Cudjoe, as Ursa's lodestar. In the end, Ursa gains a renewed cultural awareness, rooted in her history as a black woman of African descent. A long, soothing bath at the narrative's end, suffused with her grandmother's herbs, will equip Ursa for a worthy future as one of the Caribbean's new archivists, carefully chronicling slave insurgency on Triunion for publication and hence for the education of her community.

In her sixth and most recent novel, *The Fisher King*, Paule Marshall sketches a black political agenda for African Americans that respects and reveres the past, plays out the importance of the present, and focuses on the future. Respect for all generations as well as individuals' coping devices, their community successes, and their candor when it's needed—tomorrow's activists start receiving their birthright of care and attention.

Additionally, *The Fisher King* shifts the line of vision in earlier novels by presenting a young male protagonist, Sonny Carmichael Payne, raised in Paris by Hetty, an orphan from the States. The pair come to Brooklyn to attend a commemoration concert for his deceased grandfather, Sonny Rhett Payne, a famous, internationally distinguished jazz pianist. Young Sonny's uncle Edgar is transforming the diasporic community by offering its members full employment in his construction company, and by bringing Sonny home from Paris. Hence assimilation, exile, repatriation, and dislocation make their presence felt.

Having (temporarily) completed this fictional saga over the course of four decades from the 1950s to the millennium, what has Paule Marshall fictionally recorded for global readers? In a nutshell, as a second-generation Barbadian novelist, she has chronicled a post-slavery saga, an unprecedented permanent archive of a four-hundred-year history of distinct strands of the African diaspora.

Growing up in Brooklyn, Paule Marshall's cultural tour de force in African American/African Caribbean fiction derives from her personal experiences as a child of Barbadian immigrants. Marshall talks about that life in "The Making of a Writer: From the Poets in the Kitchen" (1983), in which she pays tribute to a group of housewives—"my mother included"—who spent their days "scrubbing floors." Part of Marcus Garvey's nurses' contingent, this group of strong mothers marched up Seventh Avenue to Harlem during Garvey Day parades, discussing war and their adopted home of the United States—"this man country"—as well as the people back home in Barbados or Bimshore: "I was that little girl," says Marshall, "sitting in the corner of the kitchen, in the company of poets. I was there, seen but not heard, while these marvelous poets carried on. And from way back I always wanted to see if I might not be able to have some of the same power they had with words—their wonderful oral art. I wondered if I could capture some of that same power on paper."[7]

Like the kitchen poets, Marshall weaves old and new narratives with stories about formidable ancestors and adds to the mix three significant factors that complete or synthesize these earlier scenarios: first the European setting, particularly Paris; second, a poignant view of the evolution of jazz and its relationship to race relations; and third, a study, twenty years later, of the same Brooklyn community that saturated her first and still best-selling novel *Brown Girl, Brownstones*; and last, the introduction of a male protagonist whose presence brilliantly interrogates the question of gender.

With the appearance of a second narrative set in Brooklyn two decades later, which locates an expatriate New Yorker jazz musician in Paris after World War Two and returns his great-grandson to Brooklyn from Paris—Marshall produces a canvas of global dimensions across race, class, and gender lines, the relationships both interweaving and harmonizing.

This protagonist's heritage is a mix of Caribbean, African, and African American: the great-grandparents of young Sonny (Sunny) Carmichael Payne (Pain) hail from the Caribbean and Georgia, a French émigré grandfather and grandmother, a French mother and an Algerian father. Not only that, but Hattie who raises Sonny till he is six years old is herself a city orphan, symbolizing the devastation of the triangular trade, the Middle Passage, that "Peculiar Institution" of slavery, and physical though not necessarily emotional and psychological emancipation. Thus *The Fisher King* brings Paule Marshall's saga to a splendid, possibly temporary happy ending, leaving in its wake contradictions that contain within themselves the possibility of resolution.

CHAPTER 2

Wanting Brownstones, Departing Brownstones

Set in Brooklyn during the Depression and World War Two, *Brown Girl, Brownstones* relates the life of adolescent protagonist Selina Boyce.[1] Sometimes lost, always wandering, Selina unsuccessfully tries to fit into her complex community, an everywoman in search of a cultural identity, of a geographical and spiritual home that spells security. Selina's quest begins when she is ten years old, longing to leave the sunny room in the brownstone home "for the challenge" of the outside world (4). She had come into the world, she thinks, to take her sick brother's place, "strong and well-made. . . . But they [her parents] had taken no photographs" (8). So she sets about the task of self-creation.

Selina's parents, Silla and Deighton Boyce, left Barbados "to escape the brutal colonial exploitation of blacks in the West Indies," reenact their ancestors' crossing with a goal dictated by the privations of slavery: they become an integral part of an "an employed, literate, ambitious, property-owning, upwardly mobile, tight community of first-generation immigrants. Not one person in the novel is unemployed."[2] These crossings foreshadow Selina's return to Barbados at the end.

Emigration from Barbados had an intricate history. When slavery was legal, Barbados was a launching pad for the colonization and settlement of Trinidad, Guiana, and the Windward Islands—and for runaway slaves. After emancipation in 1838, the evolving island network of communities aided the establishment of an emigration movement.[3] Eventually, laws were enacted to prevent the steady stream of departures and by 1871 when 110,000 black people were recorded in the census, seasonal migration had intensified. Deighton Boyce's decision to set off for Cuba is part of this historical continuum of immigration.[4] Few laws, besides, encouraged black men and women to stay put in Barbados. After the Franchise Act, less than five percent of the black population were enfranchised and by 1871, the vast majority was still excluded.[5] In 1930, only 6,000 out of 188,000 Barbadians could vote.[6]

In the early twentieth century, the project of building the Panama Canal appealed to the Barbadian working class. By 1914, despite the evolution of a system of poor relief in Barbados, 20,000 had left the island to work on the canal, the greatest exodus of black migration in the island's history.[7] This demographic revolution resulted in greater employment of men and women on Barbadian estates. In her youth, Silla Boyce was part of this new community of female field workers. Women became "the dominant sex in the field gangs, as well as in the [sugar cane] factory."[8] This shift in gendered power relations seems to have fostered Silla Boyce's determination to own property in the United States. From an early age, she saw that women could successfully take control.

After World War Two, Barbadians arrived in England and the United States in great numbers: "The extraordinary pull of New York was its image as a place of immense wealth and unlimited opportunity available to anyone with a business mind and an unshakable determination to 'study the dollar' and imitate the whites."[9] Recent Barbadian immigrants, besides, had already endured discrimination back home so it was nothing new to arrive in New York and face forms of racist discrimination, albeit differently configured. As a community, Barbadians gradually devised a plan to gain a foothold in U.S. society and followed common advice: "work night and day to buy house; rent out every room, overcharge if necessary; sacrifice every penny to maintain property; keep strict vigilance on the children so they will enter high-paying professions; stick close to other Bajans, and exclude American blacks who are only a 'keepback'; as soon as one house is paid for, move to the next desirable location—preferably Crown Heights; imitate the Jew."[10] Speaking of the Barbadian community in New York, Darryl Pinckney says: "Their values are those of most other immigrant groups. The hurting effort of each day is to squeeze every penny in the pay envelope, overcharge roomers, acquire property and political influence, make lawyers or doctors of their children, and have them marry among their own kind. Selina is therefore strictly brought up—rules, curfews, beatings, streets out of bounds."[11] To own a brownstone constitutes the Bajan dream. Meanwhile, whites who now live in them are discreetly dying in them. No work was too onerous to fulfill this dream, most notably the daily train trek by Bajan women to Flatbush and Sheepshead Bay to scrub floors that secured a "'few raw-mout' pennies' [that] would eventually 'buy house'" (11).

In the novel, these brownstones represent community icons; they are objective correlatives of a voluntarily dislocated people as they struggle to carve a niche for themselves in a foreign land. Resembling an army ready to do Bajan bidding, the somber, ivy-draped, tall-seeming brownstones remain impervious to "summer's heat and passion." As the war rages in Europe, the brownstones amass themselves—their ominous, looming quality complemented by hints of a European influence: "some touch that was Gothic, Romanesque, baroque or Greek triumphed amid the Victorian clutter. All seemed doomed by the confusion in their design" (3). European-style architecture underpins historical crossings, while signifying colonial conquest.[12]

On the other hand, the 'togetherness of the brownstones—their impermeable quality—is an objective correlative of the peoples' necessary bonding as they struggle not only to get by but to climb the "ladder of success." As a case in point, the community forms the Association of Barbadian Homeowners and Businessmen to focus its political agenda (143): "The banners showed two black hands in a firm handclasp against a yellow background, with the Association's full name at top, and below on the banner was embroidered the Association's motto in capital letters: 'it is not the depths from which we come but the heights to which we ascend'" (219–20). In a combination of unity, prideful nomenclature, and moral uplift, while marking a commitment to cultural nationalism, the community links up informally and participates in an early burgeoning of a Black Aesthetic and the Black Arts Movement.[13]

The Association bonds the people "in a spirit of self-help. . . . It's a sign that we has a business mind! I thank you!" (221). The goal is to claim "a right to claw their way to the top." But people are realistic: "Plenty gon have to suffer to bring it about" (225).

Buying a brownstone for herself and her family is Silla Boyce's goal, in contrast to the goals of her flamboyant, easy-going husband Deighton Boyce, who dreams of returning to Barbados. When he learns that his aunt has left him land in Barbados, he plans to implement that dream, but Silla has other plans. Their paths no longer meet.

Silla's desperate desire to expropriate her husband's modest legacy prompts Deighton Boyce to accuse her of shaming Al Capone; his wife is no better than a racketeer or gangster, he charges, a member of an organized group of criminals who obtain money dishonestly through fraud or extortion. Deighton Boyce shies from the vigorous efforts of some Barbadians to slice a piece of the American pie for themselves. He prefers the old ways, evading the fact that Silla's seeming hardheartedness results from a refusal to be deprived again; her upbringing in the fields was relentlessly strenuous.

Selina finds herself caught and confused in this parental battle between a pragmatic mother and an idealist father. Why such division exists is a murky area for Selina as she struggles to understand her parents' dissension and the need of the Barbadian community to empower itself amid bigotry. No family members, in her view, will explain things to her. So she turns for help to women outside her family in order to cope. One of them is Miss Thompson, the beautician. Selina resents the fact that Miss Thompson will not explain the origin of the festering sore in her foot, "her symbolic inheritance of the white world of the South."[14] But eventually Miss Thompson unveils the racist violence that maimed her and enables Selina to understand the historical significance of her story. It is the old familiar tale of black people at the mercy of a racist society, especially rape and violence at the hands of white men: "He didn't get to do nothing with me wrassling and hollering, but he did take a piece clean outta my foot with that rusty shovel" (216). The suppurating ulcerous sore that resulted resembles a small crater. Like white people, the sore has a hard crust, a pale center, and a fetid odor, the "unmistakable odor of putrefaction." Miss Thompson carries the mark of slavery around with her as a "life-sore," just as Selina does in wearing her silver bracelets (101). Like Miss Thompson, Selina knows she is forced to intersect with this society and is determined to survive: "She thought of Miss Thompson—the long black dress almost hiding her wound and her long thin hands on the cane handle—recounting, dispassionately, her story of violation. In each light she saw the shovel cutting like a scythe in the sunlight and, in a way, it was no different from the woman's voice falling brutally in the glare of the lamp" (292).

A historical as well as a contemporary figure, Miss Thompson represents ancestral time that predates the notorious era of the Middle Passage. Described as an ancient statue with an elongated body, her face in its contours resembling an African woodcarving, she perpetuates the women who mourned Jesus, her life on a continuum from ancient civilization through the trial of the Scottsboro Boys to the present day.[15] Admiring the fine decor of the Apollo Theater in Harlem, she tells Selina, "I got all choked up inside I was so proud to see my peoples living so swell!" (214).[16]

Selina's mentor and confidant, Miss Thompson encourages her informal ward to "start having you some good times" and connect with her community through the Homeowners Association (217). In turn, Selina confides her fear of her parents' arguments over her father's land inheritance; internal voices are warning Selina about Silla's duplicity in trying to sell Deighton's land (93). Miss Thompson tries to help Selina understand her mother's extraordinary desire to acquire a brownstone and the lengths she will go to acquire one: "West Indian peoples are sure peculiar, but you got to hand it to them, they knows how to get ahead. I don't know, maybe someday you'll understand your mamma and then you'll see why she does some of these things" (215).

Miss Thompson's nurturance affects the uncertain adolescent deeply. Even Silla reacts incredulously when Miss Thompson curls Selina's hair: "Oh God, a force-ripe woman! . . . You's too womanish" (102). Wisely discerning Selina's healthy wishes, Miss Thompson trusts her ward to grow in a good way. In the end, the physically moribund Miss Thompson returns to the South—still longing for a breeze, for the winds of change. A perpetual warrior as well as a crucial role-model for Selina, Miss Thompson enables Selina to situate herself transculturally and understand race, gender, and class issues in a new way (14).

A second, more unexpected, formative influence is the spiritual as well as the physical dying of Miss Mary. With her daughter Martizke, they hang on as obviously unwanted tenants in the brownstone that Silla claims as her own, only because they are protected in the lease agreement by a "grandfather clause of sorts. . . . Every decent white person's moving away, getting out. Except us. And they're [*sic*] so many nice places where we could live" (35). A relic who exists on the border between life and death, Miss Mary resembles her caged canary that never sings. The ugly yellow of decay stamps Miss Mary, not the sunny yellow that Deighton Boyce radiates.[17] Even her eyes have faded (20). Moreover, her lover (predictably) fought in the 1904 war (20).[18] Empathizing with Miss Mary's predicament about being displaced, a fearful Selina seeks help from Miss Mary as a last resort in the "timeless and tarnished yellow fog" of her room (79). Silla, on the other hand, smashes Miss Mary's oil painting and delft china, aiming to build anew, freed from any vestiges of a corrupt past (203).

A third influence on Selina is her close friend, Suggie Skeete, who resembles Deighton Boyce in being always associated with the sun. She hails from a small home in Barbados with a "susurrant sea of sugarcane" (18). Named after sugar and therefore symbolically associated with slavery itself, Suggie Skeete is sweet, voluptuous, and languid, a summer woman who drinks rum, while she dreams and prepares a Caribbean dish of cuckoo.[19] She lives to forget the atrocity of slavery, while her sexual ease strikes fear in Miss Mary's daughter, Martizke, who regards her as "black foreign scum."

In contrast to Suggie Skeete and her husband, Silla lets nothing stand in the way of her plans for the future. Her face reflecting bars of sunlight, Silla is "imprisoned within this contradiction of dark and light" (76),[20] a fractured person who is associated with both justice and cruelty. She evicts Skeete as a woman of too much sun and lightness, an "undesirable tenant." Is Suggie Skeete the old, easygoing other of Silla whom she temporarily is forced to bury in such a competitive racist society? Suggie Skeete disappears from the narrative since sunshine cannot exist in Silla's ambitious world. Regardless of her mother's evicting Suggie, Selina is ineluctably drawn to her mother.

A fourth influence on Selina is her friend Beryl Challenor, with whom she shares childhood illusions about a problem-free world. Together, they create an idealized female-based life, with a carefree pace and a joyful simplicity. But Beryl and Selina will, the text suggests, "grow out" of their mutual physical attraction, the muted assumption being that a lesbian relationship ranks as a viable lifestyle only among naïve adolescents. She feels comfortable exploding in front of the more complacent Beryl: "I'm bored with Tarzan. I'm tired of that old story" (15). Selina has reached the point of rejecting white values and old reenactments of slavery. But historical circumstances—lust for land, war in Europe—have dissolved the friends' childhood craving for serenity. Under her commercially minded father's influence, Beryl gradually changes into a like-minded daughter who thinks of becoming an attorney to the Association "some day," whereas Selina considers the Homeowners Association a dangerous institution for Barbadians (196). In Selina's view, it robs community members of their culture by seducing them toward white values.

Foretold in Selina's earlier killing of a fly, Selina's love for Beryl slowly fractures. After she visits the Challenor family to see Beryl's attractive new room, she witnesses Beryl's transformation into the child constructed as her parents wanted, a devotee of the Barbadian Association and its future attorney (196). Selina realizes her estrangement from this planned world, while her own life remains as formless as mist (196). When she leaves Beryl's house, she experiences the "brutal but cleansing lash" of the wind (198). New paths beckon her.

Yet she continues to wear silver bangles unquestioningly. Symbolic of slaves' handcuffs, the heavy bangles clank like chains, playing a dissonant tune (43–44). In another sense, they signify vitality, their noise empowering Selina to claim space. The bangles do double duty—that is, as positive and negative signifiers. On special occasions, Selina wears gold rather than silver bangles that convey a differently freighted symbolism. Selina wears these bangles until the time she begins college at age eighteen.

———◇———

In *Brown Girl, Brownstones*, Selina's quest takes place during wartime, not only metaphorically within the warring family, but during World War Two itself. Assumptions about Jews surface several times in relation to the lives of community members who are struggling to survive economically; Jews as people who fleece the Barbadian community is one prevailing assumption. In addition, to climb that ladder, Bajans scrub the floors of Jewish employers for a pittance and return home with their employers' cast-off clothes. Silla Boyce, for instance, works as a cleaning woman to save for a down payment on the brownstone they rent. All her life Silla has known hard times. Life in New York is no different. Growing up in cane fields "from the time God sun rise in his heaven till it set. With some woman called a Driver to wash yuh tail in licks if yuh dare look up. Yes, working harder than a man at the age of ten. . . . Her eyes narrowed as she traveled back to that time and was that child again, feeling the sun on her back and the whip cutting her legs. More than that, she became the collective voice of all the

Bajan women, the vehicle through which their former suffering found utterance" (45).

Second, Deighton Boyce dislikes how his friend, Yearwood Seifert, describes Jews.[21] Seifert's attitudes remind Deighton of racist practices he formerly endured in Barbados (38). Preferring dreams of utopia, he recoils from tension and bigotry, a man of peace and pleasure who suppresses his own victimhood. Like Jews, Yearwood would like to succeed because he respects Jews as men and women who know how to get ahead. Members of the black community like Silla want to emulate the "get up and go" of their Jewish neighbors.

Given the World War Two era, another aspect of Jewish reality surfaces during kitchen conversations among Silla and her friends concerning contemporary atrocities in Nazi Germany and Nazi-occupied Europe that people now know about. These discussions in the kitchen feed directly into old community knowledges about the historical situation of black people during and after slavery. Silla's old friend, Iris Hurley, reports gossip "that Hitler put all the Jews in a gas chamber," adding that Hitler, as the "devil-incarnate," should be shot (69). On the other hand, the genocide of European Jews offers an economic opportunity for underemployed people such as Silla to work in defense factories. Hence the issues of employment and defense play out in complicated ways.

Silla explains what she thinks, while her friends watch her industriously cook and bake to earn extra cash: World War Two, she insists, is a white people's war. Earlier in the kitchen, Florrie Trotman bemoaned the fact that her son was going to the war. People from a lower economic stratum, Silla contends, make up the frontline of combat in war; when she hears her friend Iris softening at the idea of fighting for "England and the crown," she exclaims: "But Iris, . . . you's one ignorant black woman!" "What John Bull ever did for you that you's so grateful? You think 'cause they does call Barbados 'Little England' that you is somebody?[22] What the king know 'bout you—or care? You best stop calling the man name like you and he does speak. You think the king did care when you was home heading canes? Or when the drought come and not a pot stir 'pon the stove for days . . . ?" (69–70).

Silla works in a World War Two defense factory, ironically named, for the plant is as much an economic defense of herself as the United States. The war enables Silla to defend her right to a decent livelihood, while enhancing her desire to acquire property. The issues raised by industrial labor blunt Silla's sensibilities even further as she nears her goal of buying a brownstone. In a sense, survival transforms her into a brownstone, personally hardened. Selina witnesses this metaphoric calcification of her mother when she visits her mother at work unexpectedly one evening.

Bent on protecting her father, Selina wants to confront Silla about her duplicitous behavior over the land that Deighton inherited. In doing so, Selina defies the wishes of her beloved Miss Thompson, who urges harmony at both the family and community level. To reach the factory, Selina tellingly has to follow the snow "laying a white path that could lead only to the mother" (96). When she arrives, Selina is appalled by the factory conditions in which her mother labors amid "stinking machines," helping to manufacture war material. As Selina watches her mother unseen, she thinks that only Silla's "own formidable force could match that of the machines; only the mother could remain indifferent to the brutal noise" (100). Concretely, Silla makes shells that are basically hollow tubes containing explosives (101); in a sense she is reproducing herself, a pent-up woman emptied of old days who has moved from one arena of shells—an island and an ocean—to another, more explicitly bellicose arena. In the face of intense noise and potential global destruction in this death-charged milieu, Selina shies from confrontation, whereupon Silla mocks her daughter as a "David without a sling" in the valley of Elah who is "resigned to defeat" (106–107). This helps Selina understand her mother's craving to obtain a brownstone that is partly about mourning a long-lost African home as well as acquiring a new home as a Barbadian immigrant. Put another way, craving a brownstone is an emotionally complex matter for an informally exiled Silla who lives and works in town.[23] But Silla's tough demeanor in acquiring a home also fosters a human deprivation since it anesthetizes certain basic feelings. Unlike her husband, Deighton Boyce, Silla has become associated with steel rather than sunshine. Her cold heart steals (steels) the sun, as she chimes in unison with the machine she operates (131). Not to put too fine a point on it, Silla becomes the machine: "repeatedly Silla's body rose and dropped in a threshing rhythm, the trumpet struck. She might have been a canecutter wielding a golden machete through the ripened cane or a piston rising and plunging in its cylinder" (131).

Believing solidly in the here and now as she labors in the factory and returns home to cook saleable food in her kitchen, she inaugurates a new era: "These ain ancient days" (30). She is no longer the girl whom community member Leon Brathwaite watched, who danced till "you fall out for dead right there on the grass . . . years ago on an island" (144–45).

The racist-based economic desperation that drives Silla is unfathomable to the inexperienced Selina. She loves her father so much that she has trouble understanding her mother's drive. Silla and her friends strike Selina as birds of prey that metonymize war and participate in its ugliness. Selina visualizes these kitchen women as "ominous birds, poised, beaks ready to rip her father" (75).[24] Selina also discerns that her parents are personally at war in the midst of World War Two, with no end in sight, while Selina in return is fighting wars within wars.

Following Deighton's inheritance of land in Barbados, Silla clandestinely arranges the disposition of this land by involving his relatives yet not consulting him, so that she can buy the brownstone with the proceeds. Thus Silla declares war on Deighton Boyce, a "spree boy" who longs to retire to the island of his youth. Wearing a rainbow-like halo around his head, Deighton Boyce dreams with a trumpet he cannot play, an illusory magic wand. His job matches his utopian vision. He works in a mattress (that is, dream-related) factory. But the matter runs deep. For example, when Silla hears the news about the land, she clutches the chicken feathers of the bird she is cleaning; symbolically, that is, she is permanently in tune with the Barbadian culture and the culture of her ancestors, although she opts to improve her family's present situation in the United States. Her chicken clutching adds to the constant talk of obeah in the kitchen.[25]

In contrast to Deighton's leisurely pursuits, Silla wants the Boyces to emulate the Challenor family who bought their own brownstone two years ago. She has no time for her husband's daydreams: "But what kind of man he is, nuh? Here every Bajan is saving if it's only a dollar a week and buying house and he wun save a penny. He ain got nothing and ain looking to get nothing . . ." (24). Thus she renders him "a hollow man with dead eyes" when she ends his dreams by selling the land (86).[26] Effectively, she helps to kill him.

Selina cannot halt the vanquishing of her spendthrift father's dream. After he learns that Silla sold the land behind his back, he is "broken, stripped, but delivered" (115), avenging himself by buying luxury goods with the proceeds that alienate him yet further from the community. Silla smashes the emblematic phallic trumpet that he buys for himself, thus metaphorically destroying their intimate sexual life and rendering him impotent. Unable to reconcile their "clash of cultures," Silla and Deighton Boyce have dissolved their union, as surely as the lovebirds carved out of ice on the Steeds' wedding cake are melting, while they kiss (138).[27] At that wedding, Selina thinks, "there was no place for her" in this community (141) where she and her friend Beryl are "part of a giant amoeba." In addition, the calypso sung at the celebration seems to be casting out Deighton Boyce (151): "Small island, go back where you really came from." Unbeknownst to her at the time, she takes that chant to heart.

By the time of the final confrontation between Deighton and Silla, he has already retreated to the spiritual environment of a missionary home, run by Father Peace.[28] Shortly thereafter, during the last summer of the war, his tranquility is broken by his arrest. Turned in to the police by Silla for being an illegal alien, he reacts acceptingly with an "almost radiant" smile. As Deighton Boyce prophesied, Silla plays out the actions of Brutus's faithful retainer who will kill Brutus because Brutus cannot bear to lose the battle.[29] That night, Selina beats on her mother "with the regularity of a metronome," while simultaneously denouncing Silla as Adolf Hitler (184, 186). As she strikes her mother, the bangles she always wears assist this momentary triumph: "She spat the name [of 'Hitler'] in the mother's face and brought her small fist down on Silla's shoulder. 'Hitler,' she cried and struck again. This time her bangles glanced sharply across the mother's chin" (184). From Selina's vantage point, her mother resembles an informer from the Gestapo, a brownshirt who will readily betray family members. Moreover, Selina's perception of her mother as Hitler complicates Silla's characterization of World War Two as a white people's war. Because black people are denied a stake in this war, they mark Hitler as evil because his campaign activates the community's memory of slavery and its atrocities; therefore, Nazis and plantocrats fuse. In another sense, Selina's charge that Silla resembles Hitler underscores the general complexity of Black-Jewish relations.

The upshot of the parental war is not only Silla's treachery, but also Deighton Boyce's death. En route to Barbados, he jumps or falls overboard into the ocean, "within sight of the Barbados coast" (188). His ambiguous death coincides ironically with the last days of World War

Two, with triumph imminent. Yet, though the war is over, there will be scant to celebrate: Deighton Boyce will be mourned, while men and women of color return to an underemployed status in a society flooded with G.I.s. Silla's symbolic hiring in a hospital, a site of healing and nurturance, suggests a potential softening of her character as she moves slowly toward putting down roots. On a different note, to accentuate Selina's multiple dilemmas, the journey of the mythical Ulysses reverberates throughout her adolescent's quest. Silla's name is the most striking example. (Let me outline that myth briefly to explain what I mean.)

As Ulysses and his companions approach Scylla [Silla] and Charybdis, a strait overlooked by two gaping caves, the roar and fog frighten them.[30] Circe had warned Ulysses that Scylla barks relentlessly and looks monstrous, just as Silla's behavior regarding the inherited land struck Deighton Boyce. The monster Scylla is apt to emerge suddenly from her cave—as Selina describes Silla coming into her field of vision when she returns home in the evening. Scylla kills six of Ulysses' crew who are drawn irresistibly to the cavern's mouth. Does Deighton Boyce resemble one of these mariners as he jumps overboard within sight of Barbados? Charybdis is a second sea monster that sucks on sea water three times a day and spits it out again. Ulysses is warned to stay closer to Scylla than Charybdis.

Selina's quest, by contrast, is much more loosely characterized. Lost and wandering like Ulysses, Selina steers between a machine-like mother and an easy going father, long associated with the sun. She attempts to navigate through narrow straits that represent the past and the future, war and peace. Hence Selina's ambivalence is telling as she tries to steer between the magnetic Scylla/Silla and Deighton Boyce/Charybdis whose dreams suck him into a whirlpool of disaster.

Prior to Deighton Boyce's death, Selina realizes that she has to navigate between two incomplete and dissatisfying choices and that the war which she experiences internally threatens to overwhelm her. Nor can she convince anyone of her need for help in thwarting Silla's plans that will dissolve her father's dreams: "blurring into nothingness," Selina comes perilously close to losing herself (93–94).

For a while, she joins the community as a means of finding peace through union with other Barbadians, but, on her first visit to the Association, she finds herself politically isolated and explicitly berates community members for being provincial, an accusation to which they respond angrily. Meanwhile, she meets a man named Clive Springer and plots to win a fellowship funded by the Association so that they can run away together. To this end, she asks the Association to forgive her outburst and works hard to reestablish herself in their good graces, mimicking her father's smile in the process.[31] Since battling with her mother over Deighton Boyce, Selina has earned a new gratifying respect from Silla. Nonetheless, her knowledge of the world remains uncertain: "she knew what she wanted. It was not so much a thought as something deeply felt. To flow out of herself into life, to touch and know it fully and, in turn, to be touched by it. And then, sometimes, to withdraw and be quiet within herself. . . . But how? How even to begin? She did not know" (204). The Blues singer that she and Clyde hear on a winter walk ventriloquizes how Selina feels: "Got up early this morning. But didn't have no place to go" (233). This lament paradoxically locates Selina within her community, yet she remains an outsider at the same time.

After Selina meets Rachel Fine at college, someone who has her own difficulties coming to terms with being Jewish, Selina accepts Fine's invitation to take dance lessons and eventually stages a dance performance. Mocking the equation of herself with diamonds—"all four carats of me"—Rachel chops and dyes her hair to cope with and challenge stereotypes of Jews and non-Jews (278). Rachel and Selinda, bonded by their ethnic dilemmas, seem to share what appears to be a similar experince.[32] At a party after a successful public performance of a dance that evokes the life cycle, Selina has to deal with the the host— the mother of a college friend—who insinuates that all West Indians are laborers. This bigotry infuriates Selina who feels like an animal in a long hunt, or an escaping slave (287). At this point, Selina encounters the harsh reality of life in the African diaspora by way of Barbados that her mother zealously fights and her father tried to circumvent. At this point, should Selina resign herself to life in this bigoted world of Brooklyn?[33]

As a result of personal and political interactions with Clyde, college, family, friends, and community, Selina comes to terms with the fact that no options are cut and dried. She then reconciles with her mother and leaves Brooklyn, en route to Barbados where her father headed without success.[34] Collapsing his dream into her own, temporarily at least she will migrate, closer to her roots within the diaspora. In facilitating Selina's departure, Rachel tenders a loving solution to Black-Jewish relationships.

A grudgingly admiring Silla validates Selina's decision to retrace the steps, as it were, of her ancestors. recognizing that her daughter is a survivor like herself: "'G'long! You was always too much woman for me anyway, soul. And my own mother did say two head-bulls can't reign in a flock. 'G'long!' Her hand sketched a sign that was both a dismissal and a benediction. 'If I din dead yet, you and your foolishness can't kill muh now!'" (307). In a moment of candid self-confrontation, Silla examines her own actions, understanding Selina's conviction that she killed Deighton: "Ever since the night you did call me Hitler you been waiting. You did always think I killed him. Yes. But I din do it out of hate" (305).

Leaving behind the dual worlds of Chauncey Street and Fulton Street, Selina is finally navigating on her own, Caribbean-bound: "she was one with Miss Thompson, . . . the whores, . . . the mother and the Bajan women" (292). In that freighted space of Fulton Park that is located between both streets, Selina extracts a tool for survival. Named after the steamship navigator Robert Fulton, the park in days gone by enabled Selina to experiment, in unconscious identification with Robert Fulton himself. She and Beryl enjoyed their friendship together; she and Clyde ran around the ledge of Robert Fulton's statue, trying to keep their balance (234).[35]

Now that she has found a direction of her own choosing, she can bond with people and remain steady. No surprise then that she reconsiders the wearing of the two bracelets/bangles as she stands at the site of former brownstones, "ravaged [and] . . . drawn within the darkness of themselves" (309). Blocks of these brownstones that offered a form of identity to the community as well as a site of resistance have been recently razed to the ground to make way for a new housing project where "life moved in an oppressive round within those uniformly painted walls" (310). Only fragments and rubble remain to spotlight the old confusing illusions that people cherished. Destroying brownstones destroys dreaming. Now the community will be relocated or recontained/recaged—as their slave ancestors were on the Middle Passage—in homogenized holding boxes.

But Selina refuses to be daunted. As part of that slave narrative and that wreckage in both senses, Selina marks the spot by throwing into the rubble of the brownstones one of her few permanent possessions, a solitary silver bangle (329). But she keeps the other bangle(s) as a sign of her history and her heritage. She becomes reconciled—if only symbolically and intuitively—to the historical meanings of the bangle and her old brownstone home, the site of Barbadian freedom as well as enslavement in the United States.

Finally, just as Ulysses sails toward Ithaca, managing to grasp on to the roots of a fig tree that jutted out over Charybdis's lair, Selina reaches "the islands" with Rachel's help. By playing out these mythological resonances, Marshall suggests that future possibilities are open. After Ulysses arrived safely in Ithaca, weapons were set aside and reconciliation reigned. His return marked a new era of peace. Selina remains the daughter of Silla and Barbados-bent Deighton, but her crossing to the Caribbean in search of peace, personal fulfillment, and origins also empowers her to claim an enriched, albeit fluid, cultural identity.

CHAPTER 3

Soul Clap Hands and Sing
Sadness, Resistance, Redemption

In *Soul Clap Hands and Sing*, a collection of four novellas published in 1962, a quartet of very old, all-male protagonists undertake numerous physical, emotional, political, and spiritual journeys, some diasporic. Their principal desire is to get by, but ultimately to gain ascendance over a humdrum quotidian reality. Women play a large role in their attempted transformations, arguably the co-protagonists, especially in the earlier novellas. The four stories—"Barbados," "Brooklyn," "British Guiana," and "Brazil," about old men who have endured bigotry all their lives—open with a telling quotation from William Butler Yeats that comments on the situations they confront. "An aged man is but a paltry thing, A tattered coat upon a stick, unless Soul claps its hands and sing."[1]

The first novella, "Barbados," fleshes out Yeats' quotation: in Marshall's own words, she undertook *Soul Clap Hands and Sing* "to see if I could write convincingly of men. More important, I wanted to use the relationship between the old men and the young women in the stories to suggest themes of a political nature. These were of increasing interest to me at the time."[2] She goes on to explain the particular challenges these characters represented: "They are—the men—of different backgrounds and cultures, yet they share a common predicament: their lives have been essentially empty. They have failed to commit themselves to anyone or anything in a meaningful way. When confronted with this truth or when their long-suppressed need for love finally surfaces, they reach out in a desperate, last-ditch effort to the women in the stories." But even if the women "are not major characters, they are nonetheless important as 'bringers of the truth.'" Marshall then continues: "They come to realize their own strength as a result of the encounter. I saw this as a second motif."

Marshall contends, moreover, that "Barbados" came to her in 1958, "practically ready-made"; she "never [had] it so easy." Specifically, the richly layered narrative of "Barbados" features a black protagonist cocooning himself from the Barbadian world to which he has returned after thirty diasporic years spent in Boston.[3] Pronounced intersections in *Brown Girl, Brownstones* reemerge, differently configured but still familiar.

"Barbados" stages a seventy-year-old Mr. Watford returning to the eponymous island, a wealthy but lonely bachelor who buys and tends coconut groves and doves with money salted from working in the United States. The sense of well-being that his daily labor fosters temporarily staves off an inchoate apprehension that haunts him. Watford cannot identify this frightening "spectre," but he takes prudent measures to calm himself. He seals off his bedroom, an act that appears to secure him psychologically from Barbadian reality.

As he nurtures the soothing doves, Watford's rough calloused hands illumine his internal division. So does the persistently noted signifier of whiteness. Encircled by his groves, he identifies with Barbadian people, yet he distances himself from the community by wearing a white clinical uniform and a pith helmet. His headgear familiarly tropes imperial incursions and values. Besides the uniform and helmet that match the white rheum in his eyes, a white mist floats in from the sea where fishermen appear as ghosts; the wind and the beach also seem white; further, Watford imagines his mother's white head tie as he pours canned [white] milk into his tea.

The very coconuts themselves that consume Watford's day resemble him in their "internalized" whiteness—perhaps they symbolize his divided self—while his pervasively white surroundings stress his oscillating location between the United States and Barbados. He has lost the wherewithal to fight off decades of an ascetic existence, racist conditioning, and assimilation. Hence, a contretemps erupts after Watford meets a young messenger boy who sports a button announcing "the old order shall pass." Furious at this public display of bravado, Watford fulminates at the adolescent's boss, the corpulent, sexual Mr. Goodman. Watford projects old pain as he recalls personal humiliations he endured in the past as a yard boy, forced to take orders from a white family. The boy has tapped into Watford's long-suppressed and simmering rage.

The elderly Goodman is attuned to the young man's motivation because, unlike Watford, Goodman has always lived in the community. Equably, he counters the ascetic Watford and informs him that today's black youth no longer fear white people. Goodman instructs Watford that the politically minded youth sporting the slogan will stay put in Barbados and fight for justice, rather than emigrate to Boston. He will try to implement the slogan he publicizes for the good of the community. Perhaps a modest though life-loving Mr. Goodman sets a good man's example. Goodman pleads with Mr. Watford to display a sense of civic duty by hiring a young impoverished women to assist him with domestic chores.

After reluctantly agreeing, systematically ignoring the hardworking young woman's pleas for conversation during their long, silent nights together, Watford clumsily attempts to communicate with her. Following years of isolation, speaking his thoughts let alone his desire comes hard to Watford. His diasporic experience in the United States has deadened his human feelings. He does so when she returns from local festivities with the young man who had infuriated Watford. Predictably, Watford's effort is in vain. He may be a man whose nomenclature fuses water with fording a bridge, but his experiences as a black man have denied him any "real-life" enactment of the symbolic significance of his name.[4] Limited self-knowledge about his feelings comes too late and the formerly subservient now animated domestic servant will have none of his overtures. She brushes him off like a fly, too engrossed in her relationship with the young man and a possible new and more active life. Politically coming to terms with her society, she is now beginning to articulate what she formerly repressed: "You aint people," she angrily informs her employer, disrupting his pathetic attempts to control the situation with her initiation of agency. At this point, the young woman is now sporting the very political button that angered Watford earlier.

Even Watford's doves fail him in the end, or perhaps they alone offer him some peace. They spell his origins and spotlight as well as harbor the seemingly unattainable peace that he quests. Ironically, they hail from the North African Barbary Coast where corsairs, resistant to colonial predation, kidnapped Europeans on the high seas.[5] Spiritually if not physically, blood leaves Watford's head as he dies, but not before this epiphanic episode involving the young women illumines his "inner eye." Poignantly identifying with the doves, his only friends, he recognizes the specter of bigotry that has dogged him, but change is beyond him: "For the first time it [the inner eye] gazed mutely upon the waste and pretense which had spanned his years. Flung there against the door by the girl's small blow, his body slowly crumpled from the psychological fatigue he had long denied. He sensed that dark but unsubstantial figure, which roamed the nights searching for him wind him in its chill embrace. He struggled against it, his hands clutching the air with the spastic eloquence of a drowning man. He moaned—and the anguished sound reached beyond the room to fill the house. It escaped to the yard, and his doves swelled their throats, moaning with him" (67).

The second novella, "Brooklyn," has a white academic setting, in which Professor Max Berman's life intersects with that of a quiet, talented black student, Miss Williams, who is attending his course in French literature. Chain-smoking and fastidiously dressed, Berman considers himself "something of an outcast." This sense of marginality stems from his experiences growing up as a Jew and his subsequent encounter with the House Committee on Un-American Activities that cost him his career. Ironically, Max Berman had joined the Communist Party, but had not become a political activist.

In class, Miss Williams' "loneliness interested him. He sensed its depth. . . . He saw then that she was a Negro" (32). Her calm demeanor reminds Berman of Paul Gauguin's canvas entitled *Aita Parari*, which features Paul Gauguin's lover, Anna la Javanaise. Coincidentally, neither Miss Williams nor Anna la Javanaise has a complete name, while the woman in Barbados has no name; they are collectively everywoman. So at one level, the formality of Miss Williams signifies a certain status. The famous canvas portrays the painter's lover gazing out at the world, sitting in a Berbice chair, and nominally at least associated with the Berber, a North African tribe. At her ease reclining, the lover claims roots that go back a long way. Her resemblance to Gauguin's model and lover recalls Java itself, an Indonesian island located between the Indian Ocean and the Java Sea that is associated with the discovery of "homo erectus" or the "Java man."[6] Bone fragments found in Java suggested the existence of the earliest people on earth. At Anna's feet is an energetic, warm-colored monkey—symbolizing freedom, mischief, cultural beliefs, practices, and artifacts that include the tool bag of a trickster.

Without consultation, the arrogant, unreflective Max Berman decides to use Miss Williams to regain his life, just as Watford in "Barbados" showed a similarly complex and disdainful connection to black women as symbolic bridges. Her opinion has no bearing on the matter. After Berman's none too subtle verbal propositions, inviting her to his home, she recoils. For weeks, she stays away from class until the final examination. Then she agrees to the visit, but his self-important invitation and assumptions, unbeknownst to him, have triggered old memories in Miss Williams and transformed her thinking. Before his crude proposition, Williams had maintained the pose of an obedient daughter to parents presumably wary and well aware of pitfalls faced by diasporic citizens. They have warned her to leave white and very dark-complexioned people alone: "I was confused," she eventually tells Berman, "I never really sat near anybody" (46). Now she opts on her own to dissolve his pretenses and ridicule his attitudes. Just as she defied her parents' injunctions, she also refuses the role of obedient student to arbitrary authority and masculinist self-indulgence. She will not spend her life supine, she decides, but will claim her right to agency and hence to resistance.

Frequently described by Berman in terms of amber, Miss Williams acts out the implications of that name. A hard, beautiful fossil resin found not only in the Baltic Sea but also in the Dominican Republic, its origins lie in Arabia. Amber is connected to ambergris, a substance found in whales who, figuratively speaking, swim eternally.[7] The ancestry of amber is part of Williams' own distinguished ancestral lineage, a metonymic attachment to African ancestors, borne out in Max Berman's observations about her resemblance to Gauguin's model. The discourse of amber symbolically demarcates Williams' ability to survive: "She was the one who seemed old, indeed ageless" (47). Politically wiser than her chronological years, Miss Williams assumes a rightful place on Paule Marshall's continuum of ancestral female warriors living in the diaspora, yet rooted in as well as deracinated from the African continent.

Not only does Berman decide how Miss Williams will affect his life, he also decides that he and she share "collective sufferings" (34). Her presence reminds him of his earlier self as "a boy . . . running from the occasional taunts at his yarmulke . . . impeded by the heavy satchel of books . . . proof of his scholarship" (29). Yet this mutual identification with suffering does not extend to the gay protagonist in *L'Immoraliste* by André Gide, that Berman is teaching in class. When Miss Williams discusses Gide's text, she pities the discovery by the vacillating protagonist of his homosexuality: "'what he finds out about himself is,'" she avers, "'so terrible'"[8] (44). This observation foreshadows later problematic encounters with gay men and lesbians in Paule Marshall's fiction.

The final confrontation between the aging Berman and the aspiring Williams results in Miss Williams' volteface. Where he thinks she is translucent like amber, she sees through his callow gestures. He becomes amber in her eyes as she comes to define him—or even name him— a "cup that would break in my hand" (47).

Having shattered Berman's frail illusions, she thanks him politely for his hospitality, turning her parents' injunctions about gentility into a tool of muted scorn: "it's been a nice day, all things considered." Miss Williams finds the means to become an oppositional force. Not to put too fine a point on it, she is a political activist—like her nameless sister in "Barbados"—who consciously fights race and gender bigotry, for the first but not the last time, courtesy of the jaded Berman.

A moribund Berman subsequently succumbs as Miss Williams departs, his veins resembling blue pencil markers or indecipherable scrawls. He has collapsed into emotional and political unintelligibility. By contrast, she epitomizes life as she lifts her head, proudly but serenely, to board the train that will transport her to a future of fresh possibilities.

The nameless young servant woman who displays the young man's political button on her dress and Miss Williams are political twins—in agreement that "the Old Order Shall Pass." They constitute an insurgent force, the today and tomorrow of black female power. Their oppressive counterparts, Mr. Watford and Max Berman, are victims of a different kind who avoided struggle out of fear, apathy, and a sense of futility.

In the third novella, "British Guiana," Gerald Motley similarly lives in spiritual tatters, having opted for a life of assimilation. Despite breaking a race barrier in British Guiana by accepting a job formerly available only to white people, Motley has spurned his ethnic identity. Turning colonialism against itself is not on his mind.

This story of empire in British Guiana opens with a game of cricket played by black youngsters who appear to have internalized English values and assumed colonial cultural practices. Like the boys playing cricket, Motley contents himself with merely playing the role of the "first colored program director" rather than using the job to promote greater awareness.

Motley's sartorial wardrobe constitutes an offbeat, elitist version of Watford's white uniform and pith helmet and Berman's fawn, custom-made French shoes. Clothes proclaim certain suppressed tales about the old men's lives. Motley himself wears expensive cream-colored linen suits topped by a panama hat; he drives a battered Jaguar, which is, in his friend Sidney Parrish's words, "a long expensive car." Just as ostentatiously and symbolically, he lives in a large colonial house: "a high, white, stilted monument in the darkness, its closed shutters hiding rooms where the last echoes had long been stilled" (106) . . . a white towering relic (110). A denizen of the King George Bar, Motley decries British Guiana as "this God forsaken patch of Her Majesty's Empire [where there is] nothing but Russian Bear rum giving us cirrhosis of the liver" (91).

"One of the few elite left" in the country, Gerald Motley signals an important success story to the people: "It did not matter that he had done nothing outstanding at B.G. Broadcasting. What was important was that he had been the first colored man in the West Indies to hold such a position" (97). In the long run, however, he turns out to be little more than the "puppet director" who initially thought he could make British Guiana broadcasting the "voice of the West Indies." Instead "it's still cricket, news from the B.B.C. three times a day, the governor's speeches on the Queen's birthday and funeral announcements. That's the way Frank Orly and Company [the corporate owners] want it" (117). In other words, a non-confrontational conformist, Gerald Motley declines resistance, failing to grasp that his role as the first "colored" director reinforces capitalist colonial power unless he co-opts/adapts it to his advantage. His former partner Sybil herself reacts differently to potential colonial expropriation. She assumes the very kind of insurgent role geographically elsewhere that Motley in Guiana wishes at the present time to reject. Are their divergent paths partly due to a grudge that Motley has held against Sybil for ages? Specifically, he has never forgiven her for disrupting his meditations when he journeyed as a young man to Kaieteur Falls. Accompanied by Sybil, he undertook the trip to decide whether to accept the unique job that British Guiana Broadcasting executives had offered him. At the Falls, Motley initially pondered his roots to confront who he was: "So that the branches clawed at him, the vines wound his arms, roots sprang like traps around his feet and the silence—dark from the vast shadows, brooding upon the centuries lost—wolfed down the sound of his breathing. He had felt a terror that had been the most exquisite of pleasures and at his awed cry the bush had closed around him, becoming another dimension of himself, the self he had long sought" (74). Not coincidentally, Kaieteur Falls provides a critical source of energy for Guiana from which Motley metaphorically wants to draw.[9]

This experience at Kaieteur Falls represents Motley's symbolic confrontation with a politic akin to black nationalism. As a marginalized person, he momentarily thinks of divorcing himself from the colonial scenario around him and opting for a cultural retreat. Because Sybil interrupted his meditations and urged him to stand up and fight, Motley feels justified in remaining bitter about her "intrusion." Consequently, Motley fails to recognize Sybil's choice to keep struggling against the odds. In a sense, he constructs excuses, using Sybil to evade personal accountability.

Sybil is the most obvious textual insurgent, the "first colored reporter for the *Georgetown Herald* [who] . . . had never settled in, but had remained somehow remote, restless and lonely" (84). Now assistant to the program director for Radio America, she is "doing damn well" (93).

Motley's cynical friend, Sidney Parrish, who is both resistant and partially assimilated, works as a radio announcer. Parrish sees quotidian reality as a challenge of sorts—he somewhat understands realpolitik—knowing full well that his job perpetuates colonial propaganda.

On a daily basis, Parrish announces the community obituaries so that the certainty of these announcements will always remind people that the black community is steady. Then he follows the obituaries with a commercial for Tide, a product that tries to guarantee unsurpassed whiteness. In an unconscious subversion of British colonial values, Parrish occasionally "forgets" to announce the commercial for Tide.

Resembling Parrish, Motley's servant Medford is a less than obvious fighter who helps to preserve the historical memory of the community. Embodying countermemory, she is yet another avatar of Paule Marshall's ancient female warriors, paralleling Miss Thompson in *Brown*

Girl, Brownstones and other ancestors/elders/warriors who populate later novels. She is integral to the historical continuum of slaves kidnapped in West Africa up to their ancestors in the present day.

Medford has been helping to bury the dead and has just returned from Millicent Dembo's funeral which she heard about on Sidney's program: "She usually appeared almost immediately, a thin, black, severe form, as ageless as Singh was ageless, her head wound in a silk kerchief printed with the Statue of Liberty which her daughter had sent her from America. But tonight he had to call several times before he heard her slurred tread and, when she emerged around the corner of a dim passage, he saw that she was dressed in white with a white straw hat instead of the kerchief. As she hobbled toward him—her face, arms and ancient legs lost in the shadows—she might have been an apparition" (107). Medford proves that Tide does not work; the tide cannot be turned any more than colonial efforts to "whiten" black people can work. The incident further underscores the important community role that Parrish's obituaries serve.

Motley fears that Sidney physically attracts him and acknowledges he has always been "secretly offended" by the shape of females (101): "When he finally drank and passed it over, Gerald Motley felt the warm place where Sidney's hand had rested; as he fitted the mouth of the bottle to his he tasted Sidney there—and that taste and touch, so intimate somehow in the darkness, along with the rum searing his throat, restored him" (109).

The sexual love that Motley feels for Sidney, but cannot overtly express, is double edged. Homophobically, the text suggests that Motley's realization about his sexuality is part of his degradation. Yet his attraction to Sidney tells of his sustained capacity to feel, despite a life spent evading unpleasant realities.

Motley's claim that he *is* British Guiana, that he will survive disaster because of that identification further suggests intense self-denial: "knowing suddenly that what he had sought all along had been the reflection of himself in each feature of the land. And he had been there, although he had not been able to see himself. The listing Hindu houses this morning had in some way reflected him, as had the family standing in their ruined field and the black men wielding their machetes among the gliding canes, the boys at their cricket" (99).

Having detached himself from local and international politics, Motley half-mockingly proposes bombing the government offices of

Georgetown as a political solution. That will put an end, he claims, to the People's Progressive Party (the P.P.P.), the unholy triumvirate of poverty, politics, and prejudice, which continues to rule British Guiana, a party formed in 1950, to advance Guyanese nationalism. Led by an East Indian, Cheddi Jagan, and an African, Forbes Burnham, the party won a majority of Parliamentary seats in the first election held under the new constitution. By the end of 1953, Britain had suspended the constitution, fearing—so official reports went—that the P.P.P would establish a "communist state." By 1955, Burnham and Jagan had parted ways. The more moderate Burnham, who organized the Peoples National Congress, drew black support from the P.P.P. Internal autonomy was granted in 1961, the year that "British Guiana" was published. Motley cannot countenance supporting the black progressive wing of the government, yet he wants nothing to do with Jagan's opposition party.[10] He is content to coast along, indirectly complicitous with the status quo. But his complacence is challenged at a party given for Sybil's homecoming when she invites Motley to become the coordinator of Radio Jamaica, while she will work for Radio Jamaica as the program director. Since Sybil fought hard for a person of color to secure that position, Motley understands that the job will be tough political work, not the symbolic appointment his current job was. Drinking himself into a stupor each day would be ruled out.

Shying from that challenge, Motley asks Sybil to give a job—some other job—to Parrish; he makes this unselfish offer because he prefers not to offer himself. Motley has opted out of political struggle, whereas Parrish—Motley believes—might rise to the political occasion and transcend his cynicism.

But before Motley can return home that night, he dies in a traffic accident. Metaphorically, since he can no longer navigate, he has turned the wheels over to the prophetic Sybil and Parrish, his skeptical but open-minded protégé.

Where Watford and Berman momentarily surface to play out one last sad stand, Motley has traveled beyond that possibility. He cannot even voice his sexual feelings for Sidney Parrish because he views them as socially unacceptable. But in recommending the friend he loves for a job elsewhere, Motley effects a beau geste of which he can be personally and politically proud. He tries to join Sybil's progressive continuum, at least vicariously, by bestowing on Sidney an opportunity that he cannily knows he is too personally calcified to accept.

The last novella, "Brazil," begins on stage amid a theatrical explosion. "Ladies and Gentlemen," the bilingual voice announces, "the Casa Samba presents, O Grande Caliban e a Pequena Miranda."[11] Like William Shakespeare's *The Tempest*, the story opens to a storm, with an edifice toppling and smoke billowing everywhere; people are physically and metaphorically at sea. Every night, the performance closes with Miranda carrying Caliban off stage to great ridicule. The symbolically resonating names of the characters, Miranda and Caliban, come from *The Tempest*—the former hails a brave new world, the latter is a thwarted slave.[12] As a tall, blonde, Brunhildian stage performer, Miranda contrasts with Caliban, a pint-sized elderly black man dressed as a prize fighter who is personally angry because his stage identity has subsumed his original identity as Heitor Baptista Guimares.[13] Resembling Mr. Watford's rheumy eyes, Caliban's are "opaque with [white] rheum," metonymic of his hampered vision. On stage and off he is enslaved, suffering like "some Lilliputian in a kingdom of giants who had to play the jester in order to survive" (140).[14] The show is all illusion. He has no identity except Caliban's, and that identity will disappear upon retirement. Everyone knows and loves Caliban, but no one can ever remember the earlier Heitor. But these illusions are dissolving, and even his wife reflects back his failure. Heitor's life is an act, nothing more. Thus he projects his anger onto Miranda rather than dealing with it.

From a small mining town, Caliban has played everyman in the theater for thirty-five years. But like Watford, Berman, and Motley, Caliban is insecure about who he is. For decades, he has been shadow boxing, acting as everybody's "negro"—assuming the role that everyone expects of him, from Nacimento who discovered him, Miranda herself, the boys in the street, and his cruise-ship audiences. As the black nightclub star, Caliban makes everyone in the community feel better because they live in a world of abject poverty. Caliban's poverty is the poverty of the people and their deprived lives. As the creation of others, Caliban represents hope, while simultaneously he locates himself oppositionally, seeking to reclaim who he once was.

On the road to embracing a new identity, Caliban can no longer be taken in by the comforting words of his porter-valet, Henriques. Openly he confesses: "I am an old man. Did you see me tonight? The last show especially? I could hardly move. I forgot lines so that the jokes didn't make sense. I was all right in the beginning, but once

I gave the knockout punch I was through. That punch took all my strength. I feel it here," he touched his right shoulder, his chest. "Oh, I know I could go on working at the Casa Samba for a while longer, I am an institution here, but I don't love it any more. I don't feel the crowd. And then that pig Miranda has gotten so lousy" (144–45). Caliban's frustrations contort into hatred for Miranda.

Like the specter that stalks Mr. Watford, Caliban's phantom also seems ineluctable—a vague fear or disturbance that suggests a memory of Heitor Baptista Guimares—"he had come to believe that what he felt was really a disturbance within himself" (139). The show is ending, but his past life still eludes him.

Yet while blaming Miranda for his failings, he is beginning to face the fact that he remains at odds with himself. When he finds Nacimento in dire straits during a walk to the slums, the distinction between the artifice of a nightclub audience and people's reality strikes him forcibly. Compared to a "dead palm" that no longer requires light, Nacimento foreshadows the death of Caliban; earlier Nacimento had devised the death of Heitor and given birth (as his name implies) to Caliban. The dead palm, moreover, is the palm of Caliban's hand. Since Heitor's identity was subsumed in Caliban's, there is no future—or a questionable one at best, written on his palm. At the end of the long night, Caliban destroys Miranda's apartment because her very being clothed in a gleaming facade constitutes Rio itself. Up in lights, her name conceals the horror of children prostituting themselves and eating from garbage cans, of Nacimento barely existing in a woebegone hut. In requesting his identity and blaming Rio/Miranda for his plight, Caliban creates yet another tempest. He means to dissolve the neon identity that his performances have perpetuated. Everyone sees the bright lights and Rio's facade, not the dismal poverty.

Ideologically, then, "Brazil" intersects constantly with "Barbados," "Brooklyn," and "British Guiana"—sharing with them an interrogation of moribund old men facing up to who they are, their ontological realities, after lives jeopardized by bigotry writ large; institutionalized racism, poverty, class bias, anti-communism, and anti-Semitism have jeopardized the lives of this quartet and rendered their chances of personal and political contentment unattainable. At different stages of moribundity, the first three witness the endurance and emotional strength of black women. In "Brazil," by contrast, where Marshall more graphically exhibits human degradation, another Caliban lives tempestuously with little choice, then stirs up a tempest of his own. Heitor Baptista Guimares reclaims his dignity en route to claiming himself, the last and only protagonist of the quartet to transcend the situation into which historical circumstances and his own complicity have landed him. Of the four men, he at least has positioned himself to move forward. Facing the open door of the elevator, he embraces possibility.

Watford strove unsuccessfully to utilize his inner eye—while Berman still drives, if only in pitch darkness. By recommending the friend Motley loves for a job elsewhere, he stops playing mental cricket and vindicates himself politically for one magnificent moment. At the end in a sense, he resumes his meditations at the Falls. This fourth protagonist stands ready to champion W. B. Yeats's prefatory quotation to *Soul Clap Hands and Sing* that "An aged man is but a paltry thing,/ A tattered coat upon a stick, unless/ Soul clap its hands and sing. . . ." Caliban's soul, however, having escaped ambush, now claps its hands, illuminating his earlier darkness as an entertainer for the colonial-capitalist tourist trade. He has given himself time to transcend a living death among a corrupt tourist industry for a life with his own people, cheek by jowl. He has regained entry to the diasporic community that will appreciate his rejuvenation.

But this positive reading may be to overstate the case since all four are "hollow men" [with] "dried voices, when we whisper together . . . quiet and meaningless.[15] Having been molded by others' expectations, the old men feel thwarted and helpless so they strike out at their black female counterparts.[16] But the women return fire for fire, while Miranda alone capitulates. She cannot abide the thought of life without her entertainer, 'meu negrinho'" (177). In the end, the men come face to face with themselves, their illusions inexorably caving in on them.

Other Short Pieces

Reena, from the collection *Reena and Other Stories*, suggests a profile for Merle had she not grown up in the Caribbean. Reena and Merle long to journey to Africa, Merle because her child and husband live there, and Reena so her children can understand its significance. At the end of *Reena and Other Stories*, the friends separate; the old lives morph into new ones, while new challenges involving issues of social justice, we suspect, will open up for both. "The Valley Between" displays a bickering white couple in which a husband treats his wife as private property and ridicules her return to school. Should anything go wrong with the child, the wife's to blame, and with his antediluvian mentality, he insists that the grandmother is too feeble to tend their child. As an early experiment in depicting social relations, Marshall stalwartly and bluntly covers emerging feminist issues.

Once again set in Barbados and adding the concept of "living in continuity," "To Da-Duh, In Memoriam" is in Paule Marshall's words, "the most autobiographical of the stories" (*Reena and Other Stories*, 95). From New York, a keenly observant and highly competitive child visits oldtimey grandmother Da Duh. Subtle rivalries that play out culminate in the child's citing new technology as a seeming trump card over her grandmother's old ways. This so-called triumph is eventually unveiled as the imperial "Hollow Man" whose predatory planes swoop over Barbados during WWII causing Da-Duh's death, and hence "In Memoriam." Besides its autobiographical importance, Da-Duh also functions iconically as the ubiquitous elder—revering the past, challenging colonial power by humble, personal example; Da-Duh also bespeaks one of the most solemn and violent anti-colonial moments in Paule Marshall's subtle yet edgy political repertoire. Its quiet synthesis of early cold war ideologies, competing regardless of innocent people's lives, resounds throughout Marshall's four-decades-long diasporic saga.

CHAPTER 4

A "Nation of Diabetics" Meets Empire
A Chosen Place, a Timeless People

In later fiction, Paule Marshall has not so far returned to the particular vision of *Soul Clap Hands and Sing*—the redemption of men in their old age who have not led lives that satisfied them. In Marshall's second novel, *The Chosen Place, the Timeless People* (1969), she examined a quite differently composed diasporic community—this time one that had remained in the original landing place—the point of embarkation. But even this may not be true as it is difficult to ascertain with certainty where every slave landed in *Brown Girl, Brownstones*.[1] Specifically, *The Chosen Place, the Timeless People* concentrates on U.S. interventions in the community of Bourne Hills Island and how members of the island community cope with colonial intervention. Most obviously, the population is involved in sugar production that is primarily destined for export to First World Countries.[2] Members of the Bournehills community range from the nonresident mill owner Sir John Stokes; the black politician Lyle Hutson, who is torn between the radical ideas of his youth and a pragmatic approach to politics; a serious, well-intentioned Jewish reformer from the United States, Saul Amron; his devious wife Harriet who wants to be seen as a philanthropist; and others who cater to tourists, while profiting from them. Through this economic relationship, always detrimental and even sometimes fatal to the community, the United States attempts to define and control the Bourne Island population. Workers' labor also perpetuates the colonial relationship.

The Chosen Place, the Timeless People also accentuates interactions and intersections between people, notably the politically complex protagonist Merle Kinbona and U.S. anthropologist Saul Amron, who respectively confront their African and Jewish identities. Paule Marshall describes Merle as a black woman "still seeking to reconcile all the conflicting elements to form a viable self. And she continues to search, as in the novel, for the kind of work, for a role in life that will put to use her tremendous energies and talent. Merle. She's the most passionate and political of my heroines, a Third World revolutionary spirit. And I love her."[3]

Merle lives in the part of Bournehills where the Cane Vale sugar factory is located. Having returned from several years in England that ended in sadness and a separation from her husband who took their child back to Africa to live with him, Merle remains on excellent terms with almost everyone on the island, despite her reputation as a troublemaker and an opponent of the status quo. Named after a magician, she favors creative solutions. As a case in point, she was recently fired for teaching schoolchildren about the island's authentic history and not the traditional and accepted eurocentric narrative. She told students about Cuffee Ned, Bourne's renowned revolutionary figure, and explained the need to recover the community's history of resistance. Merle keeps on trying.

At the opening of *The Chosen Place, the Timeless People*, Merle is driving on a road to the airport, accompanied by her elderly friend, Leesey Walkes, to pick up Saul Amron and his entourage arriving from the United States. To her dismay, she discovers that the route to the airport along the symbolically named Westminster Low Road has become an "unnavigable mud slough."[4] Apparently, this impasse is a common occurrence, and Merle remains cool and undaunted. Like the ancient mariner, she keeps alive old narratives about injustice (89). Her conflicts, as well as her durability, are apparent in the very car she owns—an old Bentley that belonged to a colonial governor, with several of its parts willfully damaged. Former owners of this car could not completely offset the community's slow-burning yet persistent opposition. Through her efforts at cultural regeneration, Merle attempts to subvert the symbolism of the aristocratic Bentley.

Merle's friend Leesey wears a dowdy, close-fitting, earth-brown felt hat that crowns her head, emblematic of her venerable authority on the island and her ability to harmonize. Leesey's patient waiting for a brighter world with a solution to contemporary ills frames the impasse that Merle faces. She is one of the island's warrior ancestors, appropriately named after the side of anything that is sheltered from the wind, an unruffled cove where the weary may shelter. The sibylline Leesey prophesies, "Everything's going down to grass. We are seeing the last days now" (9). The venerable Leesey foretells a vast transformation for the community—as well as for Merle, its insurgent representative.

Following their first evening on the island, Merle and the U.S. visitors end up at a nightclub belonging to a man named Sugar, whose ubiquity accentuates the island's economic base. Merle tells the recently arrived visitors about monoculture economy—its omnipresence and its consequences—in one loaded sentence: "You people aren't officially on the island until you've met Sugar" (78). She is referring to Sugar's nightclub "where in the space of one evening you can see how things stand on this side of the island." Tellingly located at the end of Whitehall Lane, named after a renowned site of empire, in its first incarnation the club was a barracoon for slaves, a notorious holding station.[5] It bespeaks the island's tumultuous history, its contemporary problems, and its uncertain future that the community tensely awaits (78).

As Merle escorts the visitors to her guesthouse, she stresses the transhistorical role that sugar has played in all their lives, regardless of origin. Sugar is, she exclaims, "our one and only national product, the thing that keeps us going in Bourne Island, that runs in our veins. . . . 'Prick me!' She thrust a dark arm across at [Saul], and as he started back in surprise, she laughed. 'Sugar,' she cried. 'That's what you'd find, Doctor. Not a drop of blood, only a little sugar water. I'm a damn diabetic, and so is everybody else in the place. A nation of diabetics. Every last one of us'" (85). Sugar enables the community to earn a livelihood, yet still concurrently enslaves them. Colonialism forces this chronic condition upon the people, all involuntarily diabetic. The canes themselves resemble "an opposing army . . . bright lances brandishing in the wind and so tall, now that they were ripe, those in the car could not see over them, . . . stretching endlessly away on both sides of the road" (95). Canes challenge workers who toil from morning till night to cut them (161). At some level, everyone cuts cane. Even time itself on Bourne Island is measured in sugar—the two seasons, lasting from June to December, the latter period following the harvest, being termed the in-crop and the out-of-crop.

Despite its pivotal role and everyday presence, however, sugar is associated with indeterminacy. Whether owners will close the Cane Vale sugar factory immediately after the crop has been cut always generates debate (7). Only after the official end of the harvest can the people harvest their personal plots of cane—Merle's friend Leesey whose "tiny half-acre of cane she owned outright" counts on that harvest for her livelihood (26).[6]

Merle denounces the white male ruling class of the island in banks and businesses as sugar kings who are bent on perpetuating the community's addiction to sugar, while Merle, by contrast, wants the community to become self-sufficient. If sugar runs in the islanders' veins and they cut down the canes, aren't they cutting down and selling themselves? Everyone has caught the sugar disease, which in turn is deliberately spread by the likes of mill owner Sir John Stokes, head of the London office of Kingsley and Sons. Plantocratic in appearance and behavior, he is described as "playing to the hilt the 18th-century absentee landlord come out to the colonies to look over his holdings." In Saul Amron's view, Sir John intends to own and control the world (225). When he comes annually to inspect the factory, he overtly sports the uniform of imperial mastery—a pith helmet and his "white hunter outfit . . . complete with swagger stick" (225). Sir John's pith helmet recalls the one that Mr. Watford wears when he returns home to Barbados: Paule Marshall's intertextual resonances encode Sir John's classic colonial behavior with Mr. Watford's almost resigned mimicking sartorial act. The former validates his authority arrogantly in front of the community, while the latter conveys a poignant assimilation—consciously or not, it is hard to say—over a long period of time.

Lyle Hutson's pro-corporate commentary signifies his own form of co-optation, certainly different from Sir John's, but profoundly invaluable to a western capitalist value system: he is "a casualty of the radicalism of my youth. . . . Another one of those who gave up for one reason or another. But I know what needs to be done" (225). Lyle Hutson had been something of an activist during his long sojourn in England as a student, due largely to Merle, who was also studying there. Lovers briefly, Lyle and Merle "had shouted about socialism and revolution at the heated parties they attended" in the company of other Caribbean students (61). Politically they were at one with former slave insurgents.[7] In London, Hutson had talked of nationalizing the sugar industry back home in Bourne Island, while driving Kingsley and Sons from the island: "But once he had returned home and married into the famous Vaughan family, once his law practice had grown and he had entered politics, he had gradually started speaking about the need for change in less radical terms. He had begun to caution moderation and time" (61). Hutson's Christian name, Lyle, furthermore, signs his attachment to the community: He is the island, Lyle being both a homonym and a variant spelling of French for island, "l'île"; he is someone thoroughly indigenous (215). The famous brand of imperial sugar, Tate and Lyle, is also embedded in his name, while his patronymic Hutson reconfirms his humble origins (hut) in/as the tropical sun.[8]

From Hutson's pragmatic standpoint, since so many people are selling themselves one way or another, diversifying production would at least create jobs. Banking on a long shot, he wants to outbid other islands in order to attract competition to his own. Later, Hutson's supporters in the new diversification scheme ardently debate the gambling concession for the island's large hotel, scheduled to be built under the new development plan (393). The threat of deeper corruption looms large and appears imminent.

As Hutson explains this pro-imperial development plan to Merle and Saul, his revelations stun them. Waiving customs duties, the plan offers a long tax-free period to new businesses—a measure that will severely injure the island's economy. The plan also assumes that the domestic government will build and bear the expense of the new industrial park by itself, without the usual benefit of outside subsidies.

As the island's informal oral historian, Hutson worries that a single crop economy will lessen the possibility of progress and financial benefit for the community. In theory, Lyle favors Saul and Merle's ideological position on Bournehills economics, but pragmatically he regards their opinions as mere political pronouncements that ignore realpolitik. In turn, Merle and Saul deny any logic to Hutson's pro-capital position that hearkens back to the old days of slavery. Pointedly labeling him Judas, Merle talks of the English selling Bournehills for thirty pounds sterling (101). Nonetheless, Lyle insists that "all o'we is one" (200), we are all one, to which Merle throws down a gauntlet: "Who says the auction blood isn't still with us? The chains are still on" (209–10).[9] Adopting an isolationist stance, Merle contends that the people should go it alone if the scheme offers no collective advantage. Subscribing to this collective approach to problems also means that Merle rejects the idea of foreign investment. Until the rollers in the sugar mill apparently break down, no immediate solution presents itself. Here, the text warns that people sometimes have to wait for external circumstances to force change.

Hutson's complicity with the establishment does not derive from imperial expropriation. Originally, he was the bright son (sun) of a humble village tailor: "He had stood among the sons of the island's leading families flawlessly reciting his [imperial] Latin—'a small boy' from the country . . . a hint of his mother's talcum powder lightening the strong, dark-umber of his face" (61). Yet Hutson is also the individual who sings in Latin of the exiled Aeneas who had to sail from his native land. Before Aeneas/Lyle could establish his destiny, he endured much (66, 67, 92).[10] Hutson, that is, empathizes with Merle and Saul during their dense political discussion, yet opts for expedience over principle, or put differently, he chooses different principles. Changing events, he declares, have mandated his revamped approach.

As the reformer who visits Bourne from the United States to "aid" the people, Saul Amron locates himself doubly: he stands in two places at once, well-intentioned on the one hand, and disagreeing with Hutson about the soundness of his strategy concerning Bourne's economic needs. An anthropologist, Amron came to the island with his wife, Harriet Shippen Amron, and his assistant, Allen Fusso. Unbeknownst to Amron, the community project to which he is wholeheartedly committed is funded by a grant from a high-toned Philadelphian agency at his wife's secret behest. Amron reminds Hutson that the country belongs to the Bournehills people: "In fact, he declares, 'all such as Kingsley and Sons and the big trading companies and banks along Queen Street should, at the very least, be owned in part by the government. It should demand a controlling interest in them'" (207). Saul's insidious role resembling that of a field worker for the Agency of International Development (A.I.D.) is implied, but not directly addressed. Proposing the need for technology and agricultural development at the grassroots level, Amron suggests that Bourne people could be more independent if they started to diversify their economy. Total dependence on sugar, he maintains, is ill advised. The trio comes to no agreement.

Amron discerns no contradiction between this political position and his research project. To improve the island's economy, he intends to assess the role that sugar plays. In pursuit of this, Saul spends a morning working in the sugar fields, observing workers who tackle the back-breaking task of harvesting as they try to keep pace with the formidable headman, Stinger (160).[11] One of them reminds Saul of a "winded wrestler being shortly *borne* down in defeat by an opponent who had proved him superior" (162). Toward the end of their shift in full tropical sun, the workers take on a "fixed flat stare . . . of someone asleep or dead" (163). Dizzy from heat and a complex historical scenario, Saul/Paul himself becomes temporarily blinded (163). Conversion or more illumination seems at hand. Saul begins to comprehend how the crop might be detrimentally affecting the islanders; furthermore, the privation and suffering he witnesses among the black workers remind him of his sephardic Jewish ancestors, who journeyed to South America after the Spanish Inquisition (163–64).[12] Saul parallels the diaspora of the Jews with that of enslaved Africans.

Unconscious of his complicity with political opponents, Amron plans to assist local people in working together. In doing so, he effectively helps to contain the community within the international world market and perpetuate the profitable criss-crossing operation. His ambiguous posture raises several questions: What about his role within the community? Why does he not see the bind he is in? With Saul around, do people have less chance of doing things for themselves? The community's role in sugar production becomes clearer as events unfold.

Saul's wife, Harriet Shippen Amron, boasts a plantocratic lineage that locates her very dubiously within Bourne society. The key character in her background is her forbearer, Susan Harbin, a slave-trade speculator who kept careful account of the "number of slaves taken on in Guinea and then just how much her portion of that cargo, both human and otherwise, had brought in crude sugar, rum and molasses in the islands" (38). Harbin carries a name ironically linked to the keeper of a lodging house (37), her very portrait revealing "calmly avaricious eyes."[13] Harriet's own name, Shippen, bespeaks a horrific shipping over killing seas that extends from Britain to West Africa and the Caribbean.

Harriet met Saul, the keynote speaker, at an event at the Philadelphia Research Institute where plans for a new overseas-and-development program were announced. Eager (it seems) to be unconventional, Harriet watched "his sword of a nose high into the light while speaking, as though to proclaim his heritage to all there. It added to his attraction, she thought, pronouncing it a 'not too extreme exotic touch'" (20).[14] Thinking she could capitalize on his vulnerability as a dedicated social reformer, she patronizingly decided to take him in hand. For Harriet, Saul had just the "right amount" of ethnic difference.

Covertly following in Aunt Susan Harbin's footsteps with Aryan arrogance, Harriet nonetheless worries about her historical lineage that plays itself out through personal anxiety about bats, eggs, and suspect philanthropic projects. The image of the bat, for instance, haunts her. First Merle expresses a hope that no one has scared Harriet away, "by telling the Lady from America about the bats and centipedes" (71). Colloquially, a bat also represents an ugly nagging woman, a shrew, and an eccentric—Harriet's oft-repeated view of Merle. At dusk, Harriet barricades the windows to control nocturnal flying animals "who had taken to flying boldly into the house from the darkness outside" (407). Her excessive precautions include filling three tilly lamps to keep bats out (447).[15]

Eggs that cannot hatch also sign Harriet and the image of an egg flags the fracture of her first marriage to boot. At breakfast one morning, "she leaned across the poached egg on her plate, maintaining a composed face and a calm voice, while she stated to her husband: 'Andrew, I've decided to leave you, dear'" (40).[16]

In her self-appointed role as community philanthropist to malnourished children and adolescents, Harriet takes it upon herself to interfere in the private domestic affairs of community members. At the home of the tireless, married field workers, Gwen and overseer Stinger, Harriet unilaterally cooks specially stored eggs that the family would exchange for a precious weekly supply of staples (180). She is above seeking permission from Gwen and Stinger. She assumes her right to do as she pleases—to cook these eggs, or anything else on hand, for the hungry children. Harriet sees herself as a Christ-like figure, bestowing omelets, instead of loaves and fishes, to the poor. To her credit, she means to feed the hungry (178). "Your values aren't necessarily the world's," an enraged Saul tells her when he finds out about her thoughtless, busybody behavior. To show Harriet's singular lack of effect, Gwen continues to sell her eggs to the postmaster despite Harriet's advice (407).

On other occasions, Harriet donates food to emaciated youngsters—"her children"—who stop by for a visit. Giving the children five eggs out of the two dozen plus she has on hand, she instructs them not to sell any of the food, "especially the eggs, but to eat everything themselves" (249). Control is all. She also buys sea eggs from the children for which they dive over and over into the cold morning sea, a high labor cost (248). Harriet represents colonialism in one of its most common disguises: "bogus philanthropy."[17]

These same children who hunt turtles also watch for the hawksbill turtle to come ashore to lay eggs. They are so poor they have to curtail the female hawksbill's life in order that they themselves might live. As reptiles with horny toothless jaws and enclosed bodies, turtles are subjected to the children's invasion, just as the community is subjected to the invasive U.S. visitors. Exigency dictates in one case and corporate profit in the other. Daphne Pollard, the sister of an "aged planter-turned-manager who rode the fields on his piebald horse," reminds Merle of Harriet, who resembles forbearer Susan Harbin of the avaricious eyes. "You never saw what she looked like. . . . She would have a servant walking along holding a big parasol over her. That woman was frightened for the sun, yes! And she was a great collector of flowers like yourself" (173). Daphne Pollard's name carries multiple associations, with her last name signifying disguise and disempowerment; Daphne, in a word, is lacking.[18] Without her seductive powers, pollard/Harriet hides who she is. Harriet's appearance also suggests secrecy and ancient rituals. Forever veiled, Harriet sports a coiffure like a monk's hood or cowl that partially hides her foremother's desire for profit and disdain for black people.

When Lyle touches Harriet, "it was not his hand resting on her, or any part of him, but rather some dark and unknown part of herself which had suddenly, for the first time ever, surfaced, appearing like stigmata or an ugly black-and-blue mark at the place he had touched" (97): Lyle flags Harriet's loathing and simultaneously represents a conjoined, repressed racism and desire—Harriet's efforts to staunch her complex feelings. Her assumed role as a philanthropist demands kindness to people whom she despises; these supercilious attitudes intensify (out of insecurity?) when a rather calculating Lyle tells Harriet that her husband Saul and Merle are lovers.[19]

This consummation occurs at the end of Carnival when they find their common ground. Cuffee's revolt, Saul confesses, made him dwell on the persecution of Jews (314). Merle then remarks on bigotry she experienced at the hands of East End Jews. Wisdom, she semi-mystically concludes, is not necessarily linked to suffering (203). Saul tells Merle about his wife Sosha, a Polish Jew who had been interned and experimented upon in Birkenau concentration camp. Following a miscarriage in Honduras during a research trip, Sosha died of complications. "I'm only now beginning to feel it all," Saul laments (323–26). He feels primarily responsible for Sosha's death because she was too far from medical aid; he had selfishly and incautiously encouraged her to come on the project without ensuring appropriate provision. After their sexual union, Ash Wednesday glides in with an "ancient calm" (339). On the heels of this bonding between Merle and Saul, the sugar mill breaks down—or so it seems. Predictably the breakdown follows the harvesting of the corporate crop, but before the community has harvested its own small, private crop. After struggling to rectify this palpable injustice, Merle suffers a severe illness and secludes herself. When Saul visits, he sees her contradictions made manifest in the memorabilia and telling artifacts, paintings, and prints among them that mark Merle's inner and outer conflicts. "It expressed her: the struggle for coherence, the hope and desire for reconciliation of her conflicting parts, the longing to truly know and accept herself (401). . . . Only an act on the scale of Cuffee's could redeem . . . the figures bound to the millwheel in the print and to each other in the packed, airless hold of the ship in the drawing" (402).

Similarly, with the symbolically warring jewelery that Merle wears, expressive pendant silver earrings in the shape of medieval European churches and numerous heavy silver bracelets, like Selina's, that jangle continually: "She moved always within the ambience of that sound. Like a monk's beads or a captive's chains, it announced her" (5). She tells Saul that her former friend—a somewhat stereotypically manipulative lesbian—"had them copied especially for me from the saints on the outside of Westminster Abbey when I told her of our hill of the same name" (327).[20] This sketch of Merle's life in England reintroduces a certain theme about same-sex relationships in Marshall's texts. The commentary matches assumptions embedded in *Brown Girl, Brownstones* and "British Guiana." In the former, friends Beryl and Selina will, the text suggests, "grow out" of their mutual physical attraction. In "British Guiana," Gerald Motley "can't help" his feelings for Sidney Parrish, wrong as he thinks they are.

The sketch of Merle's jewelery where faces strain with anxiety also returns us to the beginning where Merle halts at Westminster Low Road. When Merle becomes angry at the suspiciously timed closing of Cane Vale factory that halts community harvesting—the saints, metonymic of owners, quake in fear (386). They also shiver during Merle's final conversation with Harriet, when the Philadelphian foolishly tries to bribe Merle into leaving the island. Merle's response is decisive (437). Just as Ned Cuffee remained, so Merle will remain (442). "And stay I will. Right here in Bournehill where I belong" (442). Standing in Ned's footsteps, representing Bournehills people and all former slaves, she refuses to do Harriet's bidding: "From the way Bournehills people still go on about [Cuffee Ned], the old fellow scarcely seems dead" (422).

After various showdowns when Merle ultimately sells the Eurocentric earrings for "good money," she realizes "how different I look without them . . . the piously suffering saints were gone" (463). She has become "unburdened, restored to herself, and had even foregone the white talcum powder on her face"[21] (463). Merle is shedding the shroud of colonialism, something that Selina in *Brown Girl, Brownstones* is only beginning to learn.

Merle's bracelets, moreover, emblemize slaves' chains. Just as the earrings recall Europe's iniquitous past, so the bracelets keep Merle in tune with the Bournehills community, their clanging an ongoing colonial marker (69). Additionally, Merle's bracelets match those worn by individuals on the Bournehill Float during Carnival signifying the people who crossed the Middle Passage and (like Merle) survived to tell the tale: "The slow dragging step that carried them forward was more stated, clearly audible and regularly punctuated by the loud ring of the bracelets the women and girls wore. With each slurred step they would half-raise their arms and then, together, bring them sharply down, causing the heavy silver to fall to their wrists with a stunning clash" (282). The community reenacts the historical memory of the Atlantic Crossing/Middle Passage and the enslavement of black people over centuries:[22] "It was an awesome sound—the measured tread of those countless feet in the dust and the loud report of the bracelets, a somber counterpoint to the gay carnival celebration. It conjured up in the bright afternoon sunshine dark alien images of legions marching bound together over a vast tract, iron fitted into dank stone walls, chains— like those to an anchor—rattling in the deep holds of ships, and exile in an unknown inhospitable land—and an exile bitter and irreversible in which all memory of the former life and of the self as it had once been had been destroyed" (282). "The float displays not only Pyre Hill in flames, but also the slow rhythmic tramp and the loud ring of the bracelets [278–80], . . . spelling out on their converted oil drums the story of Cuffee and the revolt . . . the only thing they deemed worthy of their energy, the one thing to which they were willing to give themselves" (281). This rebellion inspires people yet bewilders Saul and the retinue of colonial entrepreneurs who visited Bourne before him. As U.S. agents, they deny any complicity in slavery and ignore the historical resonance of the annual float. As the float staged the ring-shout dance that spelled resistance, so slaves revolted.[23]

Following the closing of the mill by its owners after Carnival, Merle attempts to reproduce Cuffee Ned's collective spirit by condemning this callous act that shatters community complacency and disrupts their economic stability. The people, Merle believes, need to claim personal and political agency and gain a former, now long-denied autonomy.

At an informal community meeting, member Delbert vents the peoples' outrage: "We know we're not a people famous for helping out the one another," he began flatly—and there was an uncomfortable stir. "Not anymore at least. Years back when Cuffee was alive and we was running things around here ourselves we did different, maybe because we knew then that if we had lived selfish we couldn't live at all" (394). This fittingly belligerent response calls that old collective spirit into play and people start organizing to harvest their small crops (394); during this time, Saul joins the opposition to the mill owners' profiteering act energetically, but thereby pinions himself in a dangerously contradictory role—by profession, Saul trains indigenous people to enhance the profits of the project's bankrollers back in the United States. As the community representative, Delbert presents the catastrophe as a way for the community to redeem itself. "We're going to have to see whether we can't work together, help out the one another, as we did back in Cuffee's time" (395). The rollers that relentlessly crush the juice out of the cane stems' shaft, the people understand, also squeeze out their own lifeblood. Community labor benefits the exploitative capitalist international world market within which the people must function to survive.

The community uprising that followed the callous corporate act of closing the mill had been foreshadowed in a somewhat unconscious monthly resistance that took the form of a pig-sticking ritual. That event involved multiple intersections of important issues in community life—food, medicine, and ritual itself. Sow-killing feeds and nurtures people—while, as ritual, it restages the past and keeps it alive. Moreover, in medical terms, since pigs supply the insulin hormone that can cure diabetes, killing pigs can literally heal the community.[24] Pig sticking serves as an antidote to sugar.

At one of these monthly events that he witnesses, Saul senses the people's strength and solidarity as he watches them kill the sow belonging to Merle's elderly friend, Leesey. Saul's outsider status enables him to understand the "forces at their depth which he had not suspected were there" (259).[25] The humanity and collectivity around him starkly contrast with the inhumanity that Africans (and Jews) had suffered for centuries (259).

Alongside pig sticking, four other significant elements have foreshadowed the people's resistance: smoke, the sea, stones, and the cassia tree. One of these elements is the still smoldering Pyre Hill, a promontory that memorializes past slave resistance on the island. Under the leadership of the insurgent Cuffee Ned centuries ago, slaves burned the estate of Perry Bryan one night, torching the hill and adjacent cane fields: They "captured Bryan. The fire burned for five long years . . . long after Cuffee Ned was dead and the revolt put down" (102). The Pyre Hill rebels lived as a small independent nation behind a ridge that they sealed off during three years of fighting. Pyre Hill is one prominent hill among the worn range of hills that gave Bournehills its name, a recently burning "blackened heap" that might still contain embers: "You expected to see the last of the smoke drifting up from its charred sides, from its crest, blurring the air around it; and to feel the heat from it against your cheek. The ground, you were certain, would still be hot underfoot" (101).

The memory of Ned and his rebellion is indelible. Burning the pyre is another cleansing ritual, a funeral rite of the dead that constitutes a great purifying.

This smoldering fire is rekindled when Saul learns to his horror that Harriet has secretly arranged to have the grant that supported his work on the island terminated. After confronting her at home with his suspicions and an ultimatum about leaving her: "The darkness came pouring into the house: smoke, it seemed, from the final conflagration set off by the departing sun atop Westminster" (450). Reviving the earlier suggestion of insurgency, this image suggests that Saul's action bodes well.

Following Saul's outburst, Harriet foolishly visits Merle to persuade her to leave the island, and by trying to bribe her to do so, she incurs Merle's wrath. In turning the tables on Harriet, Merle ironically reminds Harriet of her mother's maid, Alberta, whose favorite spiritual was "I shall not be moved" (434).[26] No white person, that is, will easily move Merle again—not even Saul; no one will obstruct Merle's quest for herself and her family. In the name of Alberta, Merle speaks; she will leave her diasporic community, initiate a new journey that rejects colonial machinations, and return to her ancestors' roots in Africa.

The sea signifies a second mark of resistance. A constant reminder of Cuffee Ned and his rebel ancestors, the sea encircling the community is the site of the very Middle Passage itself. Early on when Merle escorts the visiting trio, Saul, his assistant Allen Fusso, and Harriet to the guesthouse, she points out the iconic Atlantic to Merle and the diasporic community: "with a sound like that of the combined voices of the drowned raised in a loud unceasing lament—all those, the nine million and more it is said, who in their enforced exile, their Diaspora, had gone down between this point and the homeland lying out of sight to the east. This sea mourned them. Aggrieved, outraged, unappeased, it hurled itself upon each of the reefs in turn and then upon the shingle beach, sending up the spume in an angry froth which the wind took and drove in like smoke over the land" (106). Harriet's reaction to this memorable sight of the sea suggests guilt (107). After solitary walks on the beach, Harriet hears "the sustained roar of outrage and grief" from the sea, but "she singly closed her mind to it" (172). She declines to confront the role that her ancestor, Susan Harbin, played in the horror of the Middle Passage journey which the sea so keenly marks. Before Harriet's drowning, the tumult of the sea thickens. In Merle's words: "the old sea's cleaning itself. It's worse this year than I've ever seen it though. The water's rougher—you don't even dare go near Horseshoe Pool, and the noise is enough to stun you. People are saying it's grieving over Vere [who has died accidentally]. But it'll be done soon" (434).

En route to suicide, Harriet cringes at the sight of people from the community because they remind her of Harbin's historical role in slavery and Harriet's own mimicking of that old role. Saul's anger at Harriet's behavior completes that offstage chorus of condemnation. Harriet recalls vividly what happens to Alberta's nephew: His "weighted body had been found at the bottom of the pond. Watched by them, borne down by their gaze, she continued on her way to the sea. And as always she heard it—the sea—long before it came into view. The massive detonation set off by the breakers on the reefs. And then the spray rising in the dazzling white toadstool of a cloud" (459).[27] The recent murder of Alberta's nephew triggers memories of the old murders on the Middle Passage, all part of an Anglocentric continuum that prioritizes profit over Africans' lives. She knows (it seems) that her death will contribute to historical redress. When the new sea comes, "it looked as though it had been endlessly filtered to remove every impurity. And all trace of the unsightly seaweed it had sloughed off like so much dead skin over the weeks was gone. Most of this had been gathered up and buried under the dunes, but some was being used as fertilizer and a small portion had been carefully washed and boiled into bush tea to be drunk as a tonic. It had lost some measure of its fury; and the high-pitched ritual keening of the lesser waves and the wind, which never ceased, had been taken to a slightly lower register. And though the sea continued to hurl itself in an excess of grief and mourning onto the shore, sending up the spume like tears, it did so with something less than its usual hysteria. Above all, the powerful undertow that had been felt even in Horseshoe Pool during the period of purification, and which everyone assumed had swept Harriet out over the low barrier of rock into the open sea, had dropped, and the water within the enclosure was manageable again" (461–62). Harriet surrenders to an obscene rest and apologizes for her self, for her ancestor, with her suicide. Significantly too, the seaweed that dissipates is a particular marine alga, not visibly with roots, that can go anywhere. The horseshoe shape of the pool—never "completed"—always suggests openness and possibility. So the seaweed healthily disperses itself as the always-open Horseshoe Pool reclaims Harriet. The elements protect the people and do the peoples' righteous work for them. The ocean insists on redemption, recompense, and retribution. Harriet's suicide by drowning, her surrender of herself to the Middle Passage, assuages the sea since one more link with slavery through Harriet's involvement in Bournehills has been severed. The resistance implied by the conflagration and a wild sea also engenders a cleansing. The fire purifies the community; the sea dies down.

A third resistance takes the form of great boulders that had roared down from Westminster (all puns intended) centuries ago and stood scattered in the sand and surf; "these, sculpted into fantastical shapes by the wind and water, might have been gravestones placed there to commemorate those millions of the drowned" (106). The boulders are revered memorials to the millions dead. These massive stones are everywhere, documenting origins and permanence that testify to human presence (251). They resemble the ancient ruins of Zimbabwe, Stonehenge, and Easter Island—sites of ancestors, colonialism, and its opposition. Collectively, they represent historically specific yet timeless transcultural crossings, just as community members and ancestors share an ancient partnership. The national break where the boulders of Horseshoe Pool formed was the only place safe to swim (156). Hence that place swallows up the invader and restores calm. Smoke, sea, and stones serve as reminders of genocide on the one hand, and the inevitability of historical retribution on the other. Smoke and bracelets cancel the power of obeah: "Smoke is one of the best protections against any form of obeah, we believe in Bournehills. These for another." She shook the noisy bracelets covering nearly her entire forearm: "Their racket is enough to keep the devil himself away" (319).

Lastly, in Merle's garden, the cassia tree symbolizes another emblem of serene rebellion. Almost constantly leafless, it suddenly flowers for a very short time. In that moment, "making the tree look as if it were always in the sunshine," the cassia tree functions as another cleanser of crimes and a marker of healing.[28] Famous for its cathartic qualities, the tree purges impurities that are plaguing the community. The elements anthropomorphically reflect the popular will. After Harriet's death, for example, the natural order slowly transforms itself. Until then, the sea has been furious, awaiting atonement for countless forced crossings and murders.

In contrast appear signs of stasis, of a quietism that relentless domination can foster. Slavery and racist practices inevitably take their toll, sometimes in self-defeating ways that Vereson Walkes, for one, exemplifies. Grandson of Leesey Walkes, the community ancestor warrior and Merle's friend, he emerges as an unwitting victim of colonialism who has internalized its values. Vereson and Saul Amron's group coincidentally arrive in Bourne on the same plane, the former hard at work for three years in the United States in a demeaning labor scheme. Wearing a large blue hat ordered from the *Ebony* mail order catalogue, Vereson Walkes is someone who displaces his ire at discrimination onto another diasporic victim (31–32). Specifically, he pursues a vendetta against the young prostitute who bore his baby. While scheming to avenge himself on the mother of his dead child, he attempts to win the Whitsun race by rebuilding a German car. The back of his trousers conceals a cane with which he eventually beats the mother. Like overseers of old or like Stinger with his invisible whip, Vere uses the (sugar) cane—product of their own labor—against his people. His dreams suffuse him. Named after "versant," the slope of a mountain, Vereson Walkes is continually sloping downward.[29] He plays out the truth (*vere*) of historical atrocity in perpetuating imperial corruption. Markers abound regarding the stasis that exists and the transformation that Leesey initially predicted when Merle and she confronted the collapse of Westminster Low Road. Hence the ubiquity of the almshouse or poorhouse in the novel, the most prominent resident of which is a young man named Seifert (whose name contains the word *cipher*, a person without influence or value).[30]

When Vereson Walkes dies, "he was staring like Seifert at the almshouse straight up into the sun through the fernlike leaves of the tamarind. Beside him in the dust, holding his head with its broken neck between her hands knelt a distraught, loudly weeping Merle" (368). Merle also holds an almshouse status, but she declines her cipher status (328, 470). The almshouse children are finally united: Vere, Seifert, their slave ancestors, and all dispossessed people. The sea grieves for the truth of history—Vereson Walkes—for its cargo from Middle Passage, for what colonial powers still perpetrate and perpetuate. The workers themselves, moreover, unwittingly advance colonialism by providing cheap labor. No decent paying jobs on the island exist for the majority of people.

Sugar and slavery, the text hints, are still inseparable since a sugar monoculture is little more than slavery dressed up in new clothes. Legal slaves may be dead, but plantocratic ghosts and a slave-owning mentality live on. The local estate manager named Pollard appears occasionally in the cane fields like "some ghost who refused to keep to his grave even during the day time" (161), his demeanor invoking overseers of the past.[31] He is a man of the people, yet economically forced to wear an overseer's costume.

By the end when Merle leaves, the irony of the novel's title, *The Chosen Place, the Timeless People*, stands sharply exposed. Saul Amron is unexpectedly divided, by no means one of the chosen people. The place called chosen is being exploited by those who did the choosing: slavery's entrepreneurs. Its people, by now deeply rooted, are subjugated historically, anything but timeless. Their lineage may be in Africa, ancient and honorable, but events constantly change them.

Yet in the end, the people transcend a plantocratic tradition and reassert Cuffee Ned's modus operandi. They act collectively and hence help dissolve historical corruption. Harriet, for example, has died in an act that helps healing, envisioned by the ancestral Leesey. The timeless Leesey herself is the sibyl who prophesies the end. But colonial co-optation has also contaminated people once again. Vere dies, although the nameless sex worker/mother whom Vere attacks victoriously survives. Merle departs to track her daughter in Africa, while Vere's daughter and the progeny of Saul and Sosha are both dead. So Merle's daughter for whom she will search in Africa represents the future. In questing for her daughter, Merle leaves the diasporic community for the African continent—the grand origin, ultimately plundered by predators.

CHAPTER 5

Water and Nomenclature
Praisesong for the Widow

At the end of *The Chosen Place, the Timeless People*, Merle Kinbona goes historically home. From the Caribbean to Brazil, the United States, and across Africa itself from Dakar to Kampala. Her mission corporealizes the constant longing of slaves themselves, forced across the Middle Passage, to go back home to Africa. Whether Merle will ultimately find her daughter remains as unknown as the future, but the possibility is imaginable.

In *Praisesong for the Widow*, protagonist Avatara (Avey) Williams Johnson initially refuses to travel to her ancestral home when she disdains the ardent advice of her radical daughter Marian: "Why go on some meaningless cruise with a bunch of white folks anyway, I keep asking you? What's that supposed to be about.... I begged you to go on that tour to Brazil, and ... to Ghana ... learn something!"[1]

Having put her life on hold, declining to face the past, Avey joins the white community in North White Plains. Estranged from family and community, and even her own name, Avey has become "a woman whose face, reflected in a window or mirror, she sometimes failed to recognize" (141). Avatara Johnson has gone; she is, as it were, absent. But despite Avey's temporary embrace of assimilation and Anglocentric values and her denial of her African-Caribbean roots, the sea exerts a pull in contradictory directions. Unconsciously, she identifies with the heritage of slavery without any direct address to the fact of its being. To her surprise, the seemingly desirable situation aboard the luxury cruise ceases to be enjoyable. Unaware of any specific cause for her discomfort, Avey embarks on an adventure that will detach her from her diasporic home emotionally and spiritually.

Praisesong for the Widow opens with Avey Johnson preparing to leave her two unsuspecting friends on board the Bianca Pride liner in the midst of a luxury cruise. Three years earlier, one year after the death of her husband, Jerome Johnson, the thought of such a cruise had captivated her, perhaps by offering her a conventional chance to escape; Avey Johnson had not only been widowed, but had become alienated from her community, her past, and her personal feelings. Loosely speaking, Avatara Johnson had lost sight of who she was: "With a strength born of the decision that had just come to her in the middle of the night, Avey Johnson forced the suitcase shut on the clothes piled inside and slid the lock into place" (9).

Yet life had not always seemed bleak during a happy childhood and adolescence on Seventh Avenue, Harlem. During her marriage to Jerome Johnson, they lived for twenty years in a fifth-floor walkup on Halsey Street where they shared small but loving rituals together during scant leisure time. These private moments fortified them against the rigors and bigotry of daily life. As a rejoinder to silent discrimination, Jay sported a lively moustache. Later they inherited an old house from Avey's father's great-aunt Cuney on the South Carolina tidewater, in the Sea Islands of Gullah. During their summers together, Cuney entrusts the then child Avey with "a mission she couldn't even name yet had felt duty-bound to fulfill" (42).[2]

Prior to sending Avey for the summer to great-aunt Cuney in Tatem, the Williams family enjoy an annual boat ride sponsored by the neighborhood social club that takes community members and tourists up the Hudson River to Bear Mountain aboard the steamship Robert Fulton:[3] "Boat rides up the Hudson were always something . . . momentous and global. As more people arrived to throng the area beside the river and the cool morning air warmed to the greetings and talk, she would feel what seemed to be hundreds of slender threads streaming out from her navel and from the place where her heart was to enter those around her. And the threads went out not only to people she recognized from the neighborhood but to those she didn't know as well, such as the roomers just up from the South and the small group of West Indians whose odd accent called to mind Gullah talk" (190).[4] Having felt solid bonds with this community, Avey tries to maintain these close connections after her marriage to Jerome, despite financial difficulties.

Times change, however, as the family grows and their circumstances straiten. In 1947, eight months pregnant with her third child, Avey threatens to leave Jerome and take the children with her for she worries daily about where Jerome is before he returns home. After this explosive episode, he transforms his life by taking on several jobs and going to school to "better" himself. Having successfully passed the CPA exams four years later, he is employed in keeping the books for large stores, businesses, and fraternal organizations. To complement his new life, he joins the freemasons in a move that is both good for business and a contribution to community solidarity. Eventually, as a result of his hard work and advancement, the couple buy a beautiful home in the symbolically named North White Plains. In a second symbolic gesture not long after, Jay shaves off his moustache. The transformation from the carefree Jay to the hard-working Jerome Johnson is complete. Having purchased a modest accounting firm on Fulton Street, he dies soon after, presumably of overwork.

At the prompting of her friend, Thomasina Moore, Avey embarks on the first of several cruises a year after her husband's death in a move, perhaps, to distance herself from that early life. With all its "dazzling white steel," the sight of the symbolically and Latinate/imperial-named liner Bianca Pride magnetizes her when she first boards. Its computer rendered the passengers "awestruck and reverent . . . there had been no resisting it" (15). Avey internalizes values that equate cruises with good living. But her seeming pleasure and internal tranquility start disintegrating during her third cruise aboard the same liner, the source of her restlessness a mystery.[5] The memories and experiences that a bigoted society has forced her to suppress start surfacing. She senses a "mysterious clogged and swollen feeling . . . like a huge tumor" (52). Has living comfortably in North White Plains enjoying indulgent holidays, out of touch with great-aunt Cuney's aspirations for her—unsettled Avey Johnson?

Nauseous and disenchanted with the spirited frivolities on board ship day and night, she identifies only with a clay pigeon that had been fired from the deck: "rushing in a straight desperate line toward the upper air, as far above the ship as possible" (57). Other passengers strike her as "padded neanderthal men clubbing each other," reminiscent, she muses, of sadistic white police officers whom she and Jay had watched many years ago as they enthusiastically applied their night sticks to a solitary black man (56).[6]

This inchoate panic erupts at dinner when a delicious dessert in the shape of the Palace of Versailles repels her;[7] a dream later in which she vigorously wars with an enraged great-aunt Cuney crystallizes this nasty experience. These two events, her repulsion at the imperial-referenced dessert and the dream, propel her to leave the cruise. Furthermore, both events are linked to Avey Johnson's earlier visit to the volcanic museum in Martinique that she took with her friends from the cruise.

Known as the "Little Paris of the West Indies," the original village of St. Pierre stood as the cultural capital of Martinique until the disastrous earthquake of 1902. Long considered a benign volcano, Mount Pelée presented no risk to the population—or so people thought—any more "than Vesuvius does to the Neapolitans."[8] At 8 a.m. on May 8, 1902, however, the southwest side of the mountain massively exploded, pelting fire and lava on the population. Two minutes later, meltdown heat, toxic gas clouds, and an arching roof of hot ash incinerated 30,000 people—the town of St. Pierre, no more, no less. A black convict incarcerated in a dungeon underground amazingly survived the power of nature.[9]

Witnessing the ruins of that earthquake affects Avey deeply: "She kept seeing with mystifying clarity the objects on display in the museum in the town of St. Pierre at the foot of Mt. Pelée, which she had visited three days previously in Martinique. There, in room after room, she had examined the twisted, scarcely recognizable remains of the gold and silver candlesticks and snuffboxes, jewelry, crucifixes and the like that had been the prized possessions of the well-to-do of St. Pierre before the volcano had erupted at the turn of the century, burying the town in a sea of molten lava and ash. She might enter the dining room tomorrow night to find everything reduced to so many grotesque lumps of metal and glass by a fire like the one she had seen raging aboard the liner for an instant that morning from the launch" (83). The meaning of these artifacts, somehow, resonates deep within her. Like Mount Pelée's victims, Avey not only feels buried alive, but seems to begin to know the pointlessness of prized possessions—of the house and goods in White Plains, New York, that she and Jay struggled so obsessively to obtain. These, she concludes, can disappear at any time.

And in just the way Avey's hard-won house could "melt," so now aboard the liner the sun is creating an eerie optical effect in which it appears to obliterate the liner—that is, Bianca or white pride. Once again, the forces of nature are palpable but this time, nature is causing the massive self-proclamation of the liner to disintegrate. Collapsing facades expose the fragility of so-called civilization:

> She turned only to have her eyes assaulted by what looked like a huge flash fire of megaton intensity and heat, as the tropical sunlight striking the liner's bow and sweeping over the hull appeared to have set it ablaze. She could almost feel over the distance the heat from the fires on the decks. Then, abruptly, as she shifted her line of vision away from the glare, it all vanished, and there was the Bianca Pride lying huge, serene and intact out in the deep water. (63)

Thus, Avey begins to match up relics from the debris with the ruin of her own life. No guarantees of permanence exist since a life of accumulation can disintegrate in two minutes. Representing ancient ways, the volcano's eruption instructs her, its lesson affirming the validity of great-aunt Cuney's actions and narrative as well as her keen sense of history.

That near annihilation prompts Avey's unfathomable desire in dreams that night to abandon the cruise: "Tired after a long day spent ashore on Martinique, during which she and her companions had traveled overland for hours to visit the volcano, Mount Pelée, she had gone to bed early that evening, only to find herself confronted the moment she dropped off to sleep by her great-aunt Cuney" (31).

Memories of great-aunt Cuney are triggered by the sight of the artifacts and the sole survivor of this involuntary "natural" genocide, and perhaps by a memory of her great-aunt's powers.[10] The need to remember old beliefs and know her historical location is affecting Avey. Since Cuney played a major role in instructing Avey on the importance of tradition and time-honored beliefs during their summers together on Tatem Island, she reappears, so to speak, to remind Avey. Cuney herself had bestowed on her the name of Avatara: "the name of someone people had sworn was crazy" (42). But Avey's state of mind induced a dream that severely distorted early experiences with her great-aunt. This dream made manifest her current angst.

During the Augusts that Avey spent as a young girl on Tatem Island where Gullah is spoken, said to be the closest linguistic relative in the United States to African languages, she and her great-aunt took the same walk every day.[12] It led them past a wood that a white man had swindled from a black man named Shad Dawson. Then they passed a church that held great significance for Cuney. Years earlier at a church ceremony, Cuney had broken a taboo by crossing her feet during a certain ritual named a Ring Shout circle dance.[13] Although only banished temporarily from the ceremony, Cuney became unable to accept such a punishment and refused to return.

The community believed that Cuney's ritualistic walks with her grand-niece past the church partly substituted for her abandoned participation at the Ring Shout circle dances: "People in Tatem said she had made the Landing her religion after that" (34). Standing secretly in the darkened road, Cuney and Avey periodically watched the dancers through an open door, while Avey clandestinely mimicked the dancers: "She performed their 'little rhythmic trudge' i.e. the ring shout dance" (35). This trudge echoes the same ancestral "slow rhythmic tramp" that Merle Kinbona and the Bourne Island community witnessed at Carnival. In the last lap of their hike, Avey and her great-aunt Cuney unconsciously connect their slave ancestry with the volcanic eruption and their contemporary lives.

After leaving the populated area, the couple reach a vast former plantation of sea-island cotton that had been destroyed during General Sherman's march "of blood and fire up from Atlanta" to the sea.[14] Like the decimated St. Pierre, the plantation remained in its original state of devastation (36), the sight invoking its given name and ancient ancestry, Gullah and Sea Islands, the latter a signifier for cotton in today's capitalist world.

The last lap of the walk, the climax of the journey, brought the pair to the place that Tatem dwellers call the Landing.[15] At this point without fail, great-aunt Cuney told Avey the same story every day in order (so we learn) to attune her niece to white society. The long but significant landing narrative concerns Ibo people from West Africa who had been transported as slaves across the Middle Passage to this very location:

> Those Ibos didn't miss a thing. Even seen you and me standing here talking about 'em. And when they got through sizing up

the place real good and seen what was to come, they turned, my gran' said, and looked at the white folks what brought 'em here. . . . And when they got through studying 'em, when they *knew* just from looking at'em how those folks was gonna do, do you know what the Ibos did? Do you. . . ? ". . . They just turned, my gran' said, all of 'em—" "and walked on back down to the edge of the river here. Every las' man, woman and chile. And they wasn't taking they time no more. They had seen what they had seen and those Ibos was stepping! And they didn't bother getting back into the small boats drawed up here—boats take too much time. They just kept walking right on out over the river. Now you wouldna thought they'd of got very far seeing as it was water they was walking on. Besides they had all that iron on 'em. Iron on they ankles and they wrists and fastened 'round they necks like a dog collar. 'Nuff iron to sink an army. And chains hooking up the iron. But chains didn't stop those Ibos none. . . . And when they got to where the ship was they didn't so much as give it a look. Just walked on past it. . . . When they realized there wasn't nothing between them and home but some water and that wasn't giving 'em no trouble they got so tickled they started in to singing. You could hear 'em clear across Tatem 'cording to her. They sounded like they was having such a good time my gran' declared she just picked herself up and took off after 'em. In her mind. Her body she always usta say might be in Tatem but her mind, her mind was long gone with the Ibos. . . ." (37–39)

Cuney is an appropriate chronicler of the Ibos landing since linguistically as well as historically, she is linked to the original crossing from Tatem Island to Africa. Only once during the twice-weekly summer recitals of this history did Avey interrupt Cuney to pose a curious question: "But how come they didn't drown, Aunt Cuney?" (39).[16]

Cuney's astounded response to what she considered an inappropriate question took Avey years to forget: "the look on the face under the field hat, the disappointment and sadness there." After Cuney reminds a mortified Avey that Jesus was not drowned when he walked on water, Cuney then quizzes her niece sternly: "you got any more questions?" Avey shakes her head, indicating "no" (40).

The significance of the Ibo crossing is not lost on Avery, but she cannot yet conceptualize what she hears though one thing is clear. She feels "entrusted with a future mission she couldn't even name yet had felt duty-bound to fulfill." That old knowledge notwithstanding, when she abandons the cruise, she still does not remember that injunction about a mission. Over the years, she has tried to slough off any sense of her responsibility to Cuney's unspoken request.

However, Avey's vivid dream on the Bianca Pride revives that sense of mission. In the dream, Cuney beckons Avey to take their usual walk—driving a wedge, as the derivation of Cuney's name implies, between Avey's diasporic present and the life she had recommended to her grand-niece on their walks. Great-aunt Cuney's name is worth pondering. It derives from the Latin *cuneus*, meaning wedge, while also giving rise to the word *cuneiform*. This latter term designates the wedge-shaped characters used in ancient Sumerian, Akkadian, Assyrian, Babylonian, and Persian writing.[17] Thus metaphorically, Cuney is a wedge between Avey and the white world that cheats Shad Dawson out of his wood as she keeps doors open and keeps history in play. *Wedge* also signifies Cuney's transcultural, transhistorical, and global character. Avey up till now has declined to follow in Cuney's footsteps. Specifically, Avey sports a new spring suit in her dream as she hurries to a fancy Masonic luncheon at the Statler Hotel where she will sit on the dais with her Master Mason husband, Jerome Johnson (45). When Avey refuses in her dream to go on the ritualistic walk, great-aunt Cuney charges toward her, in a staging of Avey's struggle to withstand great-aunt Cuney's power. Then the pair engage in a tug-of-war, witnessed by Avey's neighbors in North White Plains who feel affirmed in their racist assumptions as they watch and eavesdrop on this violent family quarrel. Cuney is transporting Gullah to the Statler Hotel, metaphorically destabilizing the imperial center in an intervention that renders Avey distraught.

The vision renders great-aunt Cuney as a preacher in a Holiness church, imploring sinners and backsliders to come forward to the mercy seat. Cuney begs Avey: "*Come/O will you come. . . ?*" (42). Avey no longer seems capable of the "two giant steps" her aunt formerly encouraged her to take (33). The Avatara who was instructed by Cuney has temporarily disappeared.

During the fight, Avey's emblematic mink stole flies up in the air and lands "with a sound like an expiring breath (44) . . . a creature [the mink] wantonly slain and flung" (44). In a sense, Avey is wearing her conditioning, the semi-aquatic stoat-like animal that always symbolizes a lavish lifestyle. Moreover, the mink is assimilation, an animal that would be considered destructive in a farming (or former farming) community like Tatem. This fur wrap represents Avey's stolen cultural birthright. Hence her incapacity to answer great-aunt Cuney's pressing but mute plea: "Come/Won't y– Come." Frozen inside and severed from her past, alienated from the dreams and rituals that she and Jay shared in their carefree early days together, she cannot yet surrender the old life that her husband died to construct.

Great-aunt Cuney, on the other hand, is a survivor who wants Avey to join the ranks of the opposition. She is trying to pry Avey loose from her role as the Master Mason's wife, from her pact with Faust that yields so little.[18] Certainly, Jerome Johnson attained the third degree of Freemasonry (are all ironies intended in this language?) and he is being buried in the white lambskin apron and white gloves of a Master Mason, which represent his entitlement (87). Visually and symbolically, his accomplishments and the sight of him at his death in his ceremonial Masonic garb spell the couple's distance from their original dreams. But the Masonic clothes also mark the couple's refusal to cut themselves off completely because they are also important members of a Masonic community effort to unite against racist organizations and practices.

Consciously or unconsciously, Jerome Johnson knows the dubious political significance of belonging to a Masonic Lodge that emphasizes a secret universal fraternity and encourages its members to study and be philanthropic. He further understands the complicity involved in passing the CPA exam and taking on "the accounts of fraternal organizations such as the Elks and the Masons, which he also thought it in his interest to join" (120). Although they purport to maintain community bonds, Masons are often equated with self-conscious Anglo-ethnicity; they are known as a white institution whose members frequently scorn and even disavow black Masonry. Many Masons belong to the Ku Klux Klan.[19] In connection with the political turnaround of Jay and herself to a more traditional viewpoint, Avey muses on their discussion, and especially on her own involvement:

> What kind of bargain had they struck? How much had they foolishly handed over in exchange for the things they had

gained?—An exchange they could have avoided altogether had they been on their guard!

Too much! " . . . Hadn't she lived through most of the sixties and the early seventies as if Watts and Selma and the tanks and Stoner guns in the streets of Detroit somehow did not pertain to her? (139–40)

In addition, Avey's dream quarrel with great-aunt Cuney invokes memories of political altercations with her youngest daughter, Marion, who politically takes after Cuney. A child of the Civil Rights movement, Marion positively and peacefully participates in the Black Power movement, eager to embrace cultural alterity. Born in the weeks following her father's transformation from Jay to Jerome Johnson on that fateful Tuesday in 1947, Marion comes of age during the politically active early sixties. She is the family's Cuney-like conscience in civil rights matters. Even as a baby, "the huge eyes that were Jay's would look in their faces in such a way at times it seemed she had come to judge them all" (118–19). Marion remonstrates with her mother, as Cuney does in the dream, for going "on some meaningless cruise with a bunch of white folks . . . What's that supposed to be about?" (27).

At one with great-aunt Cuney's mission and image, Marion pleads with her mother to dissociate herself from white [*biancan*] pride. In that respect, Marion also resembles her namesake, the black singer Marian Anderson, who defiantly sang on the steps of Independence Hall after being forbidden to sing inside by the conservative Daughters of the Revolution.[20] Marian Anderson had "poise and reserve [and] the look of acceptability about her. She would never be sent to eat in the kitchen when company came!" (49).

Committed to nonviolence and proud of her economic roots, Marion Johnson was a teenager when the Black Power movement exploded. Intrepidly, Marion joined the Poor People's March on Washington: "the great hungry roar of the thousands encamped in the mud near the Lincoln Memorial, the sound reaching out to draw her into its angry vortex, to make her part of their petition" (140). When Marion phones her mother collect from that March, Avey is so threatened by the political destabilization that she almost refuses the phone charges. Marion teaches in a community school, visits Brazil and China, and wears—not crêpe de chine and pearls like her mother—but a "noisy necklace of cowrie shells and amber she had brought back from Togo her last visit" (13–14).

Symbolically, Marion has already danced in the Ring Shout in Tennessee with great-aunt Cuney and walked to the Landing. A woman of her times, a Cuney update, Marion chooses to associate with black not white pride.

In tune with her roots and ancestry, Marion has studied both received and untraditional cultural history. As a case in point, prior to the cruise when Avey mentions the word *Versailles*, Marion leaps on the word and scorns it: *"Do you know how many treaties were signed there, in that infamous Hall of Mirrors, divvying up India, the West Indies, the world? Versailles—repeating it with a hopeless shake of her head"* (47). This remark about Versailles distinctly locates Marion on her great-aunt's global continuum. Unlike Avey, Marion will not be isolated from her ancestors. She understands how people of color were affected by the Treaty of Versailles that was signed on June 28, 1919 in the Hall of Mirrors. Technically ending World War I, the treaty further colonized people of color around the world.[21]

Germany, for example, ceded its leasehold on Shantung to Japan and renounced all its overseas colonies, which were placed under a mandate of the League of Nations. Allied forces that had occupied territories during the war received mandates to govern. Many countries in the Third World were involved in these arbitrary redistributions and expansions of land among hegemonic, white western nations. Marion's discourse, moreover, helps to precipitate the third event—alongside the museum visit and the dream—that rocks Avey.

At the dinner table the night before Avey mysteriously decides to leave the cruise, she becomes disgusted with a delicious-looking dessert, symbolically named Parfait à la Versailles. Avey does not link this disgust with Marion's remonstrations about the Anglo-centered carving-up of the "third world" at the Treaty of Versailles. Yet unconsciously she remembers. At this point, the visit to the volcanic museum, her suppressed feelings about being buried alive, her great-aunt's chastisements about living as a rich white person, and Marion's insistence on tradition collectively devastate Avey. The opening of *Praisesong for the Widow* signposts Avey Johnson's imminent eruption. Close to exploding "with a strength born of the decision that had just come to her in the middle of the night, Avey Johnson forced the suitcase shut on the clothes piled inside and slid the lock into place" (1). The vestigial fragments of her old, bottled-up life chime with something she saw at the volcanic museum—perhaps little more than a memory. The dream involving Aunt Cuney affirms this new insight and induces nausea at the dessert. Slowly, as her facade of order starts to crumble, Avey decides to leave the cruise unceremoniously, even before Clarice and Thomasina Moore awaken.

Inevitably, the friends who discover her in the act of packing think that she's "done gone and lost her mind" (24). They are unaware of Avey's self-alienation, although the occasional visibility of pink skin under Avey's lip is the hidden sign that at least minimal resistance was alive; Clarice "was met instead by the underlip Avey Johnson had left thrusting forward slightly so that the knife edge of raw pink was still visible, and by the expression in her eyes of someone who had already left the cabin and the ship and was well on her way somewhere else" (24).

After Avey arrives in Grenada, en route to her projected return to North White Plains, she approaches a perplexing sight: a pier jam-packed with happy black vacationers that serves as a reminder that Avey has been vacationing on the Bianca Pride with predominantly white tourists. The pier overflowing with people taking off for their annual visit to Carriacou also means she cannot hail a taxi. Carriacou is the largest island in the Grenadines, a forty-mile chain that leads to Grenada, populated by the descendants of African slaves. Avey's sense of being an outsider in this joyful crowd erupts in another telling memory.

As a taxi finally transports her to an opulent Grenadian hotel on the first wing of her return home from the cruise, Avey finds herself within sight of the Grande Anse beach—the great cup or handle. She is gradually signaling that she is about to grab that handle, so to speak, and climb into a new life. At that point, she catches herself thinking about certain key events from her past, especially a certain time when she was nearly in tears during a weekend trip to the Laurentians with members of Jerome's Masonic lodge and their wives. Among the guests were Thomasina Moore, her present cruise companion, and Thomasina's dentist husband. A range of Canadian mountains north of the St. Lawrence River, the Laurentians contain ancient Precambrian rocks. This ancestral trope transports Avey again to the past she is trying to recover. The sight of the mountains puts her in mind of an "esquimo" practice into which she projects herself and her own fears: old people are sent outside alone in the snow to die. Empathizing with the hunched, moribund figures of old women, Avey senses that she, too, is outliving her usefulness. She no longer knows her name, nor indulges in rituals that offset daily bigotry. Solace, alongside passion, have vanished from her life. "The names 'Avey' and 'Avatara' were those of someone who was no longer present, and she had become Avey Johnson even in her thoughts, a woman whose face, reflected in a window or mirror, she sometimes failed to recognize" (141). After Avey recapitulates this fleeting set of associations, the taxi driver deposits her at a hotel that complements, both architecturally and ideologically, the Bianca Pride: a "towering structure of stark white concrete and glass done in a 'ski slope' design," it is another bourgeois masterpiece (80).

Having fled to the beach on arrival, an exhausted Avey stops at a rum shop named Rock Haven, so fatigued by all her recent experiences that she pours her heart out to its venerable proprietor, Lebert Joseph.[22] His emblematic role in Avey's healing is apparent. When she first sees him, he is quietly mending something behind a partition, bearing the look of a St. Pierre survivor, "having undergone a lifetime trial by fire" (160–61). He has already completed the journeys that Avey now contemplates.

On a continuum with great-aunt Cuney and Marion in their efforts to regain Avey's soul, Lebert Joseph is an Old Testament prophet, warning Avey not to neglect her ancestors, nor ignore people like him: "I tell you, you best remember them!" he cried (165). But Avey is still floundering. All she can recall of her ancestry at this point is a faint memory of the word *juba*, a dance rendered by women in long skirts facing each other (177).[23]

Having reached a certain, almost comfortable level of intimacy with Avey after she confides in him, Lebert Joseph invites her to visit Carriacou during the annual celebratory community excursion from Grenada that she had witnessed at the pier. After some demurring, she accepts.

Symbolically defined as a "two-master," the schooner they will board sports an unusual figurehead in the shape of an eaten-away Christ figure, an ancestor of sorts, holding a divining rod. This schooner's name is Emanuel C. Part of an unwieldy flotilla, this boat annually carries people who work in Grenada back to Carriacou where they hail from.[24] The extravagant pageantry of the expedition includes a display of huge unfurled sails, suggesting spectacle on a ritualistic scale. But this anti-Santa Maria flotilla is afloat, not with "bianca" but with black pride. Avey has boarded a very different kind of ship.

Avey soon experiences a sense of community among the female passengers who remind Avey of the presiding mothers in her own church. These feelings of camaraderie make her think of the emptiness of her own life, how it resembles a hollow, yawning Mount Pelée crater (196). The feeling of sisterhood further reminds Avey of her radical daughter Marion's fond remembrances of visiting Ghana, "of something called a New Yam, of a golden stool that descended from the sky, and of ancestors who were to be fed" (188). Avey's new experiences are causing her to connect with her politically aware daughter. And just at that moment, not uncoincidentally, she excavates another tender, buried memory: "the annual boat ride up the Hudson River to Bear Mountain" (188).

Avey recalls conversations between her happy, sprucely attired parents about the boat always being late and the implied racial overtones of the steamship's invariable tardiness. Such loving remembrances of being among people she grew up with and dearly loved rarely moved her these days, reoccurring only when she mentally stood beside great-aunt Cuney outside the church in Tatem and watched the congregation perform the Ring Shout. On these occasions, her navel and heart seemed to radiate slender threads galore, connecting Avey with people who mattered to her life. As long as she felt those threads, she deduced, she would never be lost, alone, or in danger: "she became part of, indeed the center of, a huge wide confraternity" (191).

In line with great-aunt Cuney and even with the helpless clay pigeon on the liner, these people beckon her (196). Soon the schooner's motion as well as her memories stir up how she sometimes used to feel at church. During the Reverend Morrissey's fire and brimstone sermon, she would feel like vomiting due to overeating. On board the schooner, the pastor's sermon now churns over in her mind. Memory and feelings of affiliation enable Avey to purge herself of the "mass of overly rich, indigestible food that had lodged itself like an alien organ beneath her heart and needed to be expelled" (207). She vomits profusely, revisiting the scene onboard the Bianca Pride when she gagged at the Versailles dessert; simultaneously she revisits the nausea of Middle Passage. This epiphanic self-cleansing liberates Avey Johnson. At Lemuel's encouragement, the trip on the Emanuel C. has empowered her to evacuate years of accumulated rubbish. It comes up "through her mouth and down past her navel. Down through the maze of her intestines. Down into her bowel" (207).

Her subsequent exhaustion as she lies on a bunk inside the cramped deckhouse reminds her of millions of captive ancestors who journeyed the notorious crossing over the Middle Passage, forced to lie in their own excrement:

> She had the impression as her mind flickered on briefly of other bodies lying crowded in with her in the hot, airless dark. A multitude it felt like lay packed around her in the filth and stench of themselves, just as she was. Their moans, rising and falling with each rise and plunge of the schooner, enlarged upon the one filling her head. Their suffering—the depth of it, the weight of it in the cramped space—made hers of no consequence. (209)[25]

Emptied now, she is channelling ancestral suffering and the commonality (as well as difference) of people across centuries and continents; she starts to comprehend the magnitude of what she rejected, of speaking "from the blood" (137). Up till now, she had abandoned positive cultural practices—music, dancing, and praise song immediately spring to mind—that she shared with Jerome Johnson and church members respectively. In those moments of transformation, she experiences a sense of the hard-tempered inner metal left over from ancestral devastation; only "cast-iron hearts and muscles tempered to the consistency of steel remain" (161); only iron survives fire, ubiquitous in diverse forms in the lives of these survivors. The musical instruments made of iron unite the archipelago and draw Ogun Feraille, the stalwart god of iron, into their midst (246–47).[26] Having ventured the crossing, Avey is poised for reentry into the richness of community life. She had earned the right to join the dance that celebrates stones, the Big Drum dance; this ritual is part of a stone feast called *saraca* that marks the setting of a tombstone, when a grave is entombed or formally marked with a tombstone. The Reverend Morrissey, she recalls, sermonized about stones that have "done buried your spirit." What is happening to Avey now has long been within her.

Thus Avey becomes an active participant in a fragmented, post-slavery life that upholds and honors tradition. Metonymically, Avey is experiencing a post-volcanic life in the sense that she has survived massive eruption and the sight of the "the bare bones. The burnt out ends" (240). But that very crucial residue itself rekindles vitality: "new thoughts—vague and half-formed [were] slowly beginning to fill the emptiness. . . . Anybody that feels to [sic] can dance now" (240–41). Avey is ready to bare "the menacing sliver of pink" on her lip and join the dance and the community, "cautiously at first, each foot edging forward as if the ground under her was really water—muddy river water—and she was testing it to see if it would hold her weight. . . . She had finally after all these decades [she realized] made it across, . . . part of what seemed a far-reaching, wide-ranging confraternity." Avey performs the rhythmic trudge "designed to stay the course of history" (246–50). She has begun to repeat Cuney's stride on their walks together, "designed to cover an entire continent in a day" (242). She finally tunes into the world of the South Carolina tidewater in the Sea Islands of Gullah. Emanating from the navels and castiron hearts on board the Robert Fulton and outside the church in Tatem respectively, the threads entwine and embrace her. Indigenous ritual and resistance have cancelled the western colonial exploitation that did Jay to death and ground down her avid spirit with him. Heralded by avatar Joseph, the community bows to her, acknowledging the power of her name Avey, short for Avatara. She receives their praise song that prepares her for a new beginning "without being trapped in imitation."[27]

At one with Cuney and Jay, she can also feel a sense of unity with her friend Thomasina Moore. The trip to Carriacou has healed that division. Avey's new response to Thomasina Moore decisively marks her change, her crossing over to a location that her friend had already occupied. Specifically Thomasina Moore's actions demonstrated her love for and proud connection with the past that Avey was unable to share. Perhaps Thomasina always had more (Moore) than Avey. Avey had formerly cared much more about leaving her friend Clarice behind, despite the fact that Thomasina Moore had arranged the cruises for the last three years. Even Marion had not understood the fracture between Avey and Thomasina Moore: "'Why go on some meaningless cruise with a bunch of white folks anyway, I keep asking you?' Marion had cried. 'What's that supposed to be about? Couldn't you think of something better to do on your vacation? And since when have you started letting Thomasina Moore decide how you should spend it? You don't even like the woman'" (13–14). But the activities on Carriacou alter Avatara's knowledge of her friend.

Less conflicted than Avey Johnson about her identity, Thomasina Moore may occasionally explode, but she still plays the part expected of her on the cruise; she understands, rather than internalizes, assimilation. Dressed with flair in Pucci-print evening culottes dictated by her show-business background, Thomasina blends "easily with the hundreds of other faces at the tables" (48), while remembering the rape of her mother who then gave birth to a light-complexioned baby (19). Middle Passage memories metaphorically resonate in Thomasina Moore—she burns a night light, her sleep punctuated and disturbed with an "ominous implosive clucking at the roof of her mouth," a sound that chimes with the sound of certain African languages (12). On a nightly basis, then, Thomasina Moore may return to the hold of the notorious ancestral ship. Bewildered during the cruise, Avey has been estranged from this powerful friend who encapsulates historical harmony. She does not reconnect until the community dance begins.

In Cartagena, moreover, a stopping off point on the cruise, Thomasina had abandoned Clarice and Avey to dance animatedly in Carnival; she had disdained the stares of surprised white passengers: "White faces laughing! White hands applauding! Avey Johnson had never been so mortified. And she had returned, the woman—laughing proudly, with the jumpsuit she had on soaked through under the arms, and in her laugh, in her flushed face, something of the high-stepping, high-kicking young chorus girl she had once been. 'Girl, those drums got to me! Where's some water?'" (25–26).

A seaport in North Colombia located in a bay on the Caribbean Sea, Cartagena was an original colonial Spanish stronghold that was eventually claimed by nationalist insurgents in 1821. Thomasina's actions reaffirm that victorious event. Beyond that, Thomasina Moore embraces historical memory, perhaps recalling Cartagena's twin-named town on the southeast Spanish coast that was probably built by Carthaginians from North Africa; African lineage is alive for Thomasina.[28] Consequently, although Thomasina complains about Avey Johnson's abrupt departure from the cruise, the resistant part of her responds empathetically. She connects with sudden impulse, the ancestral memory that moves an individual: "Her anger was matched now by the look of helpless curiosity and even awe with which she fixed Avey Johnson during the short time she remained in the cabin. . . . Her wondering gaze focused on the underlip which was still slightly pursed to reveal the no-nonsense edging of pink she had never seen before" (62). But to the still unreconstructed Avey, her friends resemble children "frozen into absurd poses in a game of statues." Still somewhat unknowing, Avey Johnson nonetheless discerns a change and declines the pose of a fixed statue although she still cannot comprehend Thomasina Moore's constant dismantling of a prescribed, inflexible role. Until Carriacou, Avey Johnson is unconscious of the fact that her own soul resembles those souls she had heard about as a child when she sat with the presiding mothers of Mount Oliver: "Walled up in a darkness deeper than midnight. Giant stones have done buried your spirit. . . shutting you off" (200).

Another time, when Thomasina and friends sailed away on a hired sloop with a "worn and flimsy mainsail" after the cruise ship docked in St. Vincent, Avey was astounded (66). But on board the Emanual C., that astonishment dissolves because a similarly flimsy sail—validating Thomasina Moore's intrepidity—billows impressively, yet tenaciously. The catch is, however, that the ships sail "in the name of the Father and of the Son." In other words, these ships serve empire (195). That colonial omnipresence mandates the nightlight that Thomasina always leaves on. Thomasina strives never to be caught completely off guard.

Avey's unconnected memories of Thomasina Moore synthesize on the night of the purge, when she is recuperating and ready to reposition herself. Now she decides why she recoiled at the overindulgent dessert named after the conference at Versailles where massive colonial territorial theft was enacted. She no longer needs the "spiraling dome" of the dessert, with its French political/architectural resonances. Because of her internal, volcanic-like eruption, Avey metonymically is the new Mount Pelée.

That inner debate prompts a memory of Thomasina Moore easily jumping into the dance in Cartagena: "And for the first time ever Avey Johnson found herself thinking of her with something akin to affection" (246). At one with friend and family transhistorically, Avey reenters life as the oral historian and instructor of future generations, a new community avatar. She can reclaim her emblematic role as a woman allegedly crazy for terminating a cruise for rich capitalists. She is another ancient mariner who survives the Middle Passage in order to recite an updated slave narrative to grandchildren, or "grands" as they are called—Marion's "sweetest lepers." In allying herself ideologically with Marion, Avey affirms "black motherhood as a strategic response to racist constructs" of which the Bianca Pride is a prime example. Simultaneously, she identifies colonialism as a historical contamination.[29] These young people, the ending suggests, will know what to do when they consider the plight of the Ibos removed from the boats, "right here where we'se standing" (37). Just as the Ibos walked away when they left—"they didn't so much as give [the ship] a look" (39)—so Avey has left the slave ship behind and come home to her ancestors in great-aunt Cuney's and Tatem, and to her descendants, her "grands."

But that surge of happiness also undercuts itself, because Jay/Jerome Johnson is dead. Even more to the point, does the question that angered great-aunt Cuney still remain unanswered: "How come they didn't drown?" (39) Now at least Avatara comprehends the significance of the Ibos' crossing and the crossing she took herself as part of her self-determining mission, her reengagement in the struggle initiated by ancestors. No longer buried alive, rather she is confronting different or reconfigured situations where she will make choices.

In the end, Avey brings her daughter Marion's questions back home. As the radical, hitherto submerged part of Avey, Marion has drawn complex politico-historical issues to the surface. And now that Avey has welcomed ancestors, avatars, and supporters, she stands on her own feet. With a firm sense of her diasporic place and status and a desire to move closer to her African origins in "Gullah country, "she has replaced assimilation with new knowledge and a richer understanding of her identity.

CHAPTER 6

Paule Marshall's *Daughters*
Wars of Independence

In *Daughters*, protagonist Ursa Mackenzie echoes the experiments of prior protagonists in different formulations. More specifically *Daughters* stages a feminist intervention in empire, a charting of black women's agency both in the United States and in a fictional Caribbean island named Triunion. *Daughters* stages another war of independence.[1]

In the spirit of the island's foremost, female insurgent ancestor, Ursa Mackenzie fights back, exposing a corrupt, paternalist colonialism, exemplified by her father, Primus Mackenzie. Furthermore, the crisscrossings of astronomical constellations with slave insurgents map consistent personal and political confrontations between empire and satellite, between past, present, and future time.

Yet the tale ends on a happy note with the possibility of a new progressive order headed by Justin Beaufils. A formerly numbed Ursa begins to feel her abortion and hence starts to heal. Yet despite several healthy features, colonial logic silently undercuts these ostensibly agreeable resolutions. The final section, "Tin Cans and Graveyard Bones," resonates with the need for greater employment and better conditions on the island; ambiguously configured, "Tin Cans and Graveyard Bones" is saturated in metaphoric as well as material deaths and new starts.

The narrative of *Daughters* proceeds through a series of double exposures, both discontinuous and multiple. Ursa uses this photographic term—double exposure—to characterize diverse corruptions played out in the United States and Triunion.

> She tells Viney that life [is] a series of double exposures. Everything—"elections, roads, the South Ward, Armory Hill, the P.M., the Do-nothings, Sandy Lawson, the white people—them!—still running things in both places—everything superimposed on everything else. Inseparable. Inescapable. The same things repeated everywhere she turned." (333)

Against the grain of the island's postcolonial independence, Ursa suggests, empire replicates itself. In addition to these double exposures that Ursa identifies—impoverished neighborhoods that endure racism, corrupt politicians there are doubled. They are doubled frames she does *not* discern because she cannot access certain complicated knowledges.

Daughters is divided into four books that are respectively entitled "Little Girl of All the Daughters," "Constellation," "Polestar," and "Tin Cans and Graveyard Bones." Books one and three are set in the United States (New York and New Jersey), while books two and six play out in Triunion. Only seven out of fifty chapters are titled—and all seven are named after major characters; four are in book one and three are in book two. Consisting of flashbacks and reminiscences in time present, *Daughters* charts the orbits of traversing stars that relate back to a physical as well as symbolic gravitational force. While stars may circle in different orbits, the former colonizing power still exerts sway.

A brief synopsis helps to contextualize these complex relationships: in Triunion, the opposition leader, Primus Mackenzie, is running for reelection against an independent politician named Justin Beaufils, a working class or "ringtail" boy. As a child, Justin Beaufils used to play with Primus Mackenzie's daughter Ursa. Other Triunion notables are Mackenzie's now dead mother, Miss Mack; his mistress, Astral Dolores Forde; her impoverished friend Malvern; and the servant who dotes on Mackenzie, Celestine Marie-Claire Bellegarde.

The U.S. orbit primarily features Primus Mackenzie's radical wife Estelle who now resides in Triunion and their daughter Ursa, who lives in New York but will soon return home to support her father in the upcoming elections. Ursa presently works on a New Jersey project for Sandy Lawson who followed in Primus Mackenzie's political footsteps by selling out to corporate interests after he was elected mayor. A tireless political organizer, rebellious Mae Rylands resists Lawson's successful plan to build a convenient expressway that bypasses the black community, long considered an "eyesore" by resident whites.

Other stars in the U.S. orbit are Ursa's lover, Lowell Carruthers, and her friend Viney, who separately counteract bigotry; Estelle's brother Grady, a permanently injured hero of the Civil Rights movement; and Estelle's grandparents, victims of segregation and its aftermath.

Dominating both the Triunion and the U.S. landscapes, in the form of a massive stone sculpture on the island and through flashbacks in the United States, are Will Cudjoe and Congo Jane, slave rebels and national heroes.[2] Referred to as the Monument, this sculpture of Cudjoe and Congo Jane, accompanied by their slave allies, Alejandro and Père Bossou, was strategically built by the conservative party, Mackenzie's political opponents, far removed from the haunts of tourists. It stands in Mackenzie's seat in the North District, also known as Morlands. As the sole female, Congo Jane represents a paradigmatic model of resistance. She wears a lace shawl expropriated from her mistress and has a disfigured breast—the nub of it was torn off by an abusive owner. What's more, Jane uses the shawl to bandage Will Cudjoe's wounds. When Primus Mackenzie initially meets Estelle, he outlines some of this general history of the island. Early on, that is, he assumes the role of informal oral historian and chronicles for Estelle Triunion's many wars, popular resistance, and the island's tripartite division at one time into British, French, and Spanish sections (138). As he narrates the island's colonial history, he explains solutions that he favors. Estelle is sympathetic to Primus Mackenzie's view of what has to be done and marries him.

I want to return now to the intricate series of double exposures and crossings, the first of which concerns abortions: Ursa's own to begin with, then Astral Forde's, and third, Estelle's spontaneous abortion before she gave birth to Ursa. Accounts of the women's experiences underscore their comparative living conditions and the deleterious effect of race and gender bigotry.

Short in stature like her mother, protagonist Ursa—a "study in underdevelopment"—leaves a plush midtown New York abortion clinic, following the termination of her pregnancy; a manicured Latina worker commiserates. Feeling nothing, Ursa heads for Columbus Circle, all ironies intended. Named Ursa Beatrice Mackenzie, she is popularly known as Ursa B. At this point, she is the Little Bear who has lost her bear rings.

Ursa is symbolically named after a northern constellation, which includes Polaris or the North Star.[3] The main pattern of seven stars that form the shape of the constellation gave rise to its popular name, the Little Dipper.[4] Ursa's name also recalls her African roots. Arabs from North Africa knew Ursa Minor as Al Dubb al Asghar—the lesser Bear.[5] An even earlier designation of the name was Daughters of the Lesser Bear, Banat al Na'ash al Sughra, that was applied to the three stars in the tail of the constellation.[6]

Two other notable facts surround Ursa's name. Polaris, pole star, or stella polaris, phoenice, was erroneously thought for a long time to mark the pole—which would have rendered the "heavenly pole" a fixed entity.[7] Ursa Minor proves—or will demonstrate in *Daughters*—the relativity of things.

Subtler is the historical link between Ursa B.'s name and institutionalized slavery. The thirteenth-century Persian astronomical writer Al Kazwini narrates a community belief that staring at the North Star would cure ophthalmia, the most common disease of the desert that made eyes itch.[8] Opthalmia was also a notorious affliction endured by slaves on the Middle Passage; its high incidence en route caused many slaves to be seriously devalued by plantocrats and proslavery entrepreneurs on arrival in the Caribbean.[9] Perhaps the fact that Ursa is temporarily directionless—since the North Star is in her own constellation—suggests that she might have been staring at the polestar without knowing it.

That aside, Estelle taught Ursa as a child to spot both the constellation of the North Star and of Orion. Metaphorically, Estelle wants Ursa always to be able to reach the radical-activist home folks who live up north. Despite this sturdy instruction by her U.S. mother, Ursa has temporarily lost these bear rings; regretting that she has not yet learned to steer, Ursa maintains that life is a rowboat. She is presently considering an emergency telegram from her mother who has asked Ursa to return home to help with her father's election. Despite her present discomfort, Ursa continually draws on certain happy memories of her father that involve her meaningful nomenclature, Ursa B., in a somewhat different context. Concretely, she recalls frequent trips to the sea with her father when she was a little girl. The pair of them sat in the water, dipping mangoes in salt—the little and big dipper together—and then ate the fruit (98). They created an image of harmony.

Yet the idyllic scene of the salt/sweet mango dipping emblematizes Primus's individual conflicts and the mutual conflicts of father and daughter. Estelle's injunction to her daughter to note mentally the North Star and her father's delight in mixing sweet and salty constitute part of Ursa's store of memories that she wrestles with in New York.

Life in New York is anything but harmonious. At Mt. H. College, Professor Crowder has rejected Ursa's thesis: a study of the social, sexual, and family life of slaves among New World slave communities "and their significance for and contribution to the various forms of resistance to enslavement found in the United States and the Caribbean" (11). As sources for her research, Ursa had used "the slave narratives and oral histories, the old plantation records."[10] But Professor Crowder, a formerly amicable mentor, had dug in his heels when Ursa threatened to use authentic history to confound the kind of imperial myth making that abounds at this representative academic institution. "Foreigners," in Crowder's view apparently, cannot be permitted to articulate anti-colonial resistance. Crowder's refusal to accept Ursa's thesis induces a hallucination. She imagines herself armed with a musket—just as Congo Jane—firing between"[his] grayish blue eyes." Professor Crowder causes Ursa to lose direction; he fundamentally destabilizes her plans (9–11).

As Ursa mulls over Crowder's intransigence and her defiant mental reaction, childhood memories erupt—especially those of visiting the Monument—the sculpture of the slaves who are holding muskets. She remembers her mother punting her up to touch Congo Jane's toes: "Go ahead. Stretch! I'm not going to let you fall. . . . And make sure to touch Will Cudjoe's toes while you're at it. You can't leave him out" (13–14). Since Ursa found herself seemingly unmoved by these experiences, she sought refuge in her mantra, *ke'ram*. She finds comfort in repeating *ke'ram* over and over because it grounds her in time and space: *ke'ram* is "nothing more than a sound designed to quiet the mind and suspend all thought. Peace; be still. Ke'ram, that when it's working, takes her in her head down to Triunion and a beach there that's her favorite in all the world. A two-mile stretch of sand, sea, and sky that's so perfect and peaceful no thoughts can reach her there" (17).

The second abortion that marks the first double exposure is Astral Forde's. As a young woman in Triunion, she endures a brutal back-street experience with a doctor who treats her as if she were an animal. In contrast to Ursa's abortion, no Latina with manicured hands in a waiting room adorned with calla lily wallpaper tends Astral, who grew up as a poverty-stricken ringtail girl with her friend Malvern.

Raped by a football player, Astral Forde confides solely in Malvern who lives in dire straits with her hardworking, moonfaced husband and their ever-growing family. Malvern and her husband inhabit a two-room house on Armory Hill, a shantytown built on a ruined colonial armory (180). Malvern unselfishly encourages Astral to capitalize on her prized hair and creamy skin. She advises Astral to play up the "white people"—features that will attract men who, in turn, might economically assist Astral Forde (175). On her visits to Malvern, Astral describes the series of men who befriend her and secure her career, most significantly, Primus Mackenzie. Astral becomes Mackenzie's mistress and manages his hotel, appropriately named for white tourists—Mile Trees Colony Hotel.

In this underemployed community that lacks even a sorely needed cannery for yearlong abundant fruit, Astral has little chance to develop a career of her own. Similarly disenfranchised, Malvern is content to string a wire across the tiny living room to make two even tinier spaces that can accommodate the growing family. Betraying signs of insecurity sometimes manifested by impoverished people, Malvern fears the Black Power movement in which Estelle's brother, Grady, actively participates; any rocking of the status quo, she anticipates, will somehow rebound on her. "There's too much of this Black Power Talk" (212). Her poverty mystifies her so much that she admires the U.S. battleship, the Woody Wilson. Not surprisingly or coincidentally, Malvern has never been to see the Triunion Monument featuring the slave rebels: "They had to have a lot of old-time names after the people on the monument in Morlands I ain't never seen" (181).

The third abortion concerns Ursa's mother, Estelle, who serves as a poignant foil to Ursa and Astral in a multiple exposure. Unlike Ursa and Astral, Estelle does not desire an abortion. Apparently unable to carry a baby to term, she suffers a series of "slides" or miscarriages—perhaps projections of her own concern about life in Triunion, about peoples' everyday, trying conditions. Soon after her arrival on the island, Estelle proficiently organizes the building of a roofed market shed that provides shelter for the hawkers—women who walk miles each day to sell produce at the market and sit all day in the sun.

These juxtaposed abortions experienced by Ursa, Astral, and Estelle signify radical indeterminacy and lack of closure. Geographically and emotionally, they cross and recross one another, their different astral positions a result of gendered class difference. The women function in different orbits.

The second double exposure concerns Primus Mackenzie in conjunction with his "complements," Sandy Lawson and Justin Beaufils. Like the women, they are likewise located in different orbits, different astral positions. Just as Ursa's first-person narrative—of a traveling daughter—dominates book one, so Primus's narrative that chronicles his rise to political power dominates the first Triunion section. Unlike Ursa's first-person account, however, others in his circle ventriloquize his experiences. This narrative mode accentuates both his power behind the scenes and his dependence on others. Son of a village seamstress who ultimately became Miss Mack the shopkeeper and a father who sports white shoes, a white suit, a panama hat, drives a box Ford, chats all day, and wildly speculates, Primus refers to himself as "this country boy in his donkey cart." Estelle needs to keep him on the "straight and narrow," he claims, because of this upbringing (133). Sending him to the island's swanky school early on in life, Miss Mack wants her son to know "how things go in this world" (161). She cautions him about the company he will keep and advises him to find a classy wife who is not "blacker than yourself."

Since protagonist Ursa is named after Miss Mack, the original Ursa, Miss Mack herself is arguably Ursa Major.[11] Primus Mackenzie, in a sense then, is associated with, derives from, Ursa Major. Or does he inherit Ursa Major? Put another way, once Ursa Minor is born, Primus Mackenzie is situated in an ambiguous space between certain constellations.

After graduation, Primus Mackenzie symbolically sets out in the "early light" of the "dun-colored hour before" dawn—foreshadowing, in that patriotic resonance, his potential conflicts as Miss Mack's son *and* as an idealist. Perhaps more to the point, Primus Mackenzie's charisma "shines so brightly it blinds others to his contradictions."[12] He charms Estelle by choreographing his well-intentioned desire to change Triunion for the better: "I don't have to tell you what our situation is like, what with the people in Spanish Bay running off to Cuba and Puerto Rico in some leaky boat the first chance they get, so there's scarcely anyone left at that end of the island. And the people up Gran'

Morne behaving like they're still maroons fighting the French, refusing to even speak the official language; and the rest of us still with this colonial thinking, acting more British than the British. If only we could throw off all that, come together and start thinking, 'get up and do,' you wouldn't recognize Triunion. The place would actually begin to live up to its name. And what that would mean for the rest of these little islands! We might all finally come together—French, Dutch, English, Spanish—all o' we one! so that even Big Brother would have to respect us. It's the dream that keeps me going, Estelle" (144). Against the ideological grain of that discourse, however, is his fixation on external signs of empire; he invests in a lavish estate and swimming pool that will attract tourists.

But he begins with distinctly positive sympathies. As leader of the Parliamentary opposition, he knows that Estelle wants him to change the material conditions of the population for the better. Persevering market women, he concurs, have "some of the better business minds in the world [but] were born the wrong color, the wrong sex, the wrong class . . . in this kiss-muh-ass place" (143, 147). His astuteness about industrious market women partly stems from his knowledge of the Creole servant who raised him. An original ringtail child who was so uncared for when Miss Mack hired her that her hair had turned red from malnutrition, Celestine doted on Primus. She denounces Primus's wife Estelle as an interfering white negro—"Blanche Neg'r," she is a competing star. Celestine discerns no contradiction in her acknowledgment of Estelle's "good heart" and her contempt for Estelle.

Mackenzie's political transformation to a conservatist mode is gradual, rather than calculated. For example, when it becomes clear that his party, the National Progressives (NPP) will win the election, the conservative Democratic National Party (DNP) employ gunboat diplomacy. They stage a show of might in Triunion's harbor through the presence of the battleship Woody Wilson, then give permission for the crew to "turn the guns and bombs on us, if necessary" (222).

This naval presence does not strike everyone on the island as ominous. For Astral Forde's friend, the impoverished Malvern, Woody Wilson radiates in the harbor, like "a starfield of lights on the sea" (181). But despite the seemingly glamorous appearance that manipulates Malvern, Primus gives up. . . . He can't get over the sight of the United States Navy sitting armed to the teeth out in the harbor. . . .

All of it, he says, is a [puppet] show with no longer England, but guess who now pulling the strings" (222).

Subsequently, the DNP invites Mackenzie to sit as a token opposition member on a Planning and Development board—a joint public and private venture. Over Estelle's objections, he agrees, thus becoming fully invested in a post-colonial apparatus.

Primus's capitulation to gunboat diplomacy signals not only his personal-political defeat but also the anti-imperial resistance of his wife Estelle and daughter Ursa. His actions force suppressed contradictions into the open.

Earlier I quoted Ursa's pronouncement that double exposure characterizes her world—and that in turn it thoroughly implicates her father's U.S. counterpart, Sandy Lawson, in these intersections. Ursa knows Sandy Lawson from the time she worked in Midland City, New Jersey on his campaign to become the first black mayor.

When Ursa starts a second research project in that same place, however, she finds out immediately that Sandy Lawson, another former ringtail boy, had already capitulated to the white power structure. Specifically, he agreed on the construction of an expressway that bypasses and hence isolates the black community in the area known as the South Ward (283). The South Ward now reminds Ursa of "a bombed-out section in Beirut" (296). Prior to accepting the job, Ursa selects a new hairstyle—a woven braid that hearkens back to Celestine who favors the same style and to a Black Power hairstyle that Estelle had suggested earlier for Ursa. The trope of weaving, understood as a need for underprivileged people to unite, is also imbricated in the name of Ursa's school, the New Jersey Weaver High School, where Estelle insisted on sending her. Estelle's brother Grady, a civil rights activist, taught in that school where nomenclature signs togetherness. Ursa begins braiding the different strands of her life together.

Ursa's friend and co-worker on the original black mayor campaign in Midland City is Mae Rylands, a tireless agitator for justice in the black community. By the time Ursa returned to New Jersey for her second job, Rylands had already left Sandy Lawson's office in protest against his reactionary activities. On learning of Mae Rylands's resignation, Ursa remarks that "the Woods are on Fire" (296).

Lawson's shenanigans constitute one of the frames in the double exposure featuring Primus Mackenzie. In the United States, Lawson's activities parallel Mackenzie's co-optation in Triunion; put another way, Lawson is Mackenzie's U.S. look-alike. Justin Beaufils, on the other hand, is Mackenzie's political opponent in Triunion and an advocate of peoples' rights. In his election campaign, Beaufils foregrounds Mackenzie's "sell-out" and predicts his downfall. Yet another ringtail boy whom Estelle invited to play with Ursa as a child, Beaufils poignantly restages Primus Mackenzie's pilgrimage from shopkeeper's son to leader of the opposition. Now running as an Independent against Mackenzie, Beaufils "actually talks about class and color" (300, 360). His projected program matches Mackenzie's early idealist plans. As an agronomist who studied in Cuba, Beaufils's wife ideologically matches Estelle.

This triple braiding of Mackenzie with Beaufils and Lawson intimates that Beaufils alone can fulfill the promises of Primus Mackenzie's youth. But uncertainty still lurks so long as Beaufils resembles Mackenzie. Moreover, the "exposure" of Primus Mackenzie returns us to the abortion multiple scenarios.

Those abortions experienced in Triunion and the United States by Ursa, Estelle, and Astral Forde mimic and complement the mirrorings of Mackenzie that sicken Ursa. In tune with Astral's back-street abortionist, the DNP aborts progress in the black community and on Armory Hill where Malvern lives. Lawson and Mackenzie enable the white elite to fulfill themselves economically.

Posed oppositionally to these crisscrossing frames are a set of actions implemented by heirs of Congo Jane: these heirs are the daughters of the title—contemporary rebels who bring to life the stone Monument where Jane, Cudjoe, Alejandro, and Père Bossou, boldly stand as a united quartet under fire. These daughters are Ursa's friends and lover, Mae Rylands, Viney Daniels, and Lowell Carruthers; her mother Estelle Mackenzie; and Ursa herself. But the unity of these daughters is not immediately recognizable. Indeed, far from being a force poised to swing collectively into action, they represent individual sites of resistance, people who take risks as a matter of principle or as opportunities present themselves.

One of Ursa's guiding stars, old-time political activist Mae Rylands, inherits and occupies Congo Jane's orbit. Already she shines in the North, pointing the way for Ursa. Estelle's instructions to the young Ursa that she recognize these shining lights have materialized, so to speak, in Mae Rylands. Like Congo Jane who wears a lace shawl that symbolizes resistance to colonial expropriation, Mae Rylands also wears lace blouses. Beyond that signifying trope, Mae Rylands's very walk is discursively attached to the renowned slave rebel: she took a "few brisk Congo Jane steps over to the stage" (280). Not only is Rylands closely associated with Congo Jane's opposition to colonial violence, but she means to enact this opposition publicly on stage.

Through Sandy Lawson, Ryland's altruism intersects with Mackenzie's opportunism. Lawson is both Mackenzie's political alter ego and Rylands' opportunistic boss. Frames overlay one another; scenarios of double exposure redouble and multiply. In concrete terms, Lawson cut off Mae Rylands's funds for social programs when she refused to support him in building a freeway through the black community. But nothing fazes Mae Rylands: she continues to concentrate on New Jersey youth, calling them (Ursa included) her "grands" or grandchildren. In another harsh layering frame, Ursa notes a Triunion woman in dire straits—a prostitute who solicits U.S. sailors, "superimposed suddenly on Mae Rylands's office, the baby and the girl" (290). The doubled frame marks a telling assertion: indigent and young people in Triunion and New Jersey match their cornered leaders.

On the lookout for activists like herself, Mae Rylands obliquely fingers Ursa: "The right one's got to be out here somewheres. . . . You's one of my grands too" (299–300). With the help of her mother, and of Mae Rylands who confronts Ursa with her apathy and distance, Ursa's polestar gradually appears.

Allied to Mae Rylands via Congo Jane's metaphorical orbit is Ursa's friend, Viney or Vincereta. Her name a feminine cognate of the verb to overcome, Viney hails from a family politically refined enough to admire Paul Robeson, after whom Viney names her son Robeson: she is savvy enough to be the assistant Vice President for a major U.S. insurance corporation. The sign that hangs outside Viney's house reads: "V. Daniels and Son," alluding to Robeson as a sun/son shining on the black community as well as young Robeson's Daniel-like insurgent spirit.[13] Partly choric, Viney warns Ursa of the complacency and co-optation she discerns in the Triunion political arena: "Massa really did a job on you folks down there."

Living in Brooklyn and traveling to Triunion for holidays, Viney understands how indigent members of the ringtail community connect to Congo Jane's statue: "I know there's no escaping anything," she remarks, on her first sight of the statue when she visits Triunion, "but we should have headed straight here the minute we got off the plane, put up a tent right where I'm standing, and not budged for the entire two weeks" (109).

Like Mae Rylands and Congo Jane herself, Viney is both a clear thinker and a lover of pretty things (382). Her house makes Ursa feel "as if the small rowboat . . . [her life] has finally made it to port" (82). Viney's kitchen is Ursa's second "haven"; her principal paradise are the government lands where she and her father enjoyed mango dipping.

Having struggled to personal victory, Viney fights her son Robeson's unjust arrest. Like Mae and Estelle microcosmically, she struggles to save people from institutions that erase or thwart civil rights. Resembling Mae Rylands and Estelle standing up to Sandy Lawson and Primus Mackenzie respectively, Viney returns to her parents' home after she fought the police on behalf of her son. She returns to the symbolically named Triumphant Baptist Church. Facing a civil war battlefield, her old house replicates Viney's battle in Brooklyn.

Lowell Carruthers, Ursa's lover with whom she earlier shared good sexual relations and political harmony, is hazily superimposed on these frames of surrogate daughters. He has temporarily absented himself from Congo Jane's orbit.

Originally a civil rights activist like Viney, Mae Rylands, and Estelle's brother Grady, Carruthers has become temporarily unmoved from his political bearings. He is now someone who uses the yogic sign for peace to express pleasure for a good meal. Consumed with his own situation, he enters an orbit of marginality and rants about the effects of empire. In his impotence, he reflects Ursa's worst fears.

Like Viney, Lowell Carruthers functions as a member of the chorus warning Ursa. Physically, his widow's peak forehead resembles her father's domed one; verbally he reminds her that she is independent in name only since she still takes orders from Big Daddy England: "Quit letting them run your life by remote control," he warns (268–69).

Ursa's mother, Estelle Mackenzie, ironically represents another critical daughter (of the title) who displaces the site of resistance or, just as significantly, reenacts it in a doubling process. Having been raised in the United States, Estelle returns Congo Jane's fight against colonialism back to Triunion, the colonized land. To begin with, empathetic Estelle organizes the building of the roofed shed to shield the market women from a relentless midday sun, a soulful act that in turn affirms her right to wear Congo Jane's shawl. By establishing decent working conditions for the hawkers, she dissolves and parodies the concept of colonial philanthropy. In Paule Marshall's fiction, where roofs rank highly as a running metaphor for survival and "beating the odds," perhaps the market women's roof in *Daughters* ranks as the most poignant.

Having taught Ursa about Sojourner Truth and rebellion, Estelle locates herself in Congo Jane's orbit, although she visually belongs in the constellation of Orion: "her collar bones standing out like the wings of a crossbow" (225). Equipped as a hunter and fighter who stalks her prey, Estelle tries to right wrongs in Triunion and encourage Primus Mackenzie to cross over, to "do the right thing." The homefolks in the United States to whom she often alludes support Estelle in her ventures.

From a politically aware family, Estelle knows that her membership in a black sorority attracted an invitation from the University administration to meet Primus Mackenzie as a potential leader from the Caribbean. Nonetheless, she still strives to learn the histories of these respective countries. In doing so, she is ironically struck by the number of wars in which Triunion has been engaged.

After Estelle marries Primus Mackenzie and realizes the extent of the barriers to progress on the island, regrets set in: "I need to be marching or sitting-in or demonstrating." In Alabama, her brother Grady worked as a freedom rider who participated in the voter registration drive and was permanently injured as a result of police brutality.

Following a series of miscarriages, Estelle gives birth to Ursa, raising the child unassumingly to play with the neighborhood or ringtail children. She teaches Ursa to know the North Star and Orion, while trying to steer Primus in a steady direction. She is the "coachman" who will guide his donkey cart on the "straight and narrow." In Celestine's words, Estelle is "always getting on like she's Congo Jane marching next to him with a cutlass and a gun. The *blanche neg*'" (316). Gradually, as Orion, Estelle claims the orbit of Triunion as her own.

But Estelle's patience soon dissolves: first she is livid when she discovers that Astral Forde is Primus's mistress. In the middle of the night with baby Ursa, Estelle parks on the Triunion airport runway and refuses to leave; now she locates herself in liminality, opting for an in-between space that guarantees flexibility. In doing so, she stresses her ability to choose. This capacity sharply contrasts with the expropriation of Astral Forde, who has to remain as a subservient fixture at the Mile

Trees Colony Hotel. A sexual servant who is glad to have left the shantytown where she grew up, Forde happily receives toffee tins with snow scenes from Mackenzie. These Eurocentric vignettes recall the pretty veneer that masks the imperial hegemony running Astral Forde's life.

Second, Estelle is disquieted by Primus's response to the conservative party's strong-arm tactics over the battleship, Woody Wilson, now anchored in Triunion harbor; she recognizes that "the entire country just changed character overnight, [going] back to the time when there were all the wars here.... We woke up ... to find the Gray Eminence sitting out in the harbor with its sixteen-inch guns aimed straight at us. It had stopped by at the invitation of the government. And it had brought along a friend ... this aircraft carrier the size of a football field. ... Only Primus and one other member of his party survived [the election]" (220–21).

When Mackenzie subsequently agrees to serve on the Planning and Development Board of the conservative party and is rendered politically impotent by this compromise, Estelle expresses orion-like rage during the ensuing argument (235–39): "She sat with her breath sucked deep into the wells at the base of her throat and her collar bones standing out like the wings of a crossbow" (225). She is, as it were, about to shoot her bolt and cross aggressively into other orbits temporarily. At a cocktail party for the Board, Estelle acts out her anger by playing the child's game of statues. Metaphorically, she calcifies herself to project the condition of the imperial visitors. Her status quo protests exist in the same inchoate space as the airport runway between Triunion and the United States that she protestingly parked on with baby Ursa many years earlier. Estelle is a statue, neither alive nor dead: "A stranger to myself." With her equilibrium destabilized and her threshold uncertain, Estelle has "come to see things here and in the States in pretty much the same light" (223–24). That light is Congo Jane's. Estelle has entered that orbit, while maintaining her own independent location as Orion.

These complex activities by Congo Jane's avatars gradually affect Ursa until she takes up Congo Jane's mantle herself. Prompted by Estelle, Ursa returns to Triunion for the elections, noting on arrival: "nothings's changed." But Ursa's presence invalidates that observation.

She learns from her mother that her father has agreed to build a resort on their special mango-dipping beach that doubled as a haven on Sundays for ringtail children who had no other beach to enjoy (384–85). Obliterating the story of Congo Jane and Will Cudjoe that he recited to Ursa during these halcyon days together, Primus has surrendered the community's cultural rights to U.S. corporate interests. He has no energy left to fight for a people's cannery and for decent housing (235). In many ways, Primus Mackenzie's downfall was inevitable: like Estelle's grandparents who endured segregation, Primus is a male child set up for a fall from his very baptism when he wore a symbolic Lloyd George collar and was designated as a future minister.

Given his mother's desire to better her only son, not surprisingly he mimicked U.S. values when he first met Estelle at the luxurious U.S. corporate mansion. Even his gift to Estelle was predictably named—a Ford Anglia car. The historical odds against Primus Mackenzie's success as a reformer are so almost predictably stacked that Estelle and Ursa reach breaking point and take matters into their own hands: Ursa will give information to Primus Mackenzie's rival, Justin Beaufils, that will enable Beaufils to win the election. To this end, Ursa obtains a prospectus of the notorious resort that her father is involved in building. Beaufils is then able to use this evidence against Primus on the last day of the election campaign. Ursa, that is, has finally heeded her mother's injunction early on to "sink or swim or learn how to row" (254). No longer a duppy or a loup-garou, Ursa is back from the dead.[14]

And there is more besides. Despite the fact that these resistant actions replicate earlier battles fought by Congo Jane, Ursa still avoids looking the stone statues of the early Triunion warriors in the eye. But this frozen situation—Ursa as the statue who cannot face activist ancestors—does not last.

Congo Jane herself, at this point, undertakes a miraculous, transhistorical intervention. As Ursa journeys to deliver the prospectus to Beaufils, she watches the foam of the waves spreading "like the lace of Jane's shawl" and "breaking and receding with the sound of ke'ram" (379). Her mantra and warrior-hero mesh in a triumphalist, synaesthetic moment.

Through listening to others, taking action, and marking the site of the North Star, Ursa's senses are being restored; she is tuning into herself. This new vision of Congo Jane's shawl that fuses with the sound of *ke'ram* in turn drowns out the sound of tin cans about which Viney had warned Ursa: "You remind me of a cat with a string of tin cans and some bones from a graveyard tied to its tail when it comes to your folks. . . . The tin cans and bones keep up such a racket you can't hear your own self, your own voice trying to tell you which way to go"

(112). Following the polestar, Ursa ushers into clearer focus her relationship with Celestine, Astral Forde, and her parents. She finally finds direction.

As a result of this journey, Justin Beaufils wins the election. He pelts another rock at Primus Mackenzie in the valley of Elah, just as he did as a child when asked to leave the Mackenzie's fine yard. The ringtail children of Triunion, in that sense, have united to overthrow the comprador bourgeoisie and its complicitous opposition. But the question remains: Has Beaufils done that? Will he and his new order remain unsullied? Ambiguity hovers, but one thing is sure. Precedence is not in Beaufils's favor to remain incorruptible.

Certainly, Mackenzie's political shift since he met Estelle does not augur well for Beaufils in his role as the New Honorable Member for Morlands. Like Beaufils, Mackenzie started his career as an idealist who demanded redress for the long-subjugated black community. Will a few years in office co-opt Beaufils the same way? Given the subtle blandishments, manipulations, and compromises Beaufils will confront, could he be any different from Mackenzie who unquestionably cherished good intentions; will Beaufils remain true to Will Cudjoe's principles?

In an astronomical sense, the election of Beaufils and the defeat of Mackenzie complete another orbit; yet whether anything will change remains an open question. More than likely, the cycle will repeat itself. Corruption is a hard fact of colonial realpolitik.

On the other hand, as Ursa embarks on her journey, the servant Celestine recognizes that the new ringtail children "had finally managed to put flesh and muscle on their bones and grow up." As a former ringtail child herself, Celestine marks the fact that times are changing. There is room for hope. This new generation that includes Beaufils has grown up differently, arguably stronger than Primus Mackenzie; and since they have been more healthily nurtured, the possibility exists of a stronger response to U.S. enticements. Primus Mackenzie's most devoted follower, Celestine, recognizes what has happened. Her ambiguity has always been present in her tripled name: the first part, Marie-Claire, marks clarity and the large dark areas of the moon named mare; the second part, Belle-Garde, designates her as Primus Mackenzie's vigilant protector. Celestine muses internally, but never to others, about the turn of events: "you have to run from your own thoughts sometimes." Thus she intersects on a limited basis with the oppositional women, Ursa and Estelle, while continuing to defend Primus Mackenzie. Celestine turns out to be a distant relative of Congo Jane.

On a related note, the fading sound of the tin cans that speak Ursa's self-cleansing and newfound direction also leads to her reconciliation with Astral Forde, simultaneously her father's mistress and her mother's bête noire. Put another way, the women acknowledge their respective roles in Primus Mackenzie's orbit—and through their own efforts, they close up the distance, engendered by Mackenzie's actions that separated them. Notably, too, despite a complicated self-seclusion, Astral Dolores Forde has worn a lacy, Congo Jane handkerchief all these years. In a modest way, she disrupted assumptions about the degree to which her life and body had been appropriated (402); in that sense, Astral Forde has crossed over into the community of daughters who have survived to tell the tale of their degradation. Hence Primus Mackenzie's secret life is doubly exposed, while Ursa concedes his victimhood: "he was born on the wrong continent," she sadly asserts (405). Consequently, he is ill equipped to cope with former colonizers, now transimulated into western executives, schooled in empire.

The negotiations of these diverse daughters, both spoken and unspoken, have eclipsed Primus Mackenzie's authority. Heirs of Congo Jane, no longer secured in someone else's galaxy, they have found their own constellation with and in Congo Jane (54). She is their star.

Bearers of her musket, the multiple daughters have become critical interventionists who traverse the past and the present and open up new possibilities for the future.[15] Through Ursa's actions and her own, Estelle has transported the imprint of racial memory from the United States to Triunion. Bonded across countries, the daughters quietly retain the capacity to topple governments. At the same time, their black male counterparts intersect with the anti-colonial insurgent force. Hopefully, Lowell Carruthers will cross into the ranks of the warriors alongside Grady and Robeson, whose bear hug to Ursa evinces his association with her constellation (59). Yet for the time being, Lowell Carruthers is doubly inscribed—Ursa was too—as one who has been and may again become a rebel.[16] Meanwhile, at least for now, Justin Beaufils will work for a brighter future.

Having come to terms with her passivity and heritage, Ursa realizes the political necessity of counteracting the recalcitrant Professor Crowder who stopped her writing the island's history: she realizes that "the Janes and Will Cudjoes [are] still waiting on her to tell about them" (377). She will no longer permit the professor to "crowd her," although she realizes that the influence of empire is ineradicable for now. She may recognize that imprint of empire in Triunion and in the United States, she may have to cross over Columbus Circle, but, willy-nilly, she will validate herself and write about Congo Jane. She now acknowledges that extending her orbit is her right and duty. Better still, she knows that she has to break out of orbit and reconfigure herself in her own constellation of Ursa B.

To settle into this global/local relocation when she returns to the diasporic community in New York, Ursa buys herbs that she learned about from her grandmother. The sound of her mantra, *ke'ram*, reaffirms this gynocentric return. No longer will she need to drive her old car—a Dodge Omni, an evasion of everything. This return to her apartment at dawn's symbolic "early light," followed by a long hot bath will "get rid of the last of the soreness." Tending the two nubs of her breasts, silently she restores one-breasted Congo Jane to wholeness. Having revived herself, one abortion is complete (408). Now Ursa can instigate a new beginning and renegotiate her vantage point. She is no longer a cipher, but a threatening woman who claims personal and political agency.

CHAPTER 7

The Fisher King

A Culmination and New Beginnings

In Paule Marshall's words, within "the three great wings of the black diaspora, Brooklyn, Barbados, and Benin," her characters initiate and reenact the histories of their lives and those of their elders and ancestors.[1] I argue that Marshall's most recent novel, *The Fisher King*, recapitulates and synthesizes themes in earlier novels—just as a symphony's last movement recaps earlier themes, enabling readers to admire individual narratives as well as the overarching saga they comprise. This saga that unfolds over half a century begins and ends in diasporic Brooklyn—from *Brown Girl, Brownstones* in 1959 to *The Fisher King* in the new millennium.[2] The latter, moreover, ties *Brown Girl, Soul Clap Hands and Sing, The Chosen Place, the Timeless People, Praisesong for the Widow*, and *Daughters* to one another as well as to itself. *The Fisher King*, that is, while remaining open-ended, brings this body of fine fiction to a resting point.

Additionally, it redraws the consistently feminized angle of vision by featuring (not counting the novellas) a *male* protagonist, eight-year-old Sonny Carmichael Payne. He is raised modestly, not like Selina by biological family members, but by Hattie, a city orphan, drug addict, stripper, his grandfather's lover, and Sonny's dearest friend. The text centers on the couple's arrival in Brooklyn from Paris to attend a commemoration concert in honor of his deceased grandfather, born Everett, nicknamed Sonny Rett Payne, an internationally renowned pianist extraordinaire. In a sense, eight-year-old Sonny stands in for, or "recorporealizes" his grandfather to the Brooklyn community from which Sonny Rett as a teenager sought exile in jazz-loving Paris, itself another African diasporic community. Young Sonny's amazingly varied relatives via his parents, grandparents, great-grandparents, great-great-grandparents, and other cross-generational relatives, hail from multiple sites of slavery. Through his centrality within this human nexus of relationships, the boy epitomizes Marshall's brilliant saga of African Americans, African Caribbean, and African people. He does so because his ancestors, elders, and relatives, his non-consanguineous "stepmother" Hattie, and his Parisian minder, a madame Molineaux, are natally linked to the English- and French-speaking diaspora, from the African west and northwest (Guinea and Algerian) coasts, from different parts of the Caribbean, from the United States and France. Synaesthetic threads—of sight, hearing, taste, touch, and smell in various combinations—link the past, present, and future. The community's sensory experiences are virtually complete as Sonny Rett "reappears" in the person of his grandson. To address the novel's title, the grail knight Perceval has come to heal posthumously the maimed fisher king, his grandfather; the youngster will represent, unknowingly or not, the musical genius of the community's thrice-exiled son whose history chimes with that of countless self-exiled black musicians of his generation.[3] He is the son of Ulene, a Barbadian immigrant who shares Silla's persistent goal in *Brown Girl, Brownstones* to own a brownstone. Nothing matters more. As an inspired Sonny's piano playing matures in 1930s Brooklyn, demonstrating a prodigious talent, Ulene demeans his creativity to crush his burning spirit. Any intrusion on her brownstone dream threatens to shatter it. Plus the evident racism contaminating his daily life proffers no encouragement either. So off he flees to Paris.[4] Now decades later, Ulene lives in her fortress-like Brooklyn brownstone eager to meet her "grand"; perhaps in a displaced desire for Sonny Rett's forgiveness, she steers her grandson toward the nickelodeon/piano which he intuitively masters. Ulene's fear of jazz, drugs, of that lifestyle—whatever it was that so upset her—has long vanished into irrelevance.

Sonny Rett Payne's exodus to Paris from Brooklyn in 1949 participates in the long and complex history of African Americans following the Reconstruction era. A sketch of that history contextualizes Sonny's readiness to emigrate.

Back in 1900, the 18,367 black residents of Brooklyn constituted less than 2 percent of the borough's total population; between 1900 and 1920, New York City experienced a similar growth, most of it concentrated in Manhattan, as Harlem established itself as the black capital of the United States and the focus of black settlement.[5] In Chicago, Philadelphia, Newark, and Los Angeles, the black population doubled, tripled, and more, in the same time frame.[6]

World War I and tighter restrictions on such immigrants as Italians, Poles, and Hungarians, who had traditionally supplied the labor power to operate U.S. factories, benefited black workers who found themselves unexpectedly welcomed to the expanding postwar industrial economy. Northern employers/labor recruiters viewed Southern black residents as an untapped human resource and encouraged their migration to the Northern industrial economy.[7]

Northern urban centers with segregated churches resulted from the new racial distribution and concentration. Migrants from the Caribbean, moreover, added an important community to the population. In 1930, for example, over 60 percent of black people in Brooklyn County had been born in southeastern United States, or outside the country, while the proportion born in New York State and residing in Brooklyn had declined from 39 percent in 1910 to 30 percent in 1930. African Americans in the Bedford-Stuyvesant neighborhoods favored the Fulton Street and Atlantic Avenue residential areas.[8]

The general northward migration of black families diminished during the Depression, yet Brooklyn's black population expanded at a faster rate than most Northern urban centers. By 1940, the decade of Sonny Rett's departure, Brooklyn's 107,263 black families formed 4 percent of the borough's total population, the highest proportion in a century, but severely undeveloped by the authorities: communities lacked recreational facilities, social amenities, and had no access to a hugely developing music scene next door in Harlem.[9] Employment of any sort, let alone as a jazz musician, was in short supply, while housing was in a gross state of disrepair, not far removed (and surely this is deliberate on Marshall's part) from the scene of rubble into which Selina throws one of her bangles in 1949 at the end of *Brown Girl, Brownstones*.

Decidedly more than just churches were segregated in Bed-Stuy (as the neighborhood was and is popularly known) and glee clubs were organized into separate black and white units: Hattie's singing group and Sonny Rett's all-black jazz group are two typical cases in point.[10] However, the black community unexpectedly benefited, despite systematic attempts by white residents to deny African American neighborhoods a healthy development. How so?

Specifically, the construction of the Fulton Street subway, favored by traditionally rich white residents of Bed-Stuy as a means to modernize the area and attract tenants from Manhattan, ironically backfired on their efforts.[11] Officially opened in April 1936, the subway was an instant social and cultural boon to the black population because it provided rapid transportation to the cultural Mecca of Harlem. (Fulton Street is a favored venue in *Brown Girl, Brownstones* too.) African American youth brilliantly tuned into awesome jazz musicians just "up the road" as well as around the world. In the meantime, the construction of four two-room apartments in a single building, usually a brownstone, was both common and desirable. Add Ulene's disapproval of Sonny's love of jazz to this mix, and his self-exile becomes not only inevitable but also logical and smart. These personal circumstances notwithstanding, Sonny was one of many innovative black musicians looking to the exciting mushrooming club world of Paris, now unquestionably the jazz capital of the world, for employment in a creative milieu. Having spearheaded the new diasporic highway from the United States to Paris, Sidney Bechet and Josephine Baker attracted hosts of avid French fans, a phenomenon that in turn generated even more outlets for African American talent.[12]

In the rivalry between New Orleans Dixieland/Bechet-style jazz and bebop or "bop"/Charlie Parker-style, odds seemed to favor the latter.[13] Sonny's popularity playing bop piano in Paris lasted till the 1960s when a combination of post World War II conditions and the French-Algerian War turned the tide against black musicians in exile.[14] James Baldwin and Richard Wright, two other illustrious émigrés, and their numerous compatriots saw the writing on the wall. Unfortunately, since Sonny Rett's departure from Brooklyn made his return virtually impossible, he ended up as "the pianist" in streetcorner bars, dying somewhat mysteriously at the hands of Parisian police in 1969, his old Brooklyn community in the dark about his circumstances.

By now a serious addict, Hattie remains in Paris with Sonny and her friend Madame Molineaux, who minds Sonny while Hattie works nights as a striptease club dancer in one of the few jobs open to her. Young Sonny continues to live there happily enough in the

Algerian-populated Parisian quarter until Great-uncle Edgar invites Hattie and him to participate in his grandfather's memorial concert in Brooklyn. A suspicious Hattie reluctantly accepts, yet unaware of Edgar's ploy to keep Sonny permanently in Brooklyn. Secretly, Sonny Rett had written to Edgar, pleading with him to raise the child who, significantly, as it turns out, takes up drawing. Sonny Rett's fraternal plea and Edgar's eventual agreement raise questions about the interaction of love, loyalty, family, drugs, and possibly gender relations. Is it Sonny's right as a grandfather to put the boy's welfare before his addicted lover's obsession with raising her lover's offspring? Does she forfeit all rights as an addict? Do her circumstances count for nothing, Marshall implicitly asks readers, particularly at the novel's conclusion when Edgar threatens Hattie with a dire ultimatum.

Maybe Hattie's circumstances need fleshing out to track such intricate issues of desire and loss. Years earlier, for instance, following Sonny's exile with his wife Cherisse, Hattie had succumbed to their letters beseeching her to live with them. Eventually, after their daughter JoJo is born and Cherisse has saturated herself in the glittering world of Parisian haute couture, she surrenders the baby's welfare to Hattie. After Cherisse and Sonny Rett die, a disillusioned and emotionally battered JoJo heads for Marseilles's naval community, leaving a newborn son with Hattie who raises him lovingly. Young Sonny, the grail knight and Hattie's ward, seems to understand intuitively (we never know why exactly) that he must use his art to guard his grandfather. He draws the pianist immured and armed—within castles and fortresses, with himself as the halberd-bearing entrance-keeper.[15] The youngster keeps the self-appointed mission a secret until he meets Edgar's "grands," his second cousins, on Long Island. Why does he share the secrets of his inner life with relatives he has just met? His spontaneous confession speaks volumes about a painful, poignantly guarded loneliness.

Convivial peers render Sonny so relaxed and uninhibited that emotions gush out of him like a waterfall. By contrast, a deeply restrained Hattie tries to curtail their Brooklyn visit, fearful of losing her treasured identity as Sonny's surrogate mother.

At Sonny Rett's commemoration, the ostensible raison d'être for the visit, Hattie's reminiscences about the man and his music hold centerstage. Street-hardened Hattie, his shrewd business manager all these years, knows how to rivet her audience with tales of his awesome triumphs. Yet importantly too, registering a city orphan's traditional mettle, she marks slavery boldly in her presentation: it contextualizes Sonny Rett's exile and the threesome's eagerly awaited presence, victors and victims all, united in historical bondage. Like Ursa, Hattie connects everyone to slavery and draws for them a deeper understanding of Sonny Rett Payne's forced exile; permanently exiled people find a restoration of soul, she subtly suggests, in the French African music and culture, in their witness of her ward's careful negotiations with his great-grandmothers, and echoing his predecessors, his respect for elders. Selina feels the deep worth of Miss Thompson; Merle and Avey appreciate the soulful Leesy and Lebert Joseph; Ursa admires her mentor-elder, Mae Rylands; while Paule Marshall herself, in the autobiographical "To Da-Duh," tenderly displays her proud ancestor.

His youth promises a tonic for healing ancient wounds. Sonny Rett's stunning compositions, moreover, fittingly match her moving recollections that return her lover's international legacy to his natal community. In a certain way, the couple's presence signals to the "congregation" how the upcoming generation, prompted by elders and historical memory, might function as revolutionary victors who learn from the past: long gone and long awaited—the fisher king and the knight errant respectively, Sonny and Sonny, kindred spirits in action, a ceaseless spiral.[16] Hattie prophesies the possibility of a new world leadership by community-based people of color, recuperating from decades of fierce neighborhood feuding between Ulene and Florence Varina. No surprise, then, that the notorious saga of a defeated south, a preening, alienated wife, a flawed but steadfast lover named Hattie, a glamorous male protagonist named Rett, and rampant racism lurks in the shadows; the hope of a new day in *The Fisher King* and the cessation of warring in the hands of youth and community love easily transcend the pathetic defeat of *Gone with the Wind*. The Grail Knight has left behind the riches of diasporic Parisian culture, while simultaneously drawing other riches over to Brooklyn. With Hattie his respondee, Sonny Rett's call across the grave and Hattie's response in the opulent auditorium vindicate a people's struggle through exilic suffering.

Young Sonny affirms the beauty of an African American diasporic culture and the cruelty of Sonny Rett's alienation. Already the six-year-old demonstrates multiple talent as a line drawer, a craftsman, an architect, a colorist, a budding musician, an educator, a storyteller. He quests for elusive origins, imbued with an intuition that radiates like the ribbons aboard ship in *Praisesong* and resembles the Ibos in the same text, who take for granted that their will can vanquish inhumanity. As a transcontinental son of African slavery, he speaks from a powerful historical position: first, he is the *sans papier* foster son of orphaned Hattie and the son of lost parents. His mother's tight-packed name, JoJo, bespeaks his parents' pride in two well-placed black women in exile: the redoubtable civil rights activist and entertainer, Josephine Baker, the other, Josephine, wife of Napoleon from French-speaking Martinique, generation expatriate from Brooklyn/the Southern United States/Barbados/Florida/Georgia. His other parent, the Cameroonian street vendor from an Algerian-based arrondissement bestows on Sonny his North and Central African heritage. Then add to this Sonny's descent on his foremothers' sides of the family: grandson of Edgar, a community activist like Selina and Merle with a somewhat softer first-generation Ulene from English-speaking Barbados; Florence Varina from Florida and Georgia; Selina, also from Barbados but first generation; Merle from the Africa-facing Caribbean island of Bournehills; Brooklyn-born Avatara who settles in her great-aunt Cuney's Gullah-speaking Sea Islands and Ursa, born of a U.S. mother and a Caribbean father, who complete the child's intercontinental lineage. He has grown up bilingual in France among colonizers and colonized alike. His grandfather's death occurring amid a "disagreement" with French police haunts his imagination and spawned his artistry. Sonny is also the grandson of Edgar, a community activist like Selina and Merle with a somewhat softer edge, and great-grandson of horticulturist Florence Varina from Georgia who cultivates a radiant flowering in her grandson; and grandson too, of Ulene, a Caribbean survivor who remembers and seeks forgiveness for wrongs committed in slavery's wake.[17] If this amazing concatenation dazzles the reader—so it should, slavery respecting no boundaries. Sonny, it bears repeating, embodies a new world order dominated by people of color.

Each of Paule Marshall's novels stands in its own right, while collectively constituting a unique Pan African saga. As a daughter of two diasporic communities in Triunion and the United States, Ursa Mackenzie refuses subjection in the old battle between the alleged center and periphery. Like other female protagonists in Paule Marshall's fiction, Ursa comes to comprehend the link between preservation of identity and preservation of individual and cultural memory, in the diasporic counternarrative of origins and crossings.

As the daughter of Silla Boyce and Barbados-bent Deighton Boyce, Selina Boyce had also experienced some of Ursa's conflicts. Selina realized them by questioning what Silla and Deighton had accomplished as she leaves New York for Barbados and personal fulfillment.

Unlike Selina and Ursa, the male protagonists in *Soul Clap Hands and Sing*, with the exception of Caliban, have embraced their status as "hollow men." Mr. Watford, Professor Berman, Gerald Motley, and Caliban each reached out valiantly at the end of the book to grasp life. The unknown servant girl, Miss Williams, and Sylvia have fixed a place for themselves in the face of male mystification and obstacles. Notably too, the principal female characters have likewise claimed a solid sense of identity, *per ardua ad astra*, in Ursa's case. Merle Kimbona incarnates the determined female characters as she quests for her daughter in Africa, as well as a keener sense of her own identity and origins.

Avey Johnson begins to glean the answer to great-aunt Cuney's unspoken question about why she spent only occasional time in the Sea Islands. Avey now comprehends the importance of struggle and refusal. Like her daughter, Avey knows she can cross continents again if she chooses. Determined to cross the road (whichever road) where she pleases, Ursa "marks the convergences between the two worlds."[100]

The protagonists, moreover, select different physical routes as they journey toward a diasporic location that satisfies their need for personal and historical authenticity: Selina opts for Barbados and a genealogical quest; Merle heads for the African continent; and given Marshall's oft-quoted comments on Merle's being beyond her control, I wonder: could Merle's African journey resonate with Marshall's rapt experiences in Benin? Avey's lavish claustrophobic cruise, on the other hand, explodes into an astonishing adventure in Carriacou with dance and praise song, thanks to elder Lebert Joseph. Back in New York meanwhile, following her corporate-minded father's electoral defeat at her hands, Ursa returns to soak in her grandmother's herbs, to be the therapeutic archivist of her generation—and in place of the Caucasian-inspired "facts" foisted on the community by such colonial quislings as her university supervisor, she will proffer a grim but more accurate account. Put another way, as a mentor and artist living in New York, Ursa returns to an original Caribbean site of slavery, Triunion, deduces how colonial practices play out, and quickly disembarks, so to speak, from that old ship. In doing so, Ursa links up with a new generation of African Americans, complete with a distinct cultural identity.

The female protagonists also share distinct yet especially powerful gifts. Selina, Merle, the female leads in the short stories, Avey, and Ursa, are autodidacts—Selina's dancing, her studies, her speech at the association, Merle's political activism and sartorial creativity; Avey's ancient, deliberate dance on Carriacou; Ursa's thesis drawn from slavery's elusive archives—all their individual talents bespeak the joys and sorrows of life and keep their options open. They are ready for whatever presents itself, open to future options while mindful that memory always matters. Just as importantly, their gifts connect them to Sonny Rett's scintillating, soul-drenched jazz and Sonny Carmichael Payne's politically intuitive art.

Over all of them tower the kitchen poets who spoke their minds in a richly resonant cultural discourse signifying a hard-won self-determination and a tenacious purchase on life itself.[18] These fictional and "real-life" communities make up "a human necklace" of Marshall's life and works—its main pendant, *The Fisher King*, shot through with Payne/pain and sunshine. Additionally, at different levels of realization, the women recognize and internalize how formidable foremothers and living elders who dot Marshall's fictional landscape with their immense historical significance shaped their lives.

Sonny's diasporic search is hardwired within him, thanks to his wide-flung lineage: both the geographical journeys of slaves and former slaves worldwide, through the lived experiences of his great-grandmothers and other past relatives, as well as his illustrious archetypal grandfather. That ontological reality that constitutes young Sonny's being, enmeshed with the largesse and riches of the Parisian-Brooklyn community he knows, locates him as the embodiment of, in Stuart Hall's word, diasporization.[19] Preeminent novelist and fictional archivist of the diasporic saga, Paule Marshall casts a long shadow over the Barbadian people from whom she descends, of the Brooklyn community where she was raised—and of Benin, from whence she posits, her diasporic family originated.

Epitaph
Triangular Road: A Memoir

Paule Marshall's most recent publication, *Triangular Road: A Memoir* (2009), is a redaction of a lecture series, Bodies of Water, that she gave at Harvard University in 2005, a useful and important gloss on her fiction. It opens with an "Homage to Mr. (Langston) Hughes," who in 1965 invited Marshall to join him on a European cultural tour. The series' title echoes Marshall's view that rivers, seas, and oceans have hugely affected black history and culture in the Americas.

The tour featured two-day seminars in Paris, London, and Copenhagen, with crowded question-and-answer sessions frequently focusing on racism, black/white relations, and Hughes's controversial testimony before HUAC, the House Un-American Activities Committee. Evening meals crop up, somewhat amusingly, as another issue. She tells of their train journey from London to Oxford during which she and Hughes (something of a bon vivant) had to wait ages for their evening meal. After it finally arrived minutes before their destination, Hughes packed the corked wine in his satchel while Marshall carried "two doggie bags of half-eaten steaks."

The second chapter, "I've Known Rivers: The James River," describes a Labor Day trip that Paule Marshall took with her "energetic octogenarian" friend Virginia, "close to where it (the James) flows through the heart of Richmond." On the way, they notice a landmark, little more than a pile of ruins, that used to be not only docks, but once the largest and busiest docks on the river. She recalls its grim purpose: After sailing across the Middle Passage, enslaved and starving African men and women were herded ashore, caked in excrement, "chained together at the neck and legs," and forced on a dangerous journey in the dead of night to "Olde Richmond Towne." Traveling in the dark spared complaining townspeople from the unseemly sight of this "chattel cargo," bound for tobacco plantations, laying down a new railroad system, or constructing grand neoclassical buildings. She punctuates this reminder of Virginia's origins with a brief anecdote, told flatly, about her sister's death from chain-smoking Philip Morris cigarettes.

Marshall divides the complex third chapter, "I've Known Seas: The Caribbean Sea," into three parts: Barbados, Part I; Barbados, Part II; and Grenada, 1962. She begins with a grueling report of Barbados's connection to the slave trade, as the first piece of land sighted after Middle Passage and hence as a critical way station en route.

Maintaining an uninflected tone, Marshall goes on to introduce members of her family, her mother taking pride of place. Adriana Clement grew up in hilly Scotland on the Atlantic side of Barbados while her father, the mysterious Sam Burke, hailed from nobody knew where. Later, unknown to each other, they immigrated to the United States, Adriana having benefited from the selflessness of her brother, James Fitzroy. A riveting discussion ensues about Panama Money, a phrase referring to remittances sent home by "young men from the islands" who helped build the Panama Canal. Once again, it's a horror story about roughly five thousand Caribbean workers dying vile deaths from malaria, yellow fever, and bubonic plague. In Marshall's words, "The West Indian wing of the Great Migration North could not have taken place without Panama Money." This statement brings us to Adriana's mother, Alberta Jane Clement, who bore fourteen children, managed the family money, and was lovingly nicknamed M' Da-Duh. Here Marshall's seven-year-old self writes an italicized page and a half of personal reminiscence about Da-Duh, a charming memory of meeting the redoubtable grandmother for the first time. She later published a story about this experience, and adds that Da-Duh lives on as a significant leitmotif: she "appears, in one guise or another, in every book I've written."

Da-Duh's daughter, Adriana Clement, the daughter who emigrated, ends up in the large Barbadian community in Brooklyn where she meets, marries, and raises a family with Sam Burke. When Paule is eleven, her parents separate for good after Sam, now Brother Burke, "finds god."

In part 2, Marshall describes a year she spent in Barbados, revising her first novel, visiting remaining relatives and friends, and participating in discussions about Barbadian independence. She decides to write about the landlord (Mr. Watson in *Soul*), but almost immediately gets caught up in an exciting Jamesian moment. She witnesses an incident that instantly stimulates her imagination and a second novel is born.

The section on Grenada identifies another creative phase, wholly unexpected again, but in quite different circumstances. She is overcome with every writer's nightmare, run aground with writer's block. At the insistence of a concerned friend, she joins Grenadians on their annual excursion by boat to Carriacou where they perform ancient African rituals. Born of this experience, *Praisesong for the Widow* replaces writer's block.

In the last chapter set in 1977, a coda of sorts, Marshall recalls her experiences in Nigeria at the Second World Festival of Black and African Arts. The reception accorded an internally divided U.S. delegation astounds them: "the non-stop applause was pure *Omowale* joy—*Omowale* meaning, in the Yoruba language, 'The child has returned.'" A joyful Marshall terms this enthusiastic Nigerian response "a long traditional West African praise song."

Throughout her riveting memoir, Marshall links the circumstances and people—the source material that stoked her fiction—most strikingly the "Poets in the Kitchen" who had unknowingly introduced her to writing. Over the years, she slowly acknowledged other influential anecdotes and details. Unsurprisingly, her memoir and fiction resemble each other in illumining the connection between historical context, the formation of evolving identities, and the long shadow cast by the scourge of slavery.

Marshall's organization of her memoir is a veritable coup de grace. Beginning with origins, she pays homage to Langston Hughes, who with a great goodwill set the extraordinary tour in motion. Similarly, at the very end she pays homage to black and African creativity and camaraderie. Internationalism comes home. In between these praise songs, she historically locates Barbados, Virginia, and Grenada in the context of the slave trade and African presence.

Put another way, after the initial homage to Langston Hughes, Marshall narrates a centuries-long history of human atrocities and work-related fatal diseases borne by African and Caribbean people. Grace and resilience, honesty and calm, and most movingly, an abiding love for nine million victims, mark this narrative of a triangular road drenched in the blood and sweat of millions.

Lucky students, those privileged to attend this lecture series about rivers, seas, and oceans that have hugely affected black history and culture in the Americas, a wealth of human history and experience.

Notes

Chapter 1

1. Clan, *Culture and Nationalism in the African Diaspora* (London: Verso, 1996), 13.
2. Paul Gilroy, *Black Atlantic: Modernity and Double Consciousness* (Cambridge, MA: Harvard University Press, 1993), 1.
3. Sidney J. Lemelle and Robin D. G. Kelley, *Imagining Home: Class, Culture and Nationalism in the African Diaspora* (London: Verso, 1994), 9.
4. Paule Marshall, "The Making of a Writer," *Reena and Other Stories* (Old Westbury, NY: The Feminist Press, 1970), 3–12.
5. Sally A. Lodge, "'PW Interviews Paule Marshall': Interview with Sally Lodge," *Publisher's Weekly*, January 20, 1984, 90.

Chapter 2

1. Paule Marshall, *Brown Girl, Brownstones* (Old Westbury, NY: The Feminist Press, 1959). All references will be to this edition.
2. Mary Helen Washington, "Afterword," *Brown Girl, Brownstones*, 312. For detailed information about Barbadian immigration to New York, neighborhoods, and economic survival strategies, see Philip Kasinitz, *Caribbean New York: Black Immigrants and the Politics of Race* (Ithaca, NY: Cornell University Press, 1992), especially 19–89. See also, R. M. Lacovia, "Migration and Transmutation in

the Novels of McKay, Marshall, and Clarke," *Journal of Black Studies* 7, no. 4 (1977): 437–54.
3. Hilary McD. Beckles, *A History of Barbados: From American Indian Settlement to Nation-State* (Cambridge, UK: Cambridge University Press, 1990), 112. See also Ronald Tree, *A History of Barbados* (New York: Random House, 1972); George Hunte, *Barbados* (New York: Hastings House, 1974); Alexander Hoyos, *Barbados: A History from the Amerindians to Independence* (London: Macmillan, 1978); P. F. Campbell, ed., *Chapters in Barbados History* (St. Ann's Garrison, 1986); and J. H. Parry, P. M. Sherlock, and A. P. Maingot, *A Short History of the West Indies* (London: Macmillan, 1956). For the emigration of Barbadians to Panama, see Bonham C. Richardson, *Panama Money in Barbados 1900–1920* (Knoxville, TN: University of Tennessee Press, 1985).
4. Bonham C. Richardson, *Panama Money in Barbados*, 113, 295.
5. Ibid., 120.
6. Mary Helen Washington, "Afterword," 311.
7. Hilary McD. Beckles, *A History of Barbados*, 143. See also L. P. Fletcher, "The Evolution of Poor Relief in Barbados 1900 to 1969," *Caribbean Studies* 25, nos. 3–4 (1992): 255–75.
8. Hilary McD. Beckles, *A History of Barbados*, 143. See also Jill Hamilton, *Women of Barbados: Amerindian Era to Mid 20th Century* (Barbados: Letchworth Press, n.d.).
9. Mary Helen Washington, "Afterword," 311.
10. Ibid., 311–12.
11. For the following quotation, see Darryl Pinckney, "Roots," *New York Times Book Review*, 1983, 26.
12. In "The Absence of Writing or How I Almost Became a Spy," Marlene Nourbese Philip discusses the significance of images in maintaining hierarchies. In the case of the Barbadian community, their very presence and cultural markings dissolve the power of the images. Marlene Nourbese Philip, *She Tries Her Tongue; Her Silence Softly Breaks* (Charlottetown, Prince Edward Island, Canada: Ragweed Press, 1989), 10–25.
13. In a related context, bell hooks talks of the power of these early links between artistic output and political activity. bell hooks, "An Aesthetic of Blackness: Strange and Oppositional," *Yearning: Race, Gender and Cultural Politics* (Boston: South End Press, 1990), 103–13.

14. Wilfred Cartey, *Whispers from the Caribbean: I Going Away, I Going Home*, vol. 2: (Los Angeles: University of California, Center for Afro-American Studies, 1991), 296.
15. For the miscarriage of justice concerning the Scottsboro Boys, see Haywood Patterson and Earl Conrad, *Scottsboro Boy* (New York: Doubleday, 1950); James Goodman, *Stories of Scottsboro* (New York: Pantheon, 1994); and Dan T. Carter, *Scottsboro: A Tragedy of the American South* (Baton Rouge: Louisiana State University Press, 1969).
16. Apollo Theater was a celebrated theater in Harlem. See Jack Schiffman, *Harlem Heyday: A Pictorial History of Modern Black Show Business and the Apollo Theater* (New York: Prometheus Books, 1984), 19–40 and passim.
17. Yellow is a complex color in texts by African-Caribbean writers. See, for example, Wilfred Cartey, *Whispers*, 297–98; and Moira Ferguson, *Jamaica Kincaid: Where the Land Meets the Body* (Charlottesville: University of Virginia Press, 1993), 111–12.
18. For the Boer War and racism, see A. L. Morton, *A People's History of England* (New York: International Publishers, 1938), 483–87.
19. Sugar as a stand-in for livelihood, memory, slavery, and the history of colonial expropriation is ubiquitous in Caribbean texts. For the importance of sugar, see Noel Deerr, *The History of Sugar* (London: Chapman and Hall, 1950). See also Elsa Goveia, *Slave Society in the British Leeward Islands* (New Haven, CT: Yale University Press, 1965), especially 11–12, 144–45, and passim.
20. In the sense that Silla is the attempted absence of otherness and otherness itself simultaneously, she is also a fellow victim. See Ebele Eko, "Beyond the Myth of Confrontation: A Comparative Study of African and African-American Female Protagonists," *Ariel: A Review of International Literature* 17, no. 4 (October 1986): 146. There is a fine discussion of these issues in a book regrettably too late to be included in this one: Stelamaris Coser, *Bridging the Americas: The Literature of Paule Marshall, Toni Morrison and Gayle Jones* (Philadelphia, PA: Temple University Press, 1994), 59 and passim. For discussions of absence and otherness, see Pierre Macherey, *The Theory of Literary Production*, trans. Geoffrey Wall (London: Routledge and Kegan Paul, 1978); Trinh Minh-Ha, *Where the Moon Waxes Red: Representation, Gender and Cultural Politics* (New York: Routledge, 1991), 185–99; and Trinh Minh-Ha, "Other

from myself/my other self," George Robertson et al., eds, *Travellers' Tales: Narratives of Home and Displacement* (London: Routledge, 1994), 9–26.

21. For these attitudes, see for example, Léon Poliakov, *The History of Anti-Semitism,* trans. from the French by Miriam Kochan (New York: The Vanguard Press, 1975); Robert S. Wistrich, *Antisemitism: The Longest Hatred* (New York: Pantheon, 1991). Note also the strength of the Jewish community in Barbados with which the empire was familiar. See Ronald Tree, "The Jewish Settlements in Barbados," in *A History of Barbados* (London: Granada, 1977), 82–86.

22. Barbados is frequently referred to by tourists as little England. For the origins of that concept, see Henry Fraser et al., eds., *A-Z of Barbadian Heritage* (Jamaica: Heinemann, 1990), 21.

23. This issue of leaving home and building a home that can never replicate its origin is discussed at length in Shabnam Grewal et al., eds., *Charting the Journey: Writings by Black and Third World Women* (London: Sheba Feminist Publishers, 1988). For issues of home, displacement, and imagined communities, see Sidney J. Lemelle and Robin D.G. Kelley, eds., *Imagining Home: Class, Culture and Nationalism in the African Diaspora* (London: Verso, 1994).

24. Ironically, in voodoo, birds and chicken feathers symbolize peace and unity. Marshall may be alluding to Selina's naiveté in viewing the women from a particularly Anglocentric viewpoint. See Richard A. Loederer, *Voodoo in Haiti*, trans. Desmond Ivo Vesley (New York: The Literary Guild, 1935). Selina's view of the women in the kitchen is influenced by the love she feels for her father. Sandra O'Neale expresses it very forcefully: "where fathers are present, strained relationships with mothers exist." See "Race, Sex and Self: Aspects of Bildungsroman; Select Novels by Black American Women Novelists," *MELUS* (1982): 27. See also Michael S. Laguerre, *Voodoo and Politics in Haiti* (New York: St. Martins 1989), 22–31; Wendy Dutton, "The Problem of Invisibility: Voodoo and Zora Neale Hurston," *Frontiers* 13, no. 2: 131–52.

25. As in *Soul Clap Hands and Sing*, Paule Marshall may be intertextualizing T. S. Eliot's poem "The Hollow Man" to signify despair and emptiness. See Darwin T. Turner, "Introduction," *Soul Clap Hands and Sing*, xlv; T. S. Eliot, *The Complete Poems and Plays, 1909–1950* (New York: Harcourt, Brace, and World, 1962), 56.

26. For the importance of chickens to ancient ritual, see Loederer, *Voodoo in Haiti*, 172 and 173.
27. For the clash of cultures, see Trudier Harris, "No Outlet for the Blues: Silla Boyce's plight in *Brown Girl, Brownstones*," *Callaloo* 6, no. 2 (1983): 57–67. In Greek mythology, Iphigenia was the daughter of Clytemnestra and Agamemnon. She was offered as a sacrifice to Artemis to enable the Greek fleet to sail for Troy. For Silla's supposedly machine-like qualities compared to the seeming easygoingness of Deighton Boyce and Suggie Skeete, see Lloyd W. Brown, "The Rhythms of Power in Paule Marshall's Fiction," *Novel* 7, no. 2: esp. 161–62.
28. Father Peace is a stand-in for Father Divine, a black religious leader who was very popular in Harlem in the 1930s. He claimed to be God and exhorted his disciples to reject material goods and give them to him. He then would fund missions for the homeless and hungry. See Darwin T. Turner, "Introduction," in *Soul Clap Hands and Sing* (Washington, DC: Howard University Press, 1988), xviii.
29. Brutus, the Roman political and military leader who participated in the assassination of Julius Caesar, was assisted in his death on the battlefield by his loyal retainer.
30. For Scylla and Charybdis, see *The Aeneid of Virgil*, A Verse Translation by Allen Mandelbaum (New York: Bantam, 1961). See also Michael Grant, *Myths of the Greeks and Romans* (New York: Mentor, 1962), 66, 258.
31. In the complicated issue of mimicking, Selina is here replicating her father's ingratiating smile. He wants to be part of the community but feels treated as an outsider. For theorizing about mimicking in a number of contexts, see Jenny Sharpe, "Figures of Colonial Resistance," *Modern Fiction Studies* 35, no. 1 (Spring 1989): 143–47.
32. Regarding the issue of external construction see Sander Gilman, "Black Bodies, White Bodies: Toward an Iconography of Female Sexuality in Late Nineteenth-Century Art, Medicine, and Literature," in *"Race," Writing and Difference*, ed. Henry Louis Gates, Jr. (Chicago: University of Chicago Press, 1985), 223–61.
33. Sabine Bröck, "Transcending the 'Loophole of Retreat': Paule Marshall's Placing of Female Generations," *Callaloo* 10, no. 1 (1987): 79–90. For the issues of white racism, see also Geta J. Leseur, "*Brown Girl, Brownstones* as a Novel of Development," *Obsidian II: Black Literature in Review* 1, no. 3 (1986): 126–27.

34. For these tensions, see "Architectural Imagery and Unity in Paule Marshall's *Brown Girl, Brownstones,*" *Negro American Literature Forum* 9 (1975): 71. For a brilliant discussion of migration, see Carole Boyce Davies, *Black Women, Writing and Identity: Migrations of the Subject* (London: Routledge, 1994) especially 117, 120, 132–35, 150, and passim. See also Fiona Giles, "The Softest Disorder: Representing Cultural Indeterminancy," Chris Tiffin and Alan Lawson, eds., *De-Scribing Empire: Post-Colonialism and Textuality* (London, Routledge, 1994); Trinh Minh-Ha, "Other Than Myself," *Travellers Tales*, 9–26. For isolation and displacement, see Elaine Savory Fido, "Texture of Third World Reality in the Poetry of Four African-Caribbean Women," *Out of the Kumbla: Caribbean Women and Literature*, ed. Carole Boyce Davies and Elaine Savory Fido (Trenton, NJ: Africa World Press, 1990), 29–44.
35. Robert Fulton (1765–1815) is well known for pioneer work in steam navigation: "The power of propelling boats by steam," he said "is now fully proved." Robert Fulton made steamboats a profitable venture. See the *Encyclopedia Americana*, vol. 2. and Wallace S. Hutcheson Jr., *Robert Fulton* (Annapolis, MD: Naval History Press, 1981).

Chapter 3

1. Paule Marshall, *Soul Clap Hands and Sing*, Intro. Darwin T. Turner (Washington, DC: Howard University Press, 1988).
2. Paule Marshall, *Reena and Other Stories* (New York: The Feminist Press, 1983), 51.
3. Ibid., 51.
4. On the edge of London, Watford is used by landowners to suggest the boundaries of English culture. The name conjures up a narrow Eurocentric outlook, not unlike Berman's.
5. For a discussion of Barbary Coast slaves, see Moira Ferguson, *Subject to Others: British Women Writers and Colonial Slavery, 1678–1834* (New York: Routledge, 1992), 114–18 and passim.
7. For amber, see the *Oxford English Dictionary*, vol. 1, 217.
6. François Cachin, *Paul Gauguin* (New York: Discoveries, 1989), 93, 97–98, 191, and passim. The full title of the canvas is *Aita*

Tamari Vahiné Judith Te Parari (The Child-Woman Judith Is Not Yet Breached), or *Anna la Javanaise*.
8. André Gide, *L'Immoraliste*, trans. Dorothy Bussy (New York: Alfred A. Knopf, 1930), 133.
9. For Kaieteur Falls as a critical source of energy for Guiana, see James Rodway, *Guiana: British, Dutch, and French* (New York: Scribners, 1912), 272.
10. *Encyclopedia Americana*. International Edition, Connecticut, 1994, 632–34.
11. The Casa Samba or Samba house resonates with the name of the racist character Sambo.
12. In evaluations of Shakespeare's play, Caliban has been called everything from the proletariat to the Missing Link, or the Wild Man, The Bestial Man. There has always been a cult of Miranda-worship. Caliban is an "analogue of natural anarchism. . . . and Miranda represents the dialogue of justice and mercy." Ronald Berman, *A Reader's Guide to Shakespeare's Plays* (Glenview, IL: Scott, Foresman and Co., 1965), 139–41.
13. Brunhild is a character in Richard Wagner's Nibelungenlied. She is the legendary Queen of Iceland. As such, she depicts Aryanness.
14. For a sense of Caliban's despondence at his self-image, see Frantz Fanon, *Black Skin, White Masks* (London: Pluto, 1952), 192 and passim; W. E. B. Dubois, *The Souls of Black Folk* (New York: Bantam Books, 1903), 3.
15. T. S. Eliot, *The Complete Poems and Plays, 1909–1950*, 56. For a discussion of hollow men, see *Soul Clap Hands and Sing*, intro. Darwin T. Turner, xlv.
16. "I speak this dispossession/in the language of the master." Abena Busia, *Testimonies* (New York: Doubleday, 1994), 3.

Chapter 4

1. Paule Marshall, *The Chosen Place, the Timeless People* (New York: Vintage, 1942). All references will be to this edition.
2. For commentary on sugar in Barbados, see Beckles, *A History*, 20–23, 27–8, 69–74, and passim.
3. The novella excerpted from *The Chosen Place, the Timeless People*,

entitled "Merle," fleshes out silent aspects of the original novel. The short version also begins with the symbolic washing away of Westminster Low Road, and Merle's efforts to introduce gabions. It focuses primarily in three arenas: on Merle; on the relationship between Merle and Saul; and on Bourne, the small island. In other words, Marshall addresses the "chosen place"—Bournehills—and the "timeless people" who are represented in their ongoing colonial struggle by Merle. Merle eventually crosses back to family and to Africa—to another "timeless people" and "chosen place." Marshall almost exclusively focuses on the United States-United Kingdom-African crossings. Of "Merle" written in 1969 and 1983, Paule Marshall states that she is "in partial agreement with a reviewer who termed the protagonist part saint, part revolutionary, part obeah woman" (*Reena*, 109).
4. Westminster is the home of the Houses of Parliament; Whitehall and Buckingham Palace are residences of the Prime Minister and the Queen, respectively.
5. The Barracoon, the barracks where slaves were temporarily confined, is tellingly situated in White Hall Lane, Whitehall being the seat of the British Government (empire) in London. See note 2. Barracoon derives from the Spanish for hut and hence is related etymologically to Lyle Hutson whose activities might be recreating slave conditions.
6. Leesey is another ancestral figure in Paule Marshall's corpus: she is, Marshall says, "symbolic for me of the long line of black women—African and the New World—who made my being possible." Commentary in Paule Marshall, *Reena and Other Stories* (New York: The Feminist Press, 1983), 95.
7. For slave insurgency in Bourne/Barbados, see Michael Craton, *Testing the Chains* (Ithaca, NY: Cornell University Press, 1982), 335. In the Barbadian seventeenth-century rebellion, Cuffee was described as an "Ancient Gold Coast Negro." Hilary McD. Beckles, *A History of Barbados: From Amerindian Settlement to Nation State* (Cambridge, UK: Cambridge University Press, 1990), 38. Note, too, that Coffee or Cuffy is a West African day-name, for a male child born on a friday. See Henry Fraser et al., eds., *A-Z of Barbadian Heritage* (Kingston: Heinemann, 1990), 43.
8. For Lyle Hutson's name, see note 5. Worth remembering, in

addition to the association with barracoon is the fact that Tate and Lyle, the famous British sugar-producing company, functions to this day.

9. "All we o'one" is a common Caribbean expression about the collectivity of the people.
10. Virgil, *The Aenead of Virgil*, trans. Allen Mandelbaum (New York: Bantam, 1965), 1. Mandelbaum translates: "I sing of arms and of a man; his fate has made him fugitive . . . until he brought a city into being."
11. As a driving overseer, Stinger recalls the practices of slavery, his name's metaphorically related to death.
12. Struck blind on the way to Damascus, the biblical Saul is someone who undergoes a conversion. Saul cannot yet see his role in Bourne, nor his wife's machinations, but his conversion is imminent. The word *sephardic*, moreover, underlines that Saul belongs to one of the two major Jewish groups. He is probably a Spanish or Portuguese Jew by descent. Saul's temporary blindness again accentuates the narrative of Saul of Tarsus, en route to Damascus in the process of conversion to a "higher truth." Roger Highfield, ed., *Spain in the Fifteenth Century 1369–1516, Essays and Extracts by Historians of Spain*, trans. Frances M. Lopez-Morrillas (New York: Macmillan, 1972).
13. The name of Harriet's relative, Susan Harbin, signals Harriet's like-minded approach to the word. Harbin, from harbinger, warns in advance and brings to the reader a sense of foreboding, a knowledge of Harriet's attitudes that link her back to Susan Harbin.
14. For a discussion of the attraction of the other, see Frantz Fanon, *Black Skin, White Marks*.
15. As a nocturnal mammal, originally considered a bird which retires to dark spaces at night, bats resemble Harriet in her stealthy behavior and in the masks she wears to conceal her negativity toward the people.
16. The eggs with which Harriet was associated cannot restore life. The fact that she cooks special eggs at the house of the overseer Stinger, a name applied figuratively to death, stresses his undue hard work, but also Harriet's role in that scenario.
17. The complicitous role that alleged philanthropy, including missionary work, plays in colonized countries is legion. Among many

texts on the subject, see Barry W. Higman, *Slave Populations of the British Caribbean, 1807–1834* (Baltimore, MD: The Johns Hopkins University Press, 1984); Vincent T. Harlow, *Christopher Codrington, 1668–1710* (Oxford: Clarendon Press, 1928); Betsy Rogers, *Cloak of Charity: Studies in Eighteenth-Century Philanthropy* (London: Methuen, 1949).

18. Specifically in Greek mythology, Daphne was a nymph changed to laurel by her river god father so she could elude Apollo. Daphne Pollard cannot be who she is; her agency is removed as her last name, meaning headlessness, also signifies. A pollard is a person with an immensely shaped head, often a tree or animal with its head or horns lopped off.

19. For repressed desire and loathing in tandem, see Joseph Sandler with Anna Freud, *The Analysis of Defence: The Ego and the Mechanisms of Defence Revisited* (New York: International Universities Press, 1985). See also, Caroline Walker Bynum, *Holy Feast and Holy Fast: The Religious Significance of Food to Medieval Women* (Berkeley, CA: University of California Press, 1987).

20. The view of Merle's friend in London matches one view of lesbians and gay men in Paule Marshall's text. Saul's research assistant, Allen Fusso, who is gay, is depicted as someone with insufficient self-knowledge until it is too late (306–307 and passim).

21. Merle is casting off all the white trappings; she is erasing any form of assimilation, so carefully documented in the paraphernalia and appointments of her bedroom (398–403).

22. For details about the atrocities of the Middle Passage journey, see Eric Williams, *Capitalism and Slavery* (New York: Capricorn Books, 1944); Basil Davidson, *Black Mother* (London: Victor Gollancz, 1961); Daniel Pratt Mannix, *Black Cargoes: A History of the Atlantic Slave Trade, 1518–1865* (New York: Viking, 1962); J. D. Fage, *A History of West Africa: An Introductory Survey*, 4th ed. (Cambridge, UK: Cambridge University Press, 1969); Herbert S. Klein, *The Middle Passage: Comparative Studies in the Atlantic Slave Trade* (Princeton, NJ: Princeton University Press, 1978), 141–74. See also Olaudah Equiano's, *Equaino's Travels. His Autobiography. The Interesting Narrative of the Life of Olaudah Equiano or Gustavus Vassa the African*, ed. Paul Edwards (London: Heinemann, 1789, reprinted 1967), 25–32; Werner Sallors and Maria Deidrich, eds.

The Black Columbiad: Defining Moments in African American Literature and Culture (Cambridge, MA: Harvard University Press, 1994).

For slave importation and the population of Barbados as a sugar colony, see Noel Deerr, *The History of Sugar*, vols. 1 and 2 (London: Chapman and Hall, 1949–1950). To stress the intermediary location of an overseer, Paule Marshall chooses the name Pollard, or headless person, someone who perhaps follows order and has no thoughts of his or her own.

23. For a discussion of praisesongs and poems, see Judith Gleason, ed., *Leaf and Bone: African Praise-Poems* (New York: Penguin, 1980), esp. xiii–xxxiii.
24. Insulin can be manufactured from pig hormones, making the relationship between pig-sticking rituals and diabetes unusually helpful.
25. Pig sticking also brings Saul fact to face with his upbringing and his "difference" from the community whom he attempted to aid. For a brilliant analysis of Sunday's pig stickings and the role of carnival, see Hortense J. Spillers, "Chosen Place, Timeless People: Some Figurations on the New World," in *Conjuring: Black Women, Fiction, and Literary Tradition*, ed. Marjorie Pryse and Hortense J. Spillers (Bloomington: Indiana University Press, 1985), 151–75.
26. In a brilliant multiplicity, "I shall not be moved" refers not only to ideas about civil rights, but to Harriet's intransigance concerning these rights and the resistance that Alberta and Merle can muster in different forms.
27. Echoes in the word *toadstool*, of the eruption of tragedy after the bombings of Hiroshima and Nagasaki, are unmistakeable. Marshall reminds us how much the intervention of Harriet and her forebearers cost African people.
28. Bob and Dorothy Hargreaves, *Tropical Blossoms* (Portland, OR: Hargreaves Industrial), 45. The cassia tree is named after the verb meaning to strip off bark. The bark is thicker, coarser, and less delicate in flavor and cheaper than real cinnamon.
29. For the word *versant*, see the *Oxford English Dictionary*.
30. For the matter of internalizing the other, see Homi Bhabha, "Foreword," Frantz Fanon, *Black Skin, White Masks*, xix. See also Frantz Fanon's own discussion about internalizing otherness in *Black Skin, White Masks*.

The almshouse is a focus of the novel, meshing Merle and Seifert and ultimately King Lear. In its origin as a place that extends charitable relief to the poor, generally funded by private charity, it resembles colonialism itself. It marks dependence and an auxiliary relationship and appears to assist the supposedly "disadvantaged."

Chapter 5

1. *Praisesong for the Widow* (New York: E. P. Dutton, 1984), 14–15. All references will be to this edition.
2. Avey is temporarily refusing to journey personally and psychologically as well as geographically. See Deborah E. McDowell, "New Directions for Black Feminist Criticism," in *The New Feminist Criticism: Essays on Women, Literature, and Theory*, ed. Elaine Showalter (Pantheon: New York, 1985), 186–99.
3. By traveling on a boat named after Robert Fulton, pioneer steam navigator, Marshall stresses the need, not only for basic exploration, but for journeys to the point of origin. See *Encyclopedia Americana*. International Edition vol. 12, 158–59.
4. Note that Avey's father is a "Gullah Black." Gullah is the Creole language based on English and is still spoken by former slaves and their descendants in the part of the country where great-aunt Cuney lives, namely the Sea Islands of South Carolina and Georgia and on the mainland. Gullah fuses speech used by British colonialists and aspects of West African languages. Linguistically speaking, Gullah represents closeness to origins. See *Oxford English Dictionary*, vol. 6, 944–45. See *The New Encyclopedia Britannica*, vol. 5, 566; *The Encyclopedia American*, International Edition, vol. 15, 600.
5. For compelling analyses of Avey's gradual awakening and the process of self-confrontation and ritual, see Barbara Christian, "Ritualistic Process and the Structure of Paule Marshall's *Praisesong for the Widow*," *Callaloo* 6, no. 2 (1983): 74–84; Velma Pollard, "Cultural Connections in Paule Marshall's *Praisesong for the Widow*," *World Literature Written in English*, no. 2 (1955): 285–90; and Keith A. Sandiford, "Paule Marshall's *Praisesong for the Widow*: The Reluctant Heiress, or Whose Life is it Anyway?" *Black American Literature Forum* 20, no. 4 (Winter 1966). See also Gay Wilentz, *Binding*

Cultures: Black Women Writers in Africa and the Diaspora (Bloomington: Indiana University Press, 1992), 99–115. For Avatara, see *Oxford English Dictionary*, vol. 5, 814.

6. The incident with Rodney King in Los Angeles is just the best known and most recent in a long line of such incidents when King was beaten by the L.A. police in 1991, followed by public riots.
7. The irony of a dessert in the shape of the Palace of Versailles crops up in a later remark by Avey's radical activist daughter, Marian. The sarcastic Marian is keenly aware that Britain, France, and their allies carved up the world according to their preferences at the Treaty of Versailles following World War One. For a history of the use of Versailles to resolve western imperial antagonisms to which Marian is referring in a macro-sense, see *The Encyclopedia Americana*, International Edition, vol. 28, 44–45.
8. See Margaret Zellers, *Fielding's Caribbean, 1991* (New York: William Morrow, 1991), 439.
9. This natural genocide of a town parallels microcosmically the genocide that occurred in the Middle Passage where innocent people were also victims. Avey is unconsciously projecting her sense of living amid the wreckage of white pride or Bianca Pride. She views herself as the sole survivor. For a compelling explication of these connections, see Keith Sandiford, "Paule Marshall's *Praisesong*," 388.
10. For great-aunt Cuney's powers of conjure and spirits, see Georgia Writers Project, *Drums and Shadows: Survival Studies among the Georgia Coastal Negroes* (Athens, GA: University of Georgia Press, 1940), 65–72. For connections to African spiritual practices, see also Susan Willis, *Specifying: Black Women Writing the American Experience* (Madison: University of Wisconsin Press, 1987), 53–82.
11. For Tatem, its inhabitants, and their remembrances, see Georgia Writers Project, *Drums and Shadows*, 65–72. See also, for information about Gullah and Barbados, Warren Alleyne and Henry Fraser, *The Barbados-Carolinas Connection* (London: Macmillan, 1988); and Mary Lumsden, *The Barbados-American Connection* (London: Macmillan, 1982).
12. Gullah is the Creole dialect spoken in Charleston and Coastal South Carolina. The fact that many Barbadians settled in Charleston is said to explain some linguistic similarities.

13. The Ring Shout dance (like Gullah) echoes the African ancestry of Avey and her great-aunt. See Barbara Christian, "Ritualistic Process," 82; and Keith Sandiford, "Paule Marshall's *Praisesong*," 387–89. See also James D. Shaughnessy, ed., *The Roots of Ritual* (Grand Rapids, MI: William B. Eerdmans Publishing Company, 1973).
14. A familiar figure in U.S. history during the Civil War, General Sherman, an American commander, led Union troops to rout Atlanta. See *The Encyclopedia Americana*, International Edition, vol. 26, 706–707.
15. For a fine discussion of the significance of the Ibo Landing, see, Keith Sandiford, "Paule Marshall's *Praisesong*," 373–91.
16. Since another formulation of this sentence closes *Praisesong for the Widow*, Marshall is highlighting the importance of the mythic return to Africa. *Praisesong for the Widow* addresses the need for that return.
17. For the significance of the name Cuney from cuneiform, see *Oxford English Dictionary*, vol. 4, 128.
18. Paule Marshall suggests that, just as Faust made a pact with the devil and sold his soul, so Avey and Jerome Johnson, to their detriment because of economic straits, made an unspoken pact with establishment values.
19. By joining the originally and ironically named Freemasons, Jerome Johnson signifies his conflict and his recognition of segregation. Predominantly white at its founding, from 1717 on the Masons gradually became an avenue for blacks to succeed economically. It also offered a social haven and an informal political meeting ground. For black Freemasonry, see Donn A. Cass, *Negro Freemasonry and Segregation* (Chicago: Ezra A Cook, 1970); W. H. Grimshaw, *Official History of Freemasonry Among the Colored People in North America* (New York: Negro Universities Press, 1903).
20. Marian Anderson was banned from singing inside Independence Hall by the Daughters of the American Revolution. With a large number of supporters, she flouted and transcended the ban by singing outside the Hall on its steps, an act that proclaimed her displacement, and the displacement of all blacks, to the world. See Marian Anderson, *My Lord, What a Morning: An Autobiography* (New York: Viking, 1961).
21. For details on Versailles, see *Encyclopedia Americana*, International Edition, vol. 28.

22. For the character of Lebert Joseph, see Lucy Wilson, "Aging and Ageism in Paule Marshall's *Praisesong for the Widow* and Beryl Gilroy's *Frangipani House*," *Caribbean Studies* (1988): 191–92.
23. For Juba as a signal early dance as well as an important name historically, see *The New Encyclopedia Britannica*, vol. 6, 634–35. For Juba, see also Velma Pollard, "Cultural Connections in Paule Marshall's *Praisesong for the Widow*," 292–94.
24. For the goddess of love, femininity, and Sweet Waters, see also Marjorie Leach, *Guide to the Gods* (Santa Barbara, CA: ABC-CLIO, n.d.), 762.
25. For details on the atrocities of the Middle Passage, see several firsthand accounts by Africans themselves. Olaudah Equiano's is a notable example. See also Eric Williams, *Capitalism and Slavery* (New York: Capricorn Books, 1944); Basil Davidson, *Black Mother* (London: Victor Gollancz, 1961); Daniel Mannix, *Black Cargoes: A History of the Atlantic Slave Trade* (New York: Viking, 1962); J. D. Fage, *A History of West Africa. An Introductory Survey*, 4th ed., 141–74.
26. Ogun Feraille is the god of iron. See Leach, *Guide to the Gods*, 755; Michael Jordon, *Encyclopedia of Gods* (New York: Facts on File, 1993), 192 and passim; and Alfred Metraux, *Haiti: Black Peasants and Voodoo*, trans. Peter Lengyel (New York: Universe Books, 1960), 61.
27. See Gleason, *Leaf and Bone: African Praise-Poems*, 175; Minh-Ha, *When the Moon Waxes Red*, 161.
28. For Cartagena, see *Encyclopedia Americana*, vol. 5, 718.
29. See Davies, *Black Women, Writing and Identity*, 145.

Chapter 6

1. Paule Marshall, *Daughters* (New York: Plume, 1991). All references will be to this edition.
2. Cudjoe is a familiar name and activist in Caribbean culture. See, for example, Claude McKay, *Songs of Jamaica* (Miami, FL: Mnemosyne Publishing Inc., 1969). Not a coincidence, an important statue of Cudjoe (a slave freeing himself) stands in contemporary Bridgetown today, quite distant from the center of town.
3. Brian Jones, *Night Sky Identifier* (New York: Mallard Press, 1992).

4. For plates that trace its seasonal shape, see Ian Ridpath, *Astronomy: How We View Our Solar System and the Universe Beyond* (New York: W. H. Smith, 1991), 179–89.
5. Richard Hinckley Allen, *Star Names: Their Lore and Meaning* (New York: Dover Publications), 449.
6. Ibid., 449.
7. Ibid., 654.
8. Ibid., 457.
9. See, for example, Christopher Fyfe, *A History of Sierra Leone* (London, Oxford: Oxford University Press), 130–31, 138, 153.
10. The text is probably referring to Herbert Aptheker, *To Be Free: Studies in American Negro History* (New York: International Publishers, 1948); Angela Y. Davis, "Reflections on The Black Women's Role in The Community of Slaves," *Black Scholar* 3 (December 1971): 2–16.
11. Jacqueline Mitton, *The Penguin Dictionary of Astronomy* (London: Penguin, 1991), 396.
12. Valerie Boyd, "New York and West Indies Mixed in Marshall's Eloquent Daughters," *Focus, Lincoln Journal Star*.
13. See, for example, Paul Robeson, *Here I Stand* (Boston: Beacon Press, 1958).
14. See G. Addinton Forde, *Folk Beliefs of Barbados* (Barbados: National Cultural Foundation, 1988), 16, 23, 32, 34, 38.
15. In a statement about *Daughters*, Paule Marshall says, "my work is all about reconciling the two heritages, the two cultures that went into making me." In one way or another, all of *Daughters'* daughters do that. "Book Marks," *Essence*, October, 1991, 48.
16. Sven Birkerts, "The Black Women's Burden," *Mirabella*, October, 1991, 76. This reaction reminds me, in a quite different context, of some critical reactions to *The Color Purple*.

Chapter 7

1. Paule Marshall spoke of her ancestry in terms of these "three great wings" at a lecture entitled "Triangular Quest for Self and Community, Brooklyn-Barbados-Benin," at the Hall Center for the Humanities, University of Kansas, Lawrence, Kansas, February 29, 2003.
2. The title of the novel, *The Fisher King*, and subsequent references

identify Marshall's use of the Grail myth in a version that features the knight Perceval—young Sonny, who has come to heal his grandfather, Sonny Rett, the wounded fisher king. For an analysis of the roots of the Holy Grail legend, see Jessie L. Weston, *From Ritual to Romance* (Cambridge: Cambridge University Press, 1920).
3. For the lives of the self-exiled U.S. black musicians in the 1920s, see Tyler Stovall, *Paris Noir: African Americans in the City of Light* (Boston: Houghton Mifflin, 1996); Luke Miner, *Paris Jazz: A Guide: From the Jazz Age to the Present* (New York: The Little Book Room, 2005). (Contains lists of jazz greats.)
4. Paule Marshall stated on one occasion in Massachusetts that she modeled Sonny Rett on her cousin, Sonny Clement, who played the baritone sax; then he was drafted and died in boot camp. She went on to say that the bravery it takes to play the baritone sax fascinated her. So, since she had never met him due to a family dispute, she decided to construct a life for him. In Kansas, she mentioned that Sonny Clement left Brooklyn and played the sax in Paris. See note 1. For information about the origins of black music in Paris, see Jody Blake, *Le Tumulte Noir: Modernist Art and Popular Entertainment in Jazz-Age Paris, 1900–1930* (University Park, PA: Pennsylvania State University Press, 1999), 59–82; T. Stovall, *Paris Noir*, 135ff.; Olivier Berner, *Fireworks at Dusk: Paris in the Thirties* (Boston: Little, Brown and Company, 1993). I warmly thank Val Wilmer for several helpful discussions on jazz in that era.
5. Harold X. Connolly, *A Ghetto Grows in Brooklyn* (New York: NYU Press, 1977), 52.
6. Ibid., 52.
7. Ibid., 53.
8. Ibid., 54–55.
9. Ibid., 55.
10. For the founding of glee clubs in the late 1800s through the 1950s, see Wendell Pritchett, *Brownsville, Brooklyn: Blacks, Jews, and the Changing Face of the Ghetto*, Historical Studies of Urban America (Chicago: University of Chicago Press, 2002), 84, 85.
11. See also Philip Kasinitz, *Caribbean New York: Black Immigrants and the Politics of Race* (Ithaca, NY: Cornell University Press, 1991), 44; Connolly, *A Ghetto Grows in Brooklyn*, 54ff. For commentary on the impact of the Fulton Street subway on the black and white communities, see Connolly, ibid., 71–72. When interviewed, Mr. Wong

said quite simply, "The opening of the A train in 1936 helped attract more Blacks to the area," www.nyc-architecture.com/BES/BedStuy.htm.
12. There are numerous books and articles on Josephine Baker. See, for example, Josephine Baker and Jo Bouillon, *Josephine*, trans. Mariania Fitzpatrick (New York: Paragon House, 1988); Stovall, *Paris Noir*, 168–69; 215 ff.; and Blake, *Le Tumulte Noir*, in which Blake argues that Josephine Baker and Sidney Bechet might have had a bearing on the relationship between Africa and Europe during colonial times. See also Bechet's own *Treat It Gentle* (New York: Hill and Wang, 1960).
13. For an excellent cultural background to the rise of bebop, see Blake, *Le Tumulte*, 83–110; Stovall, *Paris Noir*, 216; David Gelly, *Masters of the Jazz Saxophone: Players and Their Music* (London: Balafon Books, 2000).
14. For the French-Algerian War, see Alistair Horne, *A Savage War of Peace: Algeria 1954–1962* (New York: Viking, 1978); Rita Moran, *Torture: The Role of Ideology in the French-Algerian War* (New York: Praeger Publishers, 1989); Martin Windrow, *The Algerian War 1954–62* (London: Osprey Publishing, 1997).
15. For a physical and historical description of the dangerous weapon, the halberd, that Sonny bears to guard his grandfather, see *Wikipedia*. Interestingly enough, the name *Carmichael* that Sonny bears (Hattie's surname) has, for its family crest a broken spear. This suggests not only Hattie's vulnerability, but also perhaps Sonny's. In the end, however, Sonny's quiet efforts to heal family rifts and rivalries, while exposing the national prejudices of his great-grandmothers, are successful (the West Indian immigrant experience in the case of Ulene versus the Northern Migration experience in which Florence Varina participated). His intuited use of the potentially lethal halberd trumps, as it were, the Carmichaels' broken spear. Note, however, just to compound the ambiguities that in 1421 at the Battle of Beauge in the Hundred Years' War, Sir John Carmichael's spear broke after he unseated the English Commander Clarence.
16. See the Fisher King and the Holy Grail in *Wikipedia* for variants of the myths. See also Weston, *From Ritual to Romance*.
17. A note on Varina in *Wikipedia* states that this first name for a

female became more popular locally following the American Civil War due to her reputation as the "First Lady of the Lost Cause." See note 15. "To Da-Duh in Memoriam" was first published in 1967 and reissued in *Reena and Other Stories*.
18. From "The Poets in the Kitchen," *Reena and Other Stories*, 3–12.
19. For diasporization, see Stuart Hall, *Critical Dialogues*, ed. Morley and Chen, 14, 447. Hall elsewhere succinctly notes: "Identity is not already 'there'; rather, it is a production, emergent, in process. It is situational; it shifts from context to context" (xi).

Bibliography

Primary Sources: The Texts of Paule Marshall

Books

Marshall, Paule. *Brown Girl, Brownstones.* New York: Random House, 1959; Chatham, NJ: Chatham Bookseller [1972, 1959]; New York: The Feminist Press, 1981.

———. *Soul Clap Hands and Sing.* New York: Atheneum, 1961; London: W.H. Allen, 1962; Chatham, NJ: Chatham Bookseller, 1971.

———. *The Chosen Place, the Timeless People.* New York: Harcourt, Brace and World, 1969. New York: Vintage Books, 1984, 1969.

———. *Praisesong for the Widow.* New York: G.P. Putnam and Sons, 1983, 1984.

———. *Reena and Other Stories.* Old Westbury, NY: The Feminist Press, 1970, 1983, 1984.

———. *Merle: A Novella and Other Short Stories.* London: Virago, 1985.

———. *Daughters.* New York: Atheneum; Toronto: Collier Macmillan; New York: Maxwell Macmillan International, 1991.

———. *The Fisher King.* New York: Simon and Schuster, 2000.

Short Stories

"Barbados." In *The Best Short Stories from 1899 to the Present.* Ed. Langston Hughes. New York: Little and Brown, 1967; *Black Writers of America.* Edited Houston A. Baker Jr., 358–69. New York:

McGraw-Hill, 1971; *Confirmation: An Anthology of African-American Women*. Ed. Amiri Baraka and Amina Baraka, 203–17. New York: Quill, 1983; *Her True True Name: An Anthology of Women's Writing from the Caribbean*. Ed. Pamela Mordecai and Betty Wilson, 164–71. London: Heinemann, 1989.

———. "Brazil." *Dark Symphony: Negro Literature in America*. Ed. James A. Emanuel and Theodore L. Gross, 402–26. New York: The Free Press, Collier Macmillan, 1969; *Cannon Shot and Glass Beads: Modern Black Writing*. Ed. George Lamming, 253–77. London: Picador, 1974.

———. "Reena." *Harper's Magazine*, October 1962: n. p.; *American Negro Short Stories*. Ed. J. H. Clarke, 264–82. New York: Hill and Wang, 1966; *Black Women*. Ed. Toni Cade, 20–37. New York: Signet, 1970; *Black-Eyed Susans: Short Stories by and of Black Women*. Ed. Mary Helen Washington, 114–37. Anchor City: Doubleday, 1975; *Solo: Women on Women Alone*. Ed. Linda Hamalian and Leo Hamalian, 264–83. New York: Dell, 1977.

———. "Return of the Native." *Freedomways* 4, no. 3 (1964): 358–66; *Sturdy Black Bridges: Visions of Black Women in Literature*. Ed. Roseann P. Bell et al., 314–21. Garden City, NY: Anchor/Doubleday, 1979.

———. "Some Get Wasted." *Harlem, U.S.A.* Ed. John Henrick Clarke. Berlin: Seven Seas, 1964.

———. "To Da-duh in Memoriam." *New World Quarterly* 3, no. 1 and 2 (1966–1967): 97–101; *Black Voices*. Ed. Abraham Chapman, 205–14. New York: Mentor, 1968; *Afro-American Writing: An Anthology of Prose and Poetry*. Ed. Richard Long and Eugenia E. Collier, 604–13. University Park: Pennsylvania University Press, 1985; *Facing the Sea: A New Anthology from the Caribbean Region*. Ed. Anne Walmsley and Nick Caistor, 29–34. London: Heinemann, 1986; *Imagining America: Stories from the Promised Land*. Ed. Wesley Brown and Amy Ling, 351–59. New York: Persea Books, 1991.

———. "Brooklyn." *The Third Woman: Minority Writers in the United States*. Ed. Dexter Fisher, 214–29. Boston: Houghton Mifflin, 1980.

Essays and Non-Fiction by Paule Marshall

Marshall, Paule. "Characterizations of Black Women in the American Novel." In *In the Memory and Spirit of Frances, Zora, and Lorraine:*

Essays and Interviews on Black Women and Writing. Edited Juliette Bowles, 76–79. Washington, DC: Institute for the Arts and Humanities, Howard University, 1979.

———. "Fannie Lou Hammer: Hunger Has No Color Line." *Vogue*, June 1970, 136–27.

———. "Kenya: Variety and Spice on Africa's East Coast." *Essence*, July 1982, 51–52.

———. "The Negro Woman in American Literature." *Freedomways* 6, no. 1 (1966): 20–25.

———. "Shaping the World of My Art." *New Letters*, October 1973, 97–112.

———. "Shadow and Act." *Mademoiselle*, June 1974, 82–83, 87.

———. "The Making of a Writer: From the Poets in the Kitchen." *New York Times Book Review*, January 9, 1983, 3, 34–35; *Callaloo* 6, no. 2 (1983): 21–30.

———. "Ties That Bind." *Essence 16* (May 1, 1985), 64, 66.

———. "A Black Woman Writer Thinks Back Through Her Mothers." Speech Given at the Second National Conference on Women and the Arts. Wisconsin University, Madison, June 3–6, 1985.

———. "Black Immigrant Women in *Brown Girl, Brownstones*." In *Female Immigrants to the United States, Caribbean, Latin American, and African Experience*, Eds. Delores M. Mortimer and Roy S. Bryce-Laporte. RIIES Occasional Papers No 2, 3–13. Washington, DC: Smithsonian Institution, 1981.

———. "Great Books We Never Finished Reading." *New York Times Book Review*, June 3, 1984, 47.

———. "How the City Shapes Its Writer: Gone to Heaven at the Apollo," *The New York Times Magazine* (April 28, 1985), 33, 60.

———. "Reading." *Mademoiselle* 79 (June 1974): 82–83.

———. "Rising Islanders of Bed-Stuy." *The New York Times Magazine*, November 3, 1985, 66–67, 78, 80–82.

Interviews

Bröck, Sabine. "'Talk As a Form of Action': An Interview with Paule Marshall." In *History and Tradition in Afro-American Culture*. Ed. Günther H. Lenz, 194–206. Frankfurt/New York: Campus Verlag, 1984.

Dance, Daryl Cumber. "An Interview with Paule Marshall." *The Southern Review* 28 (Winter 1992), June 14, 1991.

DeVeaux, Alexis. "Paule Marshall: In Celebration of Our Triumph." *Essence*, May 1979; 68, 71, 96, 98, 123–24, 126, 128, 131, 133, 135.

"Speaking of Books: *Daughters*. Sally Lodge's Interview with Paule Marshall." *Publishers Weekly* 238, no. 35 (Fall 1991): 19–20.

Ogundipe-Leslie, Omolara. "'Recreating Ourselves All over the World': Interview with Paule Marshall." *Matatu* 3, no. 6 (1989): 25–38.

"A Talk with Mary Helen Washington." In *Writing Lives: Conversations Between Women* Writers. Ed. Mary Chamberlain, 161–67. London: Virago, 1988.

Russel, Sandi. "Interview with Paule Marshall." *Wasafiri* 8 (Spring 1988): 14–16.

Williams, John. "Return of a Native Daughter: An Interview with Paule Marshall and Maryse Condé." *Sage* 3, no. 2 (Fall 1986): 52–53.

"The Book List Interview: Paule Marshall. Interview with Seaman Donna." *Booklist* 88, no.4 (October 15, 1991): 410–11.

"'Holding Onto the Vision': Sylvia Baer Interviews Paule Marshall," *The Women's Review of Books* 8, no. 10 and 11 (July 1991): 24–25.

"'I Sign My Mother's Name': Alice Walker, Dorothy West and Paule Marshall." In *Mothering the Mind: Twelve Studies and Their Silent Partners*. Ed. Ruth Perry and Martine W. Brownley, 142–63 (New York: Holmes and Martine, 1984).

"'Paule Marshall's Resonant Novel Explores the Balance between Cultures': Roger Bishop's Interview with Paule Marshall." *The Little Professor Bookshop* (October 1991): 6.

"Paule Marshall: Stages in a Writer's Life. Interview with Kate Rushin." *Sojourner* 10, no. 6 (April 1985): 16–17.

Pettis, Joyce. "A MELUS Interview: Paule Marshall." *MELUS* 17 (Winter 1991–1992).

"'PW Interviews Paule Marshall': Interview with Sally Lodge." *Publisher's Weekly* 225 (January 20, 1984): 90–91.

Broadcasts

(Radio broadcast). June 20, 2008, Susan Stamberg's talk on NPR with Paule Marshall, www.npr.org/programs/morning/features/2001/jun/010605.books.html#marshall.

Literary Biographies, Bibliographies, and Encyclopedic Entries

Barksdale, Richard. *Black Writers of America: A Comprehensive Anthology.* New York: Macmillan, 1972.

Bruck, Peter, and Wolfgang Karrer. *Afro-American Novel since 1960.* Amsterdam: B.R. Grunner, 1982

Campbell, Dorothy W. "Paule Marshall." *Index to Black American Writers in Collective Biographies.* Littleton: Libraries Unlimited, 1983, 108–09.

Christian, Barbara. "Paule Marshall: A Literary Biography" (Abridged Version). In *Black Feminist Criticism: Perspectives on Black Women Writers.* New York: Pergamon Press, 1985, 103–117.

"Paule Marshall: A Literary Biography." *Dictionary of Literary Biography of Afro-American Writers.* Chapel Hill, NC: University of North Carolina Press, 1978; *Black Feminist Criticism.* New York: Pergamon Press, 1985, 103–117; "Paule Marshall." *Dictionary of Literary Biography. Afro-American Fiction Writers after 1955.* Ed. Thadious M. Davis and Trudier Harris, 161–70. Detroit, MI: Gale Research Company, 1984.

Davies, Carole Boyce. "Paule Marshall." *Fifty African and Caribbean Women Writers.* Ed. Anne Adams. Westport, CT: Greenwood Press, forthcoming.

Davis, Arthur P., and Saunders Redding. *Cavalcade: Negro American Writing from 1960 to the Present.* Boston: Houghton Mifflin, 1971.

Denniston, Dorothy Lee. "Paule Marshall." In *American Women Writers: A Critical Reference Guide from Colonial Times to the Present,* vol 3. Ed. Linda Mainiero, 125–27. New York: Frederick Unger, 1981.

Evans, Mari, ed. *Black Women Writers (1950–1980): A Critical Evaluation.* New York: Anchor, 1984, 335–36.

Fairbanks, Carol, and Eugene A. Engeldinger. "Paule Marshall." In *Their Black American Fiction: A Bibliography.* Metuchen, NJ: The Scarecrow Press, 1978, 206–208.

Fairbanks, Carol. *More Women in Literature: Criticism of the Seventies.* Metuchen, NJ: Scarecrow Press, 1979, 237–38.

Gaiownik, Melissa. "Paule Marshall." *Black Writers: A Selection of Sketches from Contemporary Authors.* Ed. Linda Metzger et al., 384–86. Detroit, MI: Gale Research, 1989; In *Contemporary Authors.* Ed. May Hal and Deborah H. Straub, 310–12. New Series, 25. Detroit, MI: Gale Research, 1989.

Glikin, Ronda. "Paule Marshall." In *Black American Women in Literature: A Bibliography, 1976 through 1987*. Jefferson, NC: McFarland and Co., 1989, 112–14.

Houston, Helen Ruth. "Paule Marshall." In *The Afro-American Novel 1965–1975*. Troy, NY: The Whitston Publishing Company, 1977. 117–22.

Hutcheson, Wallace S., Jr. *Robert Fulton*. Annapolis, MD: Naval History Press, 1981.

Kallenbach, Jessamine. "Paule Marshall." *Index to Black American Literary Anthologies*. Boston: G. K. Hall, 1979. 78.

Kubayanda, J. Bekunuru. "Notes on the Impact of African Oral-Traditional Rhetoric on Latin American and Caribbean Writing." *Afro-Hispanic Review* 3, no. 3 (1984): 5–10.

Kulkarni, Harihar. "Paule Marshall: A Bibliographical Essay." New York: Institute of International Education, 1990.

Langscheid, Linda. "Paule Marshall: A Selected Bibliography." New Brunswick, NJ: Rutgers University, 1987.

Locher, Frances Carol, ed. *Contemporary Authors Volume*. Detroit, MI: Gale Research Company, 1979. 356–57.

Low, W. Augustus, and Virgil A. Clift. "Paule Marshall." *Encyclopedia of Black America*. New York: McGraw-Hill Books, 1981. 546.

Margolies, Edward, and David Bakis. "Paule Marshall." *Afro-American Fiction 1853–1976*. Detroit, MI: Gale Research Company, 1979. 27.

Metzger, Linda, et al. *Black Writers: A Selection of Sketches from Contemporary Authors*. Detroit, MI: Gale Research Company, 1989. 384–86.

Nelson, Emmanuel S. "Black America and the Anglophone Afro-Caribbean Literary Consciousness." *Journal of American Culture* 12, no. 4 (Winter 1989): 53–57.

Page, James A. *Selected Black American Writers: An Illustrated Bio-Bibliography*. Boston: G. K. Hall, 1977. 187.

Page, James A., and Jae Min Roh. "Paule Marshall." *Their Selected Black American African and Caribbean Authors: A Bio-Bibliography*. Littleton: Libraries Unlimited, 1985. 188–89.

Ploski, Harry A., and James Williams, eds. "Paule Marshall: Novelist, Short Story Writer." In *The Negro Almanac: A Reference Work on the African Americans*. Detroit, MI: Gale Research Company, 1989. 1005–06.

Rush, Theressa Gunnels. *Black American Writers Past and Present: A*

Biographical and Bibliographical Dictionary, vol 2. Methuen, NJ: The Scarecrow Press, 1975. 527–28.
Rushin, Kate. "Paule Marshall: Stages in a Writer's Life." *Sojourner* 10, no. 6 (April 1985): 16–17.
Sale, Faith. "Editing Fiction." In *Editors on Editing*. Ed. Gerald Gross, 186–99. New York: Harper, 1985.
Schwartz, Narda Lacey. *Articles on Women Writers 1976–1984: A Bibliography*. Oxford: Santa Barbara, 1986. 157.
Shockley, Ann. *Living Black American Authors: A Biographical Dictionary*. New York: B. R. Bowker, 1977. 106.
Wakeman, John. "Paule Marshall." In *World Authors 1970–1975*. New York: The H. W. Wilson Co., 1980. 540–41.
Werner, Craig. "Paule Marshall." *Black Women Novelists: An Annotated Bibliography*. Englewood Cliffs, NJ: Salem Press, 1989. 162–74.
Yancy, Preston M. "Paule Marshall." In *The Afro-American Short Story*. Westport, CT: Greenwood Press, 1986, 126–27.

Secondary Sources

Books

Allen, Richard Hinckley. *Star Names: Their Lore and Meaning*. New York: Dover, 1963. Original title: *Star-Names and Their Meanings*.
Alleyne, Warren. *Historic Bridgetown*. Bridgetown: Barbados National Trust, 1978.
Alleyne, Warren, and Henry Fraser. *The Barbados-Carolinas Connection*. London: Macmillan, 1988.
Aptheker, Herbert. *To Be Free: Studies in American Negro History*. New York: International Publishers, 1948.
Ashcroft, Bill, Gareth Griffiths, Helen Tiffin, eds. *The Empire Writes Back: Theory and Practices in Post-Colonial Literatures*. London: Routledge, 1989.
Baker, Robert H. *Introducing the Constellations*. New York: The Viking Press, 1937.
Balibar, Etienne, and Immanuel Wallerstein. *Race, Nation, Class: Ambiguous Identities*. Trans. Chris Turner. London: Verso, 1991.
Berner, Olivier. *Fireworks at Dusk: Paris in the Thirties*. Boston: Little, Brown and Company, 1993.

Beckles, Hilary McD. *A History of Barbados from Amerindian Settlements to Nation-States*. Cambridge, UK: Cambridge University Press, 1990.
———. *Natural Rebels: A Social History of Enslaved Black Women in Barbados*. London: Zed Books, 1989.
Berman, Ronald. *A Reader's Guide to Shakespeare's Plays*. Glenview, IL: Scott, Foresman and Co., 1965.
Bindoff, S. T. *Tudor England*. Hammondsworth, UK: Penguin, 1975.
Blake, Jody. *Le Tumulte Noir: Modernist Art and Popular Entertainment in Jazz-Age Paris, 1900–1930*. University Park: Pennsylvania State University Press, 1999.
Bourne, M. J., G. W. Lennox, and S. A. Seddon. *Fruits and Vegetables of the Caribbean*. London: Macmillan Caribbean, 1988.
Braziel, Jana Evans, and Anita Mannur, eds. *Theorizing Diaspora*. London: Blackwells, 2003.
Bruck, Peter, and Wolfgang Karrer. *The Afro-American Novel since 1960*. Amsterdam, The Netherlands: Gruner, 1982.
Busia, Abena. *Testimonies*. New York: Doubleday, 1994.
Cashin, Francois. *Paul Gauguin*. New York: Discoveries, 1989.
Campbell, P. F., ed. *Chapters in Barbados History*. St. Ann's Garrison, Barbados: The Barbados Museum and Historical Society, 1986.
Carter, Dan T. *Scottsboro: A Tragedy of the American South*. Baton Rouge, LA: Louisiana State University Press, 1969.
Cartey, Wilfred. *Whispers from the Caribbean*, vol. 2. Afro-American Culture and Society Series. Los Angeles, CA: Center for Afro-American Studies, 1991.
Césaire, Aimé. *A Tempest*. Trans. Richard Miller. New York: Theater Publications, 1969.
Chamberlin, J. Edward. *Come Back to My Language: Poetry and the West Indies*. Urbana, IL: University of Illinois Press, 1993.
Christian, Barbara T. *Black Women Novelists: The Development of a Tradition, 1892–1976*. Westport, CT: Greenwood, 1980.
———. "Ritualistic Process and the Structure of Paule Marshall's *Praisesong for the Widow*." *Callaloo* 6, no. 2 (Spring-Summer 1983): 74–84; *Black Feminist Criticism*. New York: Pergamon Press, 1985, 149–58.
Connolly, Harold X. *A Ghetto Grows in Brooklyn*. New York: NYU Press, 1977.
Coser, Stelamaris. *Bridging the Americas: The Literature of Paule Marshall,*

Toni Morrison and Gayle Jones. Philadelphia, PA: Temple University Press, 1994.

Craton, Michael. *Testing the Chains*. Ithaca, NY: Cornell University Press, 1982.

Davies, Carole Boyce. *Black Women, Writing and Identity: Migrations of the Subject*. New York: Routledge, 1994.

Davies, Carole Boyce, and Elaine Savoy Fido, eds. *Out of the Kumbla: Caribbean Women and Literature*. Trenton, NJ: Africa World Press, 1990.

Deerr, Noel. *The History of Sugar*. London: Chapman and Hall, 1950.

DeLamotte, Eugenia C. *Places of Silence, Journeys of Freedom: The Fiction of Paule Marshall*. Philadelphia: University of Pennsylvania Press, 1998.

Denniston, Dorothy Hamer. *The Fiction of Paule Marshall: Reconstructions of History, Culture, and Gender*. Knoxville: The University of Tennessee Press, 1995.

Diop, Cheikh Anita. *The Cultural Unity of Black Africa: The Domains of Patriarchy and of Matriarchy in Classical Antiquity*. Chicago: Third World Press, 1978.

Dubois, W.E.B. *The Souls of Black Folk*. New York: Bantam Books, 1903.

Eliot, T. S. *The Complete Poems and Plays, 1909–1950*. New York: Harcourt, Brace, and World, 1962.

Fage, J. D. *A History of West Africa: An Introductory Survey*, 4th ed. Cambridge, UK: Cambridge University Press, 1969.

Fanon, Frantz. *Black Skin, White Masks*. London: Pluto, 1952.

Ferguson, Moira. *Jamaica Kincaid: Where the Land Meets the Body*. Charlottesville: University of Virginia Press, 1993.

———. *Subject to Others: British Women Writers and Colonial Slavery, 1678–1834*. New York: Routledge, 1992.

Ferguson, Russell, et al., eds. *Out There: Marginalization and Contemporary Cultures*. New York: Museum of Contemporary Art, 1990.

Forde, G. Addinton. *Folk Beliefs of Barbados*. Barbados: National Cultural Foundation, 1988.

Fraser, Henry, et al., eds. *A-Z of Barbadian Heritage*. Kingston: Heinemann, 1990.

Freud, Anna. *The Analysis of Defence: The Ego and the Mechanisms of Defence Revisited*. New York: International Universities Press, 1985.

Fyfe, Christopher. *A History of Sierra Leone*. Oxford: Oxford University Press, 1963.
Gide, Andre. *L'Immoraliste*. Trans. Dorothy Bussy. New York: Alfred A. Knopf, 1930.
Gilroy, Paul. *The Black Atlantic: Modernity and Double Consciousness*. Cambridge, MA: Harvard University Press, 1993.
Gleason, Judith, ed. *Leaf and Bone: African Praise-Poems*. New York: Penguin, 1980.
Goethe, Johann Wolfgang von. *Faust*. New York: Appleton-Century-Crofts, 1946.
Goodman, James. *Stories of Scottsboro*. New York: Pantheon, 1994.
Goveia, Elsa. *Slave Society in the British Leward Islands at the End of the Eighteenth Century*. New Haven, CT: Yale University Press, 1965.
Grant, Michael. *Myths of the Greeks and Romans*. New York: Mentor, 1962.
Grewal, Shabnam, et al., eds. *Charting the Journey: Writings by Black and Third World Women*. London: Sheba Feminist Publishers, 1988.
Hall, Stuart. "Cultural Identity and Diaspora." *Colonial Discourse and Postcolonial Theory: A Reader*. Ed. Patrick Williams and Laura Chrisman. Harvester: Wheatsheaf, 1993.
Hamilton, Jill. *Women of Barbados: American Era to Mid 20th Century*. Barbados: Lotchworth Press, n.d.
Hargreaves, Dorothy, and Bob Hargreaves. *Tropical Blossoms of the Caribbean*. Lahaina, HI: Ross Hargreaves, 1965.
———. *Tropical Trees*. Lahaina, HI: Ross Hargreaves, 1965.
Harlow, Vincent T. *A History of Barbados 1625–1685*. Oxford: Clarendon Press, 1926.
Harris, Trudier. *From Mammies to Militants—Domestics in Black American Literature*. Philadelphia, PA: Temple University Press, 1982.
Hathaway, Heather. *Caribbean Waves: Relocating Claude McKay and Paule Marshall*. Bloomington, IN: Indiana University Press, 1999.
Highfield, Roger. *Spain in the Fifteenth Century 1369–1516. Essays and Extracts by Historians of Spain*. Trans. Frances M. Lopez-Morrillas. New York: Macmillan, 1972.
Higman, Barry W. *Slave Populations of the British Caribbean, 1807–1834*. Baltimore, MD: The Johns Hopkins University Press, 1984.
hooks, bell. *Yearning: Race, Gender, and Cultural Politics*. Boston, MA: Southend Press, 1990.

Horne, Alistair. *A Savage War of Peace: Algeria 1954–1962*. New York: Viking, 1978.

Hoyos, Alexander. *Barbados: A History from the Amerindians to Independence*. London: Macmillan, 1978.

Hunte, George. *Barbados*. New York: Hastings House, 1974.

Irele, Abiola. *The African Imagination: Literature in Africa and the Black Diaspora*. New York: Oxford University Press, 2001.

Jones, Brian, ed. *Night Sky Identifier*. New York: Mallard Press, 1992.

Jordon, Michael. *Encyclopedia of Gods*. New York: Facts on File, 1993.

Kasinitz, Philip. *Caribbean New York: Black Immigrants and the Politics of Race*. Ithaca, NY: Cornell University Press, 1992.

Kelley, Robin D. G. "But a Local to 1950 Phase of a World Problem." *Black History's Global Vision, 1883–1950*. The Journal of American History 86, no.3: 1045–1107.

Kindell, Roy. *Night Sky: Star Lore*. Ashland, OR: Ursa Naper, 1989.

King, Henry C. *The World of the Moon*. New York: Thurman Y. Crowell, 1967.

Klein, Herbert S. *The Middle Passage: Comparative Studies in the Atlantic Slave Trade*. Princeton, NJ: Princeton University Press, 1978.

Kopal, Zdenek. *The Moon: Our Nearest Celestial Neighbour*. New York: Academic Press, 1966.

Laguerre, Michael S. *Voodoo and Politics in Haiti*. New York: St. Martins, 1989.

Leach, Marjorie. *Guide to the Gods*. Santa Barbara, CA: ABC-CLIO, n.d.

Lemelle, Sidney J., and Robin D. G. Kelley. *Imagining Home: Class, Culture and Nationalism in the African Diaspora*. London: Verso, 1994.

Lloyd, Craig. *Eugene Bullard: Black Expatriates in Jazz-Age Paris*. Athens: University of Georgia Press, 2000.

Loederer, Richard A. *Voodoo in Haiti*. Trans. Desmond Ivo Vestey. New York: The Literary Guild, 1935.

Lumsden, Mary. *The Barbados-American Connection*. London: Macmillan, 1982.

Lynch, Louis. *The Barbados Book*, rev. ed. New York: Coward, McCann and Geoghegan, 1973.

Macherey, Pierre. *The Theory of Literary Production*. Trans. Geoffrey Wall. London: Routledge and Kegan Paul, 1978.

Mackanson, David H. *Barbados: A Study of North-American-West-Indian Relations 1735–1789*. London: Mouton and Co., 1964.

Mandelbaum, Allen. *The Aeneid of Virgil: A Verse Translation*. New York: Bantam, 1961.

Meeks, Brian, ed. *Culture, Politics, Race and Diaspora: The Thought of Stuart Hall*. Kingston: Ian Randle, 2007.

Metraux, Alfred. *Haiti: Black Peasants and Voodoo*. Trans. Peter Lengyel. New York: Universe Books, 1960.

Miner, Luke. *Paris Jazz: A Guide: From the Jazz Age to the Present*. New York: The Little Book Room, 2005. (Contains lists of "jazz greats.")

Minh-Ha, Trinh T. *When the Moon Waxes Red: Representation, Gender, and Cultural Politics*. London: Routledge, 1991.

Mitton, Jacqueline. *The Penguin Dictionary of Astronomy*. London: Penguin, 1991.

Mitton, Simon, ed. *The Cambridge Encyclopedia of Astronomy*. London: Jonathan Cape, 1977.

Moran, Rita. *Torture: The Role of Ideology in the French-Algerian War*. New York: Praeger Publishers, 1989.

Morley, David, and Kuan-Hsing Chen, eds. *Stuart Hall: Critical Dialogues in Cultural Studies*. London: Routledge, 1996.

Morton, A. L. *A People's History of England*. New York: International Publishers, 1938.

Nasta, Susheila, ed. *Motherlands: Black Women's Writing from Africa, the Caribbean and South Asia*. New Brunswick, NJ: Rutgers University Press, 1991.

O'Callaghan, Evelyn. *The Earliest Patriots Being the True Adventures of Certain Survivors of 'Bussa's Rebellion' (1816), in the Island of Barbados and Abroad*. London: Karia Press, 1986.

Paget, Henry, and Paul Buhle, eds. *C.L.R. James's Caribbean*. Durham, NC: Duke University Press, 1992.

Parry, J. H., P. M. Sherlock, and A. P. Maingot. *A Short History of the West Indies*. London: Macmillan, 1956.

Patterson, Haywood, and Earl Conrad. *Scottsboro Boy*. New York: Doubleday, 1950.

Pettis, Joyce. *Toward Wholeness in Paule Marshall's Fiction*. Charlottesville and London: University Press of Virginia, 1995.

Pritchett, Wendell. *Brownsville, Brooklyn: Blacks, Jews, and the Changing Face of the Ghetto*. Historical Studies of Urban America. Chicago: University of Chicago Press, 2002.

Poliakov, Leon. *The History of Anti-Semitism*. Trans. from the French by Miriam Kochan. New York: The Vanguard Press, 1975.

Porter, Darwin. *Frommers Comprehensive Travel Guide. Caribbean '91.* New York: Prentice Hall, 1991.

Rahming, Melvin. "Towards a Caribbean Mythology: The Function of Africa in Paule Marshall's *The Chosen Place, the Timeless People.*" *Studies in the Literary Imagination* 26 (Fall 1993).

Richardson, Bonham C. *Panama Money in Barbados 1900–1920.* Knoxville: University of Tennessee Press, 1985.

Ridpath, Ian. *Astronomy: How We View Our Solar System and the Universe Beyond.* New York: W. H. Smith (Gallery Books), 1991.

Robertson, George, et al., eds. *Travellers' Tales: Narratives of Home and Displacement.* London: Routledge, 1994.

Robeson, Paul. *Here I Stand.* Boston: Beacon Press, 1958.

Rodway, James. *Guiana: British, Dutch, and French.* New York: Scribners, 1912.

Rutherford, Jonathan. *Identity: Community, Culture, Difference.* London: Lawrence and Wishart, 1990.

Schenck, Mary Jane. "Ceremonies of Reconciliation: Paule Marshall's *The Chosen Place, the Timeless People.*" *MELUS* 19, no. 4 (Winter 1994): 49–60.

Schiffman, Jack. *Harlem Heyday: A Pictorial History of Modern Black Show Business and the Apollo Theater.* New York: Prometheus Books, 1984.

Seddon, S.A., and G. W. Lennox. *Trees of the Caribbean.* London: Macmillan, 1980.

Stovall, Tyler. *Paris Noir: African Americans in the City of Light.* Boston: Houghton Mifflin, 1996.

Sundiata, Ibrahim. *Brothers and Strangers: Black Zion, Black Slavery, 1914–1940.* Durham, NC, and London: Duke University Press, 2003.

Tiffin, Chris, and Alan Lawson, eds. *De-Scribing Empire: Post-colonialism and Textualities.* London: Routledge, 1994.

Toland, Shirley. *The Works of Paule Marshall.* Tuskegee: Tuskegee Institute, 1975.

Tree, Ronald. *A History of Barbados.* New York: Random House, 1972.

Virgil. *The Aeneid of Virgil.* Trans. Allen Mandelbaum. New York: Bantam, 1965.

Wade-Gyles, Gloria. *No Crystal Stair: Visions of Race and Sex in Black Women's Fiction.* New York: The Pilgrim Press, 1984.

Weston, Jessie L. *From Ritual to Romance.* Cambridge, UK: Cambridge University Press, 1920.

Whipple, Fred L. *Earth, Moon, and Planets.* Cambridge, MA: Harvard University Press, 1968.
Wilentz, Gay. *Binding Cultures: Black Women Writers in Africa and the Diaspora.* Bloomington: Indiana University Press, 1992.
Willis, Susan. *Specifying: Black Women Writing the American Experience.* Madison: University of Wisconsin Press, 1987.
Wistrich, Robert S. *Anti-Semitism: The Longest Hatred.* New York: Pantheon, 1991.
Zellers, Margaret. *Fielding's Caribbean 1991.* New York: William Morrow, 1991.

Articles

Barksdale, Richard. "Castration Symbolism in Recent Black American Fiction." *CLAJ* 29, no. 4 (June 1986): 400–13.
Baxter, Miller R., ed. "Three Black Women Writers and Humanism: A Folk Perspective." In *Black American Literature and Criticism.* Lexington: United Press of Kentucky, 1981, 50–74; Philadelphia, PA: Temple University Press, 1982.
Benson, Kimberly. "Architectural Imagery and Unity in Paule Marshall's *Brown Girl, Brownstones.*" *Negro American Literature Forum* 9, no. 9 (1975): 67–70.
Billingslea-Brown, Alma Jean. "The Folk Aesthetic in Contemporary African-American Women's Fiction and Visual Art." *Dissertation Abstracts International* 51, no. 3 (September 1990): 894A. [University of Texas at Dallas, 1989. 275]
Brathwaite, Edward. "West Indian History and Society in the Art of Paule Marshall's Novel." *Journal of Black Studies* 1, no. 2 (1970): 225–38.
Brice-Finch, Jacqueline LaVerne. "The Caribbean Diaspora: Four Aspects, in Novels from 1971–1985." *Dissertation Abstracts International* 48, no. 11 (May 1988): 2872A.
Bröck, Sabine. "Transcending the 'Loophole of Retreat': Paule Marshall's Placing of Female Generations." *Callaloo* 10, no. 1 (Winter 1987): 79–90.
Brown, Elisa Barkley. "Mothers of Mind." In *Double Stitch: Black Women Write about Mothers and Daughters.* Ed. Patricia Bell-Scott et al., 74–93. Boston: Beacon Press, 1991.

Brown, Lloyd W. "The Rhythms of Power in Paule Marshall's Fiction." *Novel* 7, no. 2 (1974): 159–67.

———. "Mannequins and Mermaids: The Contemporary Writer and Sexual Images in the Consumer Culture." *Women's Studies* 5, no. 1 (1977): 1–12.

———. "Beneath the North Star: The Canadian Image of Black Literature." *Dalhousie Review* 50 (Autumn 1970): 317–29.

Buncombe, Marie H. "From Harlem to Brooklyn: The New York Scene in the Fiction of Meriwether, Petry, and Marshall." *MAWA Review* 1, no. 1 (Spring 1982): 16–19.

Busia, Abena. "What is Your Nation? Reconnecting Africa and Her Diaspora through Paule Marshall's *Praisesong for the Widow*."In *Changing Our Own Words: Essays on Criticism, Theory, and Writing by Black Women*. Ed. Cheryl Wall, 196–211. New Brunswick, NJ: Rutgers University Press, 1989.

———. "Words Whispered Over Voids: A Context for Black Women's Rebellious Voices in the Novel of the African Diaspora." In *Black Feminist Criticism and Critical Theory*. Ed. Joe Weixlmann and Houston A. Barker, 1–41. Greenwood, FL: Penkeville Publishing Co., 1988.

Christian, Barbara. "Paule Marshall." In *Black American Writers*. Ed. Valerie Smith, 289–304. New York: Charles Scribner's Sons, 1990.

———. "Ritualistic Process and the Structure of Paule Marshall's *Praisesong for the Widow*." *Callaloo* 6, no. 2 (Spring-Summner 1983): 74–84; *Black Feminist Criticism*. New York: Pergamon Press, 1985, 149–58.

Christol, Hélène. "'The Black Women's Burden': Black Women and Work in *The Street* and *Brown Girl, Brownstones*." *Les Etats-Unis: Images de travail et des loisirs*. Aix-en-Provence: Université de Provence, 1989, 145–59.

———. "Paule Marshall's Bajan Women in *Brown Girl, Brownstones*." In *Women and War: The Changing Status of American Women from the 1930s to the 1940s*. Ed. Maria Diedrich, and Dorothea Fischer-Hornung. Oxford: Berg, 1990, 141–53; West Indian Literature and its Social Context: Proceedings of the Fourth Annual Conference on West Indian Literature, University of the West Indies, Cave Hill, Mona, St. Augustine, College of the Virgin Islands, University of Guyana, Volume 1984.

Collier, Eugenia. "'Selina's Journey Home': From Alienation to Unity in Paule Marshall's *Brown Girl, Brownstones.*" *Obsidian* 8, no. 2–3 (1982): 6–19.

———. "'The Closing of the Circle' Movement from Division to Wholeness in Paule Marshall's Fiction." *Black Women Writers (1950–1980).* Ed. Mari Evans, 295–315. Anchor City: Doubleday, 1985.

Cooke, John. "Whose Child? The Fiction of Paule Marshall." *CLA Journal* 24, no. 1 (1980): 1–15.

Cooper, Carolyn. "The Oral Witness and the Scribal Document: Divergent Accounts of Slavery in Two Novels of Barbados." In *West Indian Literature and Its Social Context:* Proceedings of the Fourth Annual Conference on West Indian Literature, University of the West Indies, Cave Hill, Mona, St. Augustine, College of the Virgin Islands, University of Guyana. Ed. Mark A. McWatt, 3–11. 1985.

Davis, Angela Y. "Reflections on the Black Women's Role in the Community of Slaves." *Black Scholar* 3, no. 4 (December 1971): 2–15.

Davies, Carole Boyce. "Black Women's Journey into Self: A Womanist Reading of Paule Marshall's *Praisesong for the Widow.*" *Matatu* 1 (October 1987): 19–34.

———. "Mothering and Healing in Recent Black Women's Fiction." *Sage* 2, no. 1 (Spring 1985): 1.

Denniston, Dorothy Lee Hamer. "Cultural Reclamation: The Development of a Pan-African Sensibility in the Fiction of Paule Marshall." *Dissertation Abstracts International* 44, no. 7 (January 1984): 2147A. [Brown University, 1983]

———. "Early Short Fiction of Paule Marshall." *Callaloo* 6, no. 2 (1983): 31–45.

Dutton, Wendy. "The Problem of Invisibility: Voodoo and Zora Neale Hurston," *Frontiers* 13, no. 2: 131–52.

Eko, Ebele. "Beyond the Myth of Confrontation: A Comparative Study of African and African-American Female Protagonists." *Ariel* 17, no. 4 (October 1986): 139–52.

Emmanuel, James, and Theodore Gross. "Paule Marshall–1929." In *Dark Symphony: Negro Literature in America.* New York: The Free Press, 1968. 400–401.

Farred, Grant. "You Can Go Home Again, You Just Can't Stay: Stuart Hall and the Caribbean Diaspora." *Research in African Literatures* 27, no. 1 (1996): 28–48.

Fido, Elaine Savory. "Texture of Third World Reality in the Poetry of Four African—Caribbean Women." In *Out of the Kumbla: Caribbean Women and Literature*. Ed. Carole Boyce Davies and Elaine Savory Fido, 29–44. Trenton, NJ: Africa World Press, 1990.

Fletcher, L. P. "The Evolution of Poor Relief in Barbados 1900 to 1969." *Caribbean Studies* 25, nos. 3 and 4 (1992): 255–75.

Friedman, Susan Stanford. "Women's Autobiographical Selves: Theory and Practice." In *The Private Self: Theory and Practice of Women's Auto Biographical Writings*. Chapel Hill: University of North Carolina Press, 1988. 34–62.

Giddings, Paula. "A Special Vision, a Common Goal." *Encore American and Worldwide News* 23 (June 1975): 44–48.

Giles, Fiona. "The Softest Disorder: Representing Cultural Indeterminancy." In *De-Scribing Empire: Post-Colonialism and Textuality*. Ed. Chris Tiffan and Alan Lawson. London: Routledge, 1994. 141–51.

Gilman, Sander. "Black Bodies, White Bodies: Toward an Iconography of Female Sexuality in Late Nineteenth-Century Art, Medicine, and Literature." In *"Race," Writing and Difference*. Ed. Henry Louis Gates, Jr., 223–61. Chicago: University of Chicago Press, 1985.

Greene, Sue N. "The Use of the Jew in West Indian Novels." *World Literature Written in English* 16, no. 1 (Spring 1986): 150–69.

Hanchard, Michael. "Identity, Meaning and the African-American." *Social Text* 24, no. 8: 31–42.

———. "Black Transnationalism, Africana Studies, and the 21st Century." *Journal of Black Studies* 35, no. 2, 139–53.

Harris, Trudier. "From Exile to Asylum: Religion and Community in the Writings of Contemporary Black Women." In *Women's Writing in Exile*. Ed. Mary LynnBroe and Angela Ingram, 152–69. Chapel Hill: University of North Carolina Press, 1989.

———. "No Outlet for the Blues: Silla Boyce's Plight in *Brown Girl, Brownstones*." *Callaloo* 6, no. 2 (Spring-Summer 1983): 57–67.

———. "Three Black Women Writers and Humanism: A Folk Perspective." In *African-American Literature and Humanism*. Ed. R. Baxter Miller, 50–74 (Lexington: University Press of Kentucky).

Harris, Wilson. "Metaphor and Myth." In *Myth and Metaphor*. Ed. Robert Sellick, 1–14. Adelaide, Australia: Centre for Research in the New Literatures in English, 1982.

Hawthorne, Evelyn. "Ethnicity and Cultural Perspectives in Paule Marshall's Short Fiction." *MELUS* 13, no. 3–4 (Fall-Winter 1986): 37–48.

hooks, bell. "An Aesthetic of Blackness: Strange and Oppositional." In *Yearning: Race, Gender and Cultural Politics*, 103–113. Boston: South End Press, 1990.

Hull, Gloria. "'To Be a Black Woman in America': A Reading of Paule Marshall's 'Reena.'" *Obsidian* 4, no. 3 (1978): 5–15.

Ingram, Elwanda D. "Selina and Reena: Paule Marshall's Assertive Black Women." *MAWA Review* 2, no. 1 (1986): 25–27.

Kapai, Leela. "Dominant Themes and Techniques in Paule Marshall's Fiction." *CLA Journal* 16 (1972): 45–59.

Katrak, Ketu. "Decolonizing Culture: Toward a Theory for Post-colonial Women's Texts." *Modern Fiction Studies* 35, no. 1 (1989):157–79.

Keizs, Marcia. "Themes and Style in the Works of Paule Marshall." *Negro American Literature Forum* 9 (1975): 67–76.

Kelley, Robin D. G. "'But a Local Phase of a World Problem': Black History's Global Vision, 1883–1950." *The Journal of American History* 86, no. 3 (December 1999): 1045–77.

King, Rosamond S. "The Flesh and Blood Triangle in Paule Marshall's *The Fisher King*." *Callaloo* 26, no. 2: 543–45.

Kubitschek, Missy Dehn. "Paule Marshall's Witness to History." In *Claiming the Heritage: African-American Women Novelists and History*. Jackson: University Press of Mississippi, 1990, 1–23.

———. "Paule Marshall's Women on Quest." *Black American Literature Forum* 21, no. 1–2 (Spring-Summer 1987): 43–60.

Kulkarni, Harihar. "The Novels of Paule Marshall: A Poetics of Prophecy." *The Indian Jounal of American Studies* 20.1 (Summer 1990): 29–33.

Lacovia, R. M. "Migration and Transmutation in the Novels of McKay, Marshall, and Clarke." *Journal of Black Studies* 7, no. 4 (June 1977): 437–54.

LeSeur, Geta. "The Afro-American and the Afro-Caribbean Female Bildungsroman." *The Black Scholar* 17, no. 2 (1986): 26–33.

———. "*Brown Girl, Brownstones* as a Novel of Development." *Obsidian II* 1, no. 3 (Winter 1986): 119–29.

McCluskey, John. "And Called Every Generation Blessed: Theme, Setting, and Ritual in the Works of Paule Marshall." In *Black Women Writers (1950–1980): A Critical Evaluation*. Ed. Mari Evans, 316–34. Anchor City: Doubleday, 1985.

McDowell, Deborah E. "New Directions for Black Feminist Criticism." In *The New Feminist Criticism: Essays on Women, Literature, and Theory*, ed. Elaine Showalter, 186–99. New York: Pantheon.

Nazareth, Peter. "Paule Marshall's Timeless People." *New Letters* 40 (1973): 116–31.

Nowak, Hanna. "The Wild Zone in Paule Marshall's Fiction." *Fur eine offene Literaturwissenschaft: Erkundungen un Eroprobungen am Besipiel US-amerikanischer Texte (*Opening Up Literary Criticism: Essays on American Prose and Poetry*).* Salzburg, Austria: Neugebauer, 1986, 69–87.

O'Banner, Bessie Marie. "A Study of Black Heroines in Four Selected Novels (1929–1959) by Four Black American Women Novelists: Zora Neale Hurston, Nella Larsen, Paule Marshall, Anne Lane Petry." *Dissertation Abstracts International* 43, no. 2 (August 1982): 447A. [Southern Illinois University at Carbondale, 1981]

Ogunemi, Chikwenye O. "The Old Order Shall Pass: The Examples of 'Flying Home' and 'Barbados.'" *CLA Journal* 25, no. 3 (1981): 303–314.

———. "Womanism: The Dynamics of Contemporary Black Female Novel in English." *Signs* 11, no. 2 (Autumn 1985): 63–80.

O'Neale, Sandra. "Race, Sex and Self: Aspects of Bildungsroman; Select Novels by Black American Women Novelists." *MELUS* (1982): 27.

Pannill, Linda. "From the 'Wordshop': The Fiction of Paule Marshall." *MELUS* 12, no. 2 (Summer 1985): 63–73.

Paravisini, Lizabeth, and Barbara Webb. "On the Threshold of Becoming: Contemporary Caribbean Women Writers." *Cimarrón* 1, no. 3 (Spring 1988): 106–132.

Paravisini, Lizabeth. "Authors Playin' Mas': Carnival and the Following in the Contemporary Caribbean Novel." In *History of the Literatures of the Caribbean*, vol. 3. Ed. A. James Arnold. Cross Cultural Studies. Amsterdam, The Netherlands and Philadelphia, PA: John Benjamins, 1997.

———. "'The Chosen Place, the Timeless People': Race, Colonial Power, and the Absence of Sisterhood." Extra Mural Dept. of the University College of the West Indies. Mona, Jamaica. *Caribbean Quarterly* 48, no. 4 (2002): 41–53.

———. "Neverending Cycles and Revolutionary Ends: Revolt and Rebirth in the Contemporary Caribbean Novel." *Sargasso* 6 (1989): 29–39.

Philip, Marlene Nourbese. *She Tries Her Tongue; Her Silence Softly Breaks*. Charlottetown, Prince Edward Island, Canada: Ragweed Press, 1989.

Pollard, Velma. "Cultural Connections in Paule Marshall's *Praisesong for the Widow.*" *World Literature Written in English* 25, no. 2: 285–97.
Rahming, Melvin B. "The Rejection of the West Indian Stereotype." In Rahming, *The Evolution of the West Indian's Image in the Afro-American Novel.* Millwood, NY: Associated Faculty Press, Inc., 1986, 96–139.
Reyes, Angelita Dianne. "Crossing the Bridge: The Great Mother in Selected Novels of Toni Morrison, Paule Marshall, Simone Schwarz-Bart, and Mariama Bâ." *Dissertation Abstracts International* 46, no. 6 (1985): 1618A. [University of Iowa, 1985]
———. "Politics and Metaphors of Materialism in Paule Marshall's *Praisesong for the Widow* and Toni Morrison's *Tar Baby.*" *Politics and the Muse: Studies in the Politics of Recent American Literature.* Ed. Adam J. Sorkin. Bowling Green, OH: Bowling Green Popular Press, 1989, 179–205.
Rodríguez, María C. "The Narrative Work of Three West Indian Women." *Sargasso* 4 (1987): 56–67.
Rowell, Charles H. "Paule Marshall: The Fiction Writer (A Special Marshall Issue)." *Callaloo* 6.2 (Spring-Summer 1983): 21–84.
Sandiford, Keith A. "Paule Marshall's *Praisesong for the Widow*: The Reluctant Heiress; or Whose Life Is It Anyway?" *Black American Literature Forum* 20, no. 4 (Winter 1986): 371–92.
Scarboro, Ann Armstrong. "The Healing Process: A Paradigm for Self-Renewal in Paule Marshall's *Praisesong for the Widow* and Camara Laye's *Le Regard du roi.*" *Modern Language Studies* 19, no. 1 (Winter 1989): 28–36.
Schneider, Deborah. "A Search for Selfhood: Paule Marshall's *Brown Girl, Brownstone.*" In *The Afro-American Novel since 1960.* Ed. Peter Bruck and Wolfgang Karrer, 53–73. Amsterdam, The Netherlands: Gruner, 1982.
Sharpe, Jenny. "Figures of Colonial Resistance." *Modern Fiction Studies* 35, no.1 (Narratives of Colonial Resistance): 143–47.
Shattuck, Sandra Dickinson. "Personal and Political Histories: The Hard Work of Remembering in Paule Marshall's *The Chosen Place, the Timeless People* and Christa Wolf's *Kindheitsmuster.*" *Dissertation Abstracts International* 49, no. 7 (January 1989): 1794A. [University of Texas at Austin, 1988.]
Skerrett, Joseph T., Jr. "Paule Marshall and the Crisis of the Middle

Years: *The Chosen Place, the Timeless People.*" *Callaloo* 17–19 (1983): 69–73.

Spillers, Hortense J. "*The Chosen Place, the Timeless People.* Some Figurations on the New World." In *Conjuring: Black Women, Fiction, and Literary Tradition.* Ed. Marjorie Pryse and Hortense Spillers, 151–75. Bloomington: Indiana University Press, 1985.

Stevenson, Peggy Lee Denise. "Conflicts of Culture, Class and Gender in Selected Caribbean-American and Caribbean Women's Literature." *Dissertation Abstracts International* 50, no. 10 (April 1990). [Howard University, 1989].

Stine, Jean, ed. "Paule Marshall: Collected Criticism." *Contemporary Literary Criticism.* vol. 27. Detroit, MI: Gale Research, 1984, 308–16.

Stoelting, Winifred L. "Time Past and Time Present: The Search for Viable Links in *The Chosen Place, the Timeless People.*" *CLA Journal* 16 (1972): 60–71.

Talbert, E. Lee. "The Poetics of Prophecy in Paule Marshall's *Soul Clap Hands and Sing.*" *MELUS* 5, no. 1 (Spring 1978): 49–56.

Thorpe, Marjorie. "Feminism and the Female Authored West Indian Novel: Paule Marshall's *Brown Girl, Brownstones.*" In *Gender in Caribbean Development.* Ed. Patricia Mohammed and Catherine Shepherd, 318–29. Women in Development Studies Project. St. Augustine, Trinidad: University of the West Indies, 1988.

Tree, Ronald. "The Jewish Settlements in Barbados." In *A History of Barbados,* 82–86. London: Granada, 1977.

Troester, Rosalie Riegler. "Turbulence and Tenderness: Mothers, Daughters, and 'Othermothers' in Paule Marshall's *Brown Girls, Brownstones.*" *Sage* 1 (Fall 1984): 13–16.

Waniek, Marilyn Nelson. "Paltry Things: Immigrants and Marginal Men in Paule Marshall's Short Fiction." *Callaloo* 6, no. 2 (Spring-Summer 1983): 45–56.

Wade-Gyles, Gloria. "'The Truths of Our Mothers' Lives: Mother-Daughter Relationships in Black Women's Fiction." *Sage* 1, no. 2 (Fall 1984): 8–12.

Washington, Mary Helen. "I Sign My Mother's Name: Alice Walker, Dorothy West, Paule Marshall." In *Mothering the Mind: Twelve Studies of Writers and Their Silent Partners.* Ed. Ruth Perry and Martine Watson Brownley, 142–63. New York: Holmes and Meier, 1984.

———. "Black Women Image Makers." *Black World* 23 (August 1974): 10–18.

———. "New Lives and New Letters: Black Women Writers at the End of the Seventies." *College English* 43 (January 1981): 1–11.

———. "Introduction." In Washington, *Black-Eyed Susans*. New York: Anchor Books, 1975, ix–xxii.

———. "These Self-Invented Women: A Theoretical Framework for a Literary History of Black Women." In Bunting Institute Working Paper, Radcliff College, 1980, 306.

———. "Afterword." In Marshall. *Brown Girl, Brownstones*. New York: The Feminist Press, 1981.

Waxman, Barbara Frey. "The Widow's Journey to Self and Roots: Aging and Society in Paule Marshall's *Praisesong for the Widow*." *Frontiers* 9, no. 3 (1987): 94–99.

Willis, Susan. "Paule Marshall's Relationship to Afro-American Culture." In Willis, *Specifying: Black Women Writing the American Experience*. Madison, WI: University of Wisconsin Press, 1987, 53–82.

———. "Black Women Writers: Taking a Critical Perspective." *Making a Difference: Feminist Literary Criticism*. Ed. Greene Gayle and Coppelia Kahn, 211–37. New York: Metheuen, 1985.

Wilson, Lucy. "Aging and Ageism in Paule Marshall's *Praisesong for the Widow* and Beryl Gilroy's *Frangipani House*." *Journal of Caribbean Studies* 7, no. 2–3 (1989–1990): 189–99.

Reviews

BROWN GIRL, BROWNSTONES

Allen, W. H. "A Review of *Brown Girl, Brownstones*." *The Times Literary Supplement*, August 19. 1960.

Bell, G. O. "*Brown Girl, Brownstones*: A Review." *BIM* 8, no.30 (Jan-June 1960): 134–36.

Benston, Kimberly W. "Architectural Imagery and Unity in Paule Marshall's *Brown Girl, Brownstones*." *Black American Literature Forum* 9, no. 3 (Fall 1975): 67–70.

Bond, Jean Carey. "*Brown Girl, Brownstones*: A Review." *Freedomways* 22, no. 2 (1982): 110–12.

Bovoso, Carole. "Reclaiming the Motherland: A Review of *Brown Girl,*

Brownstones and The Living is Easy." *Village Voice Literary Supplement*, April 1982. 16.

Brown, Lloyd W. "The Calypso Tradition in West Indian Literature." *Black Academy Reviews* 2, no. 1–2 (Spring-Summer 1971): 127–43.

"*Brown Girl, Brownstones*: A Review." *San Francisco Sunday Chronicle*, January 28, 1962, 32.

Buckmaster, Henrietta. "Search for Status: A Review of *Brown Girl, Brownstones.*" *Saturday Review*, August 29, 1959, 14.

Buncombe, Marie H. "From Harlem to Brooklyn: The New York Scene in the Fiction of Merriwether, Petry and Marshall." *MAWA Review* 1, no.1 (Spring 1982): 16–19.

Butcher, Phillip. "The Younger Novelists and the Urban Negro." *CLA Journal* 4, no.3 (March 1961): 196–203.

Byerman, Keith. "Gender, Culture and Identity in Paule Marshall's *Brown Girl, Brownstones.*" *Redefining Autobiography in Twentieth Century Woman's Fiction*. Ed. Janice Morgan et al. New York: Garland, 1991. 135–47.

Christol, Helene. "The Black Woman's Burden: Black Women and Work in The Street (Ann Petry) and *Brown Girl, Brownstones* (Paule Marshall)." In *Les Etats-Unis: Images du travail et des loisirs*. de Provence: Aix-en-Provence University, 1989, 145–58.

———. "Paule Marshall's Bajan Women in *Brown Girl, Brownstones.*" In *Women and War: The Change Status of American Women from the 1930s to the 1950s*. Ed. Maria Diedrich and Dorothea Fischer-Hormung. New York: St. Martin's Press, 1990. 141–53.

Cinquemani, Frank."A Review of *Brown Girl, Brownstones.*" *Library Journal* (September 1, 1959): 2522.

Collier, Eugenia. "Selina's Journey Home: From Alienation to Unity in Paule Marshall's *Brown Girl, Brownstones.*" *Obsidian* 8, no. 2–3 (1982): 6–19.

Davison, Dorothy P., ed. *Book Review Digest: March 1960 to February 1961*. New York: The H.W. Wilson Co., 1961. 892.

Eko, Eble. "Beyond the Myth of Confrontation: A Comparative Study of African and African-American Female Protagonists." *Phylon* 48, no. 3 (Fall 1986): 219–29.

Field, Carol. "Fresh, Fierce and 'First': A Review of *Brown Girl, Brownstones.*" *The New York Herald Tribune Book Review*, August 16, 1959, 5.

Gallo, Donald R., and Ellie Barksdale. "'Using Fiction in American History': A Review of *Brown Girl, Brownstones*." *Social Education* 47, no. 4 (April 1932): 289.

Govan, Sandra Y. "Woman within the Circle: Selina and Silla Boyce." *Callaloo* 6 (Spring-Summer 1983): 148–52.

Greene, Brenda M. "A Cross-cultural Approach to Literarcy: The Immigrant Experience." *English Journal* 77, no. 5 (September 1988): 45–48.

Harris, Trudier. "No Outlet for the Blues: Silla Boyce's Plight in *Brown Girl, Brownstones*." *Callaloo* 6, no. 2 (Spring-summer 1983): 57–67.

Hutchens, John K. "*Brown Girl, Brownstones*: A Review." *The New York Herald Tribune*, August 18, 1959, 17.

Ingram, Elwanda. "Selina and Reena: Paule Marshall's Assertive Black Women." *MAWA Review* 2, no. 1 (1986): 25–27.

Jefferson, Margo. *Nation*, December 26, 1981, 713.

Lash, John S. "Expostulation and Replay: A Critical Summary of Literature by and about Negroes in 1959." *Phylon* 21, 2 (Summer 1960): 111–23.

LeSeur, Geta. "*Brown Girl, Brownstones* as a Novel of Development." *Obsidian* 2.1 (Winter 1986): 119–29.

Miller, Adam David. "A Review of *Brown Girl, Brownstones*." *Black Scholar* 3 (May 1972): 56–58.

Neumark, Victoria. "'Voices Round the World': *Brown Girl, Brownstones*." *Times Literary Supplement*, October 15, 1982, 32.

Parker, Dorothy. "A Review of *Brown Girl, Brownstones*." *Esquire* 52, no. 5 (November 1959), 26–28.

Pinckney, Darryl. "Roots: Review of *Brown Girl, Brownstones* and *Praisesong for the Widow*." *New York Review of Books*, April 28, 1983, 26–30.

Pochoda, Elizabeth. "Critical Comments on *Brown Girl, Brownstones* and *The Chosen Place, the Timeless People*." *Nation* 245, December 26, 1987, 795.

"A Review of *Brown Girl, Brownstones*." *Booklist*, October 15, 1959, 119.

"A Review of *Brown Girl, Brownstones*." *Harvard Educational Review* 58, no. 3 (1988): 417.

"A Review of *Brown Girl, Brownstones*." *The New Yorker*, September 19, 1959, 191–92.

Schneider, Deborah. "A Search for Selfhood: Paule Marshall's *Brown Girl, Brownstones.*" In *Afro-American Novel since 1960.* Ed. Peter Bruck and Wolfgang Karrer. Amesterdam: G.R. Grunner, 1982, 53–73.

Serebnick, Judith. "New Creative Writers." *Library Journal* (June 1959): 1870.

Southgate, Robert L. *"Brown Girl, Brownstones."* Southgate, *Black Plots and Black Characters: A Handbook for Afro-American Literature.* Syracuse: Gaylord Professional Publishers, 1979, 49–51.

Troester, Rosalie Riegie. "Turbulence and Tenderness: Mother, Daughter and Other Mothers in Paule Marshall's *Brown Girl, Brownstones.*" *Sage* 1, no.2 (Fall 1984): 13–16; In *Double Stitch: Black Women Write about Mothers and Daughters.* Ed. Patricia Bell-Scott et al., 163–72, Boston: Beacon Press, 1991.

Wade-Gayles, Gloria. "The Truths of Our Mothers' Lives: Mother-Daughter Relationships in Black Women's Fiction." *Sage* 1, 2 (Fall 1984): 8–12.

Walters, Ray. "A Review of *Brown Girl, Brownstones.*" *New York Times*, November 22, 1981, 7, 51.

Washington, Mary Helen. "Afterword." *Brown Girl, Brownstones.* Feminist Press, 1981. 311–24.

Zlotnick, Joan. *Portrait of an American City: The Novelists' New York.* Port Washington: Kennikat Press, 1982, 177–78.

SOUL CLAP HANDS AND SING

Allen, W. H. "Ruined Lads: A Review of *Soul Clap Hands and Sing.*" *New Statesman*, April 13, 1962, 535.

Apthekar, Bettina. "Race and Class: Patriarchal Politics and Women's Experience." *Women's Studies International Quarterly*, no. 9 and 10 (1982): 10–15.

Buckmaster, Henrietta. "Inner Tensions." *New York Times Book Review*, October 1, 1961, 37.

Hassan, Ihab. "A Circle of Loneliness." *Saturday Review*, September 16, 1961, 30.

Ogunyemi, Chikwenye Okanja. "'The Old Order Shall Pass: The Example of Flying Home' and 'Barbados.'" *CLA Journal* 25 (March 1982): 303–14: *Studies in Short Fiction* 5 (Winter 1983): 23–32.

Pettis, Joyce. "*Soul Clap Hands and Sing*: A Review of 1988 Edition." *Obsidian II* 4, no. 2 (Summer 1989): 114–18.

"A Review of *Soul Clap Hands and Sing*." *The New Yorker*, September 23, 1961, 180.

Reckely, Ralph, Sr. "*Soul Clap Hands and Sing*: A Review." *The Reprint Bulletin Books Review* 34, no. 1 (1989): 12.

Sealy, Karl. "*Soul Clap Hands and Sing*: A Review." *BIM* 9, no. 35 (July–December 1962): 225–28.

Sullivan, Richard. *Chicago Sunday Tribune Magazine of Books*, October 1, 1961, 3.

Talbert, Lee. "The Poetics of Prophecy in Paule Marshall's *Soul Clap Hands and Sing*." *MELUS* 5.1 (1977): 49–56.

Turner, Darwin T. "Introduction." In Paula Marshall, *Soul Clap Hands and Sing*. Washington, DC: The Howard University Press, 1988. xi–xlviii.

Walcott, Derek. "The Story of Lust in Four Lands." *Trinidad Guardian*, September 12, 1962.

Wanek, Marilyn Nelson. "Paltry Things: Immigrant and Marginal Men in Paule Marshall's Short Fiction." *Callaloo* 6, 2 (Spring-Summer 1983): 47–56.

Williams, Joanne. "A Review of *Soul Clap Hands and Sing*." *Freedomways* 2, no. 3 (Summer 1962): 328–29.

Winslow, Henry F., Sr. "'A Stellar Performance': A Review of *Soul Clap Hands and Sing*." *The New York Herald Tribune*, September 17, 1961, 6.

BRAZIL

Berman, Ronald. *A Reader's Guide to Shakespeare's Plays: A Discursive Bibliography*. Glenview: Scott, Foresman and Co., 1965.

Harbage, Alfred. *As They Liked It: A Study of Shakespeare's Artistry*. New York: Harper, 1947.

Retamar, Roberto Fernandez. *Caliban and Other Essays*. Trans. Edward Baker. Minneapolis: University of Minnesota Press, 1989.

Traversi, Derek A. *An Approach to Shakespeare*, vol. 2. New York: Anchor, 1969.

Wilson, Edwin, ed. *Shaw on Shakespeare*. New York: E.P. Dutton, 1961.

The Chosen Place, the Timeless People

Bell, Gale Chevigny. "A Review of *The Chosen Place, the Timeless People.*" *The Village Voice* 15, 41 (October 8, 1970): 6. 30–31.

Bennet, Alice Kizey. "A Review of *The Chosen Place, the Timeless People.*" *Dallas Texas News*, January 4, 1970.

Bond, Jean Carey. "Allegorical Novel by Talented Storyteller." *Freedomways* (1970): 76–78.

Bone, Robert. "'Merle Kinbona Was Part Saint, Part Revolutionary, Part Obeahwoman': A Review of *The Chosen Place, the Timeless People.*" *The New York Times Book Review*, November 30, 1969, 4, 54.

Braithwaite, Edward K. "The African Presence in Caribbean Literature." *Daedalus* 103, no. 2 (Spring 1974): 73–109.

Braithwaite, Edward K. "Rehabilitation." *Critical Quarterly* 13 (Summer 1971): 175–83; *Caribbean Studies* 10, 2 (July 1970): 125–34; *BIM* 13, no. 51 (July-December 1970): 174–84.

Burroway, Janet. "Golden Cut." *New Statesman*, October 2, 1970, 426.

Chevigny, Bell Gale. "A Review of *The Chosen Place, the Timeless People.*" *The Village Voice*, October 8. 1970, 6–8.

Chupa, Ann Maria. *Anne, the White Woman in Contemporary African-American Fiction: Archetypes Stereotypes and Characterizations*. Westport: Greenwood Press, 1990. 32–33, 48, 52, 97.

Collins, Martha. "Paule Marshall's *The Chosen Place.*" *Sojourner* 10, no. 6 (April 1985): 34.

Frecilicher, Lila P. "A Review of *The Chosen Place, the Timeless People.*" *Publisher's Weekly*, August 11, 1969), 41.

Giovanni, Nikki. *Negro Digest* 19, no. 3 (1970): 51–52, 84.

Harris, Wilson. "Metaphor and Myth." *Myth and Metaphor*. Adelaide, Australia: Center for Research in the New Literature in English, 1982, 1–14.

———. "The Womb of Space: The Cross-Cultural Imagination." Westport, CT: Greenwood Press, 1983, 57–66.

Kaufman, James. "The Chosen Place." *Christian Science Monitor*, December 7, 1984, B16.

Lask, Thomas. "Promise and Fulfillment: A Review of *The Chosen Place, the Timeless People.*" *The New York Times*, November 8, 1969, 31.

Michaelson, Judy. "Black Before Its Time." *New York Post*, December 6, 1969, 5.

Nazareth, Peter. "Colonial Institutions Colonized People: A Review of *The Chosen Place, the Timeless People*." *Busara* 6 (1974): 49–64.

Nazareth, Peter. "Colonial Relationships, Colonized People." In *The Third World Writer: His Social Responsibility*. Nairobi: Kenya Literature Bureau, 1978. 31–49.

———. "Paule Marshall's Timeless People." *New Letters* 40 (Autumn 1973): 116–31.

Purcell, Donald. "A Review of *The Chosen Place, the Timeless People*." *Library Journal* (September 15, 1969): 3085.

Rhodes, Richard. "A Serious Matter." *Washington Post Book World*, December 28, 1969, 10.

Samudio, Josephine, ed. *Book Review Digest: March 1970 to February 1971*. New York: The H.W. Wilson Company, 1971, 935.

Skerrett, Joseph T., Jr. "Paule Marshall and the Crisis of Middle Years: *The Chosen Place, the Timeless People*." *Callaloo* 6.2 (Spring-Summer 1983): 69–73.

Spillers, Hortense J. "*The Chosen Place, the Timeless People*: Some Figurations on the New World." In *Conjuring: Black Women in Fiction and Literature*. Ed. Marjorie Pryse, 151–75. Bloomington, IN: Indiana University Press, 1985.

Stoelting, Winfred N. "Time Past, Time Present: The Search for Viable Links in *The Chosen Place, the Timeless People*." *CLA Journal* 16 (September 1972): 60–71.

Talmor, Sascha. "Merle of Bournehills." *Durham University Journal* 80, no. 1 (December 1987): 125–28.

Waugh, Auberon. "The Love Life of the Third Bron: A Review of *The Chosen Place, the Timeless People*." *Spectator* (January 2, 1971): 23.

———. "'Pukka Sahib': A Review of *The Chosen Place, the Timeless People*." *Spectator*, December 26, 1970, 848.

———. "A Review of *The Chosen Place, the Timeless People*." *Spectator*, December 17, 1970, 811.

Whalem, Gretchen. "The Long Search for Coherence and Vision." *Callaloo* 8 (Fall 1985): 667–69.

PRAISESONG FOR THE WIDOW

Ascher, Carol. "Caught in the Middle: A Review of *Praisesong for the Widow*." *Village Voice* 28, March 22, 1983, 42.

Benet, Mary Kathleen. "The White Death." *Times Literary Supplement*, September 16, 1983, 1002.

Bonney, Mary Anne. "A Review of *Praisesong for the Widow*." *Punch*, November 30, 1983,: 71–72.

Borenstein, Marian K. "*Praisesong for the Widow*: A Review." *Freedomways* 24, no. 1 (1984): 56–57.

Bovoso, Carole. "A Review of *Praisesong for the Widow*." *Essence* 13 (April 12, 1983).

Busia, Albena P. "What is Your Nation? Reconnecting Africa and Her Diaspora through Paule Marshall's *Praisesong for the Widow*." In *Changing Our Own Words: Essays on Criticism, Theory, and Writing by Black Women*. Ed. Cheryl Wall, 196–211. New Brunswick, NJ: Rutgers University Press, 1989.

———. "Words Whispered Over Voids: A Context for Black Women's Rebellious Voices in the Novels of African Diaspora (Abridged)." *MAWA Review* 2, no.1: 25–27; In *Black Feminist Criticism and Critical Theory*. Ed. Houston A. Baker, Jr., and Joe Weixlmann, 1–41. Greenwood: Penkeville, 1988.

Carpenter, Lynette, and Wendy K. Kolmar. *Haunting the House of Fiction: Feminist Perspectives and Ghost Stories by American Women*. Knoxville, TN: The University of Tennessee Press, 1991, 10, 13, 142, 145–46, 153, 159–164.

Christian, Barbara. "Ritualistic Process and the Structure of Paule Marshall's *Praisesong for the Widow*." *Callaloo* 6.2 (Spring-Summer 1983): 74–84; In *Black Feminist Criticism: Perspectives on Black Women Writers*. New York: Pergamon Press, 1985, 149–58.

Davis, Carole Boyce. "Caribbean Folk Elements in Paule Marshall's *Praisesong for the Widow*." *CLA Journal*.

———. "Black Woman's Journey into Self: A Womanist Reading of Paule Marshall's *Praisesong for the Widow*." *Matatu* 1, no.1 (1987): 19–34.

Diriam, Sharon. "A Hard-Working Woman in West Indies Purgatory: A Review of *Praisesong for the Widow*." *Los Angeles Times Book Review*, February 27, 1983, part 8.

Eko, Ebele. "Oral Tradition: The Bridge to Africa in Paule Marshall's *Praisesong for the Widow*." *The Western Journal of Black Studies* 10 (Fall 1986): 143–47.

Holloway, Clayton G. "A Review of *Praisesong for the Widow*." *CLA Journal* 27, no. 4 (June 1984): 460–61.

Holloway, Karla F.C. *Moorings and Metaphors: Figures of Culture and Gender in Black Women's Literature*. New Brunswick: Rutgers University Press, 1992. 100–101, 113–40, 150, 158, 178.

hooks, bell. *Yearning: Race, Gender and Cultural Politics*. Boston: South End Press, 1990. 34–36.

Hooper, William Bradley. "A Review of *Praisesong for the Widow*." *Booklist* 79, no.7 (December 1, 1982): 466.

Jefferson, Margo. "A Black Woman's Odyssey." *The Nation*, April 2, 1983, 403–404.

Kazi-Ferrouillet, Kuumba, and Karima A. Belle. "A Review of *Praisesong for the Widow*." *Black Collegian* 15, no.1 (September-October 1984): 64.

Killens, John Oliver. "A Review of *Praisesong for the Widow*." *Crisis* 90 (August-September 1983): 49–50.

Kauffmann, James. "*Praisesong for the Widow*." *Christian Science Monitor*, May 4, 1984. B8.

———. "Novelist Marshall Sang an Early 'Praisesong' for Black Discovery." *Los Angeles Times*, May 18, 1983, part 5: 1, 4.

Lee, Pelicia. "Author Stresses Need to Forge Link with Past." *USA Today*, March 28, 1983.

Lehmann-Haupt, Christopher. "Books of the Times: A Review of *Praisesong for the Widow*." *The New York Times*, February 1, 1983, 7.

Magill, Frank N. "*Praisesong for the Widow*." In *Masterplots: American Fiction Series*, vol. 3. Englewood, NJ: Salem Press, 1986, 1286–1290.

Mooney, Martha, ed. *Book Review Digest: March 1983 to February 1984*. New York: The H.W. Wilson, 1984, 942.

Nazareth, Peter. "A Review of *Praisesong for the Widow*." *World Literature Today* 57, no. 4 (Autumn 1983): 637–38.

Newmark, Victoria. "A Review of *Praisesong for the Widow*." *The Times Educational Supplement*, June 15, 1984, 35.

Nicholson, Delores. "A Study of Ritual Behavior: A Review of *Praisesong for the Widow*." *Journal of Women's Ministries*, no. 3 (Fall 1984): 17.

Otto, Bill. "A Review of *Praisesong for the Widow*." *American Libraries* 17, no. 3 (March 16, 1986): 167.

Pettis, Joyce. "The Ancestor in Paule Marshall's *Praisesong for the Widow*." Paper presented at Conference on Black Writers and Their Sources. North Carolina Central University, September 25, 1985.

Pinckney, Darryl. "Roots: A Review of *Brown Girl, Brownstones* and

Praisesong for the Widow." *The New York Review of Books*, April 28, 1983, 26–30.

Pollard, Velma. "Cultural Connections in Paule Marshall's *Praisesong for the Widow.*" *World Literature Written in English* 25, no. 2 (Autumn 1985): 285–98.

Ravel-Pinto, Thelma. "A Review of *Praisesong for the Widow.*" *Journal of Black Studies* 17, no. 4 (June 1987): 509–11.

Reyes, Angelita. "Politics and Metaphors of Materialism in Paule Marshall's *Praisesong for the Widow* and Toni Morrison's *Tar Baby.*" In *Politics and the Muse: Studies in the Politics of Recent American Literature.* Ed. Adam Sorkin, 179–205. Bowling Green, OH: Popular Press, 1989.

Richardson, Marilyn. *Presence Africaine*, no. 132 (1984): 147–49.

Samuels, Wilfred D. "Return of the Native: A Review of *Praisesong for the Widow.*" *American Book Review* 6, no. 3 (March–April 1984): 15.

Sandiford, Keith A. "Paule Marshall's *Praisesong for the Widow*: The Reluctant Heiress or Whose Life is it Anyway?" *Black American Literature Forum* 20, no. 4 (Winter 1986): 371–92.

Scarboro, Ann Armstrong. "*Praisesong for the Widow*: A Review." *International Fiction Review* (Winter 1988): 53–57.

Sheffey, Ruthe T. "A Review of *Praisesong for the Widow.*" *Langston Hughes Review* 4.1 (1986): 55–57.

Smith-Wright, Geraldine. "In Spite of the Klan: Ghosts in the Fiction of Black Women Writers." In *Haunting the House of Fiction: Feminist Perspectives on Ghost Stories by American Women.* Ed. Lynette Carpenter and Wendy K. Kolmar, 142–65. Knoxville: The University of Tennessee Press, 1991.

Trescott, Jacqueline. "The Daughter of the Mother Poets; Novelist Paule Marshall, Exploring The World of Black Immigrants." *The Washington Post*, October 8, 1991.

Tyler, Anne. "A Widow's Tale: A Review of *Praisesong for the Widow.*" *The New York Times Book Review*, February 20, 1983, 7, 34.

Waxman, Barbara Frey. *From the Hearth to the Open Road: A Feminist Study of Aging in Contemporary Literature.* Westport: Greenwood Press, 1990, 16–20, 120–36.

———. "The Widow's Journey to Self and Roots: Aging and Society in Paule Marshall's *Praisesong for the Widow.*" *Frontiers* 9.3 (1987): 94–99.

Wilentz, Gay. "Towards a Spiritual Middle Passage Back: Paule

Marshall's Diasporic Vision in *Praisesong for the Widow*." *Obsidian* 5, no. 3 (Winter 1990): 1–21.

Wilson, Lucy. "Aging and Ageism in Paule Marshall's *Praisesong for the Widow* and Beryl Gilroy's *Frangipani House*." *Journal of Caribbean Studies* 7, no. 2–3 (Spring-Winter 1989–1990): 189–99.

Yardley, Jonathan. "Sea Journeys and Soul Searches." *Washington Post Bookworld*, January 30, 1983, 3.

DAUGHTERS

Ascher, Carol. "Compromised Lives." *The Women's Review of Books* 9.2 (November 1991): 7.

"The Black Woman's Bruden." *Mirabella* (October 1991): 78.

Boyd, Valerie. "Savoring the Bitter and Sweet of Women's Lives: A Review of *Daughters*." *The Atlanta Journal*, October 20, 1991, N-10.

Broussard, Sharon. "Fictional Women Live Real Lives." *Cleveland Plain Dealer*, September 23, 1991, x.

Cole, Diane. "*Daughters* Shows Strength in Sisterhood." *U.S.A. Today*, October 11, 1991, x.

Engeler, Anne. "Paule Marshall: Slave Girls No More." *Newsweek*, November 11, 1991, x.

Harrington, Maureen. "Marshall Had Last Laugh over Publisher's Remark." *The Denver Post*, November 3, 1991, x.

Jordon, Shirley M. "*Daughters*: The Unity that Binds Us." *American Visions*, 6, no. 5 (October 1991): 38–39.

McCabe, Carol. "A Colorful, Eventful Novel Set in the Caribbean." *The Providence Sunday Journal*, November 10, 1991, E-11.

McHenry, Susan. "Generations When Home-Folks Have No Answers You Can Use." *Emerge* (October 1991), 67.

Meritt, Robert. "Marshall Paints Canvas of Images: A Review of *Daughters*." *Richmond Times*, October 13, 1991, 67.

Miner, Valerie. "Black Women Held in a Net of Friendship." *The Philadelphia Inquirer*, November 5, 1991, E-3.

Prose, Francine. "Another Country: A Review of *Daughters*." *The Washington Post Book World*, September 22, 1991, 1, 4.

Romano, Nancy Forbes. "Suns and Lovers: A Review of *Daughters*." *Los Angeles Times Book Review*, October 6, 1991, 1, 8.

Schaeffer, Susan Fromberg. "Cutting Herself Free: A Review of *Daughters*." *The New York Times Book Review*, October 27, 1991, 3, 29.

Seaman, Donna. "*Daughters*: A Review." *Booklist* 27, no. 21 (July 1991): L 2011–12.

Smiley, Jane. "Caribbean Voices: Paule Marshall Explores the Nexus of Self, Success, Politics and Culture." *Chicago Sunday Tribune*, October 6, 1991, *Books*, 3.

Stanley, Bonnie Newman. "Paule Marshall: Sharing the World Inside Her Head." *Richmond News*, November 15, 1991, 21.

Trescott, Jacqueline. "The Daughter of the Mother Poets: Novelist Paule Marshall, Exploring the World of Black Immigrants." *The Washington Post*, Style Section, October 8, 1991, C1, C2.

Washington, Elsie B. "Paule Marshall: Merging Our Cultures." *Essence* 22, no. 6 (October 1991): 48.

White, Emily. "Daughters: A Review." *Village Voice*, November 12, 1991, 6–7.

THE FISHER KING

Newson-Horst, Adele S. "Paule Marshall's People: Meeting the Relatives." *The New Crisis*, March/April 2001.

Prado, Nereida. "Review of *The Fisher King* by Paule Marshall." *Sargasso* 2002, 2: 152–153.

Reviews of Collections

MERLE AND OTHER STORIES

Barnes, Hugh. "Return of the Native: A Review of *Merle and Other Stories*." *London Review of Books*, 7, no. 4 (March 1985): 20.

Willis, Chris. *West Africa*, no. 3536, June 3, 1985, 1119–20.

REENA AND OTHER STORIES

Denniston, Dorothy Lee. "Early Short Fiction by Paule Marshall." *Callaloo* 6, no. 2 (Spring-Summer 1983): 31–45.

Freeman, Suzanne. "From Roots to Full Bloom." *Washington Post*, February 17, 1984, E2.

Gusson, Adam. "A Review of *Reena and Other Stories*." *Village Voice*, May 15, 1984, 47.

Hawthorne, Evelyn. "Ethnicity and Cultural Perspective in Paule Marshall's Short Fiction." *MELUS*, 13, no. 3–4 (Fall-Winter 1986): 37–48.

Harris, Laurie Lanzen, and Sheila Fitzgerald, eds. *Short Story Criticism*, vol. 3. Detroit, MI: Gale Research Company, 1988.
Hull, Gloria T. "To Be a Black Woman in America: A Reading of Paule Marshall's '*Reena.*'" *Obsidian* 4, no. 3 (1978): 5–15.
Kaufmann, James. "*Reena and Other Stories.*" *Christian Science Monitor*, March 23, 1984, 20.
Simmons, Sheila M. "A Review of *Reena and Other Stories.*" *Sojourner* 9, no. 8 (April 1984), 21.
Spigner, Nieda. *Freedomways* 24, no. 2 (1984): 148–49.
———. "*Reena and Other Stories*: A Review." *Freedomways* 24, no. 2 (1984): 148–49.
Sternhell, Carol. "*Reena and Other Stories.*" *New York Times*, February 19, 1984, 22.
Taylor, Linda. "The Weapon of Laughter." *Times Literary Supplement*, April 5, 1985, 376.

Dissertations

Adams, Ann Josephine. "Sisters of Light: The Importance of Spirituality to the Afro-American Novel." Indiana University, 1989.
Backes, Nancy N. "An Adolescence of Their Own: Feminine Coming of Age in Contemporary American Literature." University of Wisconsin, Milwaukee, 1990.
Billingslea-Brown, Alma J. "The Folk Aesthetic in Contemporary African-American Women's Fiction and Visual Art." University of Texas at Dallas, 1989.
Coleman, Robert Louis. "A Literary Study of the Novels of Paule Marshall." Teacher's College, Columbia, 1990.
Cooper, Barbara Eck. "The Difficult Arts of Family of Life: The Creative Force in the Domestic Fictions Six Contemporary Women Novelists." University of Missouri, Columbia, 1986.
Denniston, Dorothy Lee Ha. "Cultural Reclamation: The Development of a Pan-African Sensibility in the Fiction of Paule Marshall." Brown University, 1983.
Ingram, Elwanda Deloris. "Black Women: Literary Self-Portraits." University of Oregon, 1980.
Japtok, Martin. "Contrast as a Structural Principle in Paule Marshall's *The Chosen Place, the Timeless People.*" Master's Thesis, Johannes Gutenberg-Universität Mainz, 1988.

Johnson, Gloria Carniece. "The Folk Tradition in the Fiction of Black Women Writers." The University of Tennessee, 1991.

Koza, Kimberly Ann. "Women as Images of History: Contemporary-Anglophone Fiction by Minority and Post-Colonial Women Writers." *Dissertation Abstracts International* 50, no. 4 (October 1989): 953A. [Indiana University, 1988]

LeSeur, Geta J. "The 'Bildungsroman' in Afro-American and Afro-Caribbean Fiction: An Integrated Consciousness." Indiana University, 1982.

Malone, Gloria Snodgrass. "The Nature and Causes of Suffering in the Fiction of Paule Marshall, Kristin Hunter, Toni Morrison, and Alice Walker." Kent State University, 1979.

O'Banner, Bessie Marie. "A Study of Black Heroines in Four Selected Novels (1929–1959) by Four Black American Women Novelists: Zora Neale Hurston, Nella Larsen, Paule Marshall, Ann Lane Petry." Southern Illinois University at Carbondale, 1981.

Reyes, Angelita Dianne. "Crossing the Bridge: The Great Mother in Selected Novels of Toni Morrison, Paule Marshall, Simone Schwarz-Bart and Mariama Ba." The University of Iowa, 1985.

de Romanet, Jerome. "The Narrative Creation of Self in the Fiction by African-American and African Caribbean Women Writers." The Louisana State University of Agricultural and Mechanical College, 1990.

Sample, Maxine J. Cornish. "The Portrayal of the Black Woman in the Works of Paule Marshall." Master's Thesis. Atlanta University, 1977.

Schreiber, Sheila Ortego. "Art and Life: The Novels of Black Women." The University of Mexico, 1981.

Shattuck, Sandra Dickinson. "Personal and Political Histories: The Hard Work of Remembering in Paule Marshall's *The Chosen Place, the Timeless People* and Christa Wolf's *Kindheitsmuster*." The University of Texas at Austin, 1988.

Stevenson, Peggy Lee Denise. "Conflicts of Culture, Class and Gender in Selected Caribbean-American and Caribbean Women's Literature." Washington, D.C.: Howard University, 1988.

Wilentz, Gay Alden. "From Africa to America: Cultural Ties that Bind in the Works of Contemporary African and African-American Women Writers." The University of Texas at Austin, 1986.

Index

Abortion, 4, 75, 77, 79, 80, 81, 84
Africa: colonialism in, 2; need for spiritual return to, 1, 55; as point of origin, 4
Afro-American(s): affected by rivers, seas, and oceans, 103; bonds with Afro-Caribbeans, 1; in club world of Paris, 96; fragmented history of, 1; migration history, 95, 96; need for spiritual return to Africa, 1; tide turns against musicians in exile, 96
Afro-Caribbean(s): bonds with Afro-Americans, 1; upwardly mobile, 7
Agency: black women's, 2, 75; right to, 27
Amber, 27
Amron, Harriet *(The Chosen Place, a Timeless People),* 37; ancestral role in slavery, 50; antipathy toward Merle, 43; appearance suggesting secrecy, 44; attempts to bribe Merle, 46, 49, 50; duplicitous behavior by, 42; follows in Aunt Susan's footsteps, 42, 43; interference with community members domestic affairs, 43; representative of colonialism, 43; repressed racism of, 44; suicide by drowning, 50, 51; superciliousness of, 44; wish to be unconventional, 42
Amron, Saul *(The Chosen Place, a Timeless People),* 37, 38, 41; anger with Harriet, 43; bonding with Merle, 45; confronts Jewish identity, 38; double location of, 42; dwells on persecution of Jews, 44; joins community in opposition to mill owners profiteering, 48; suggest diversification of economy to islanders, 42; threatens to leave Harriet, 49
Ancestors: attachment to, 27; formidability of, 6; narratives of, 6; slave, 8, 9, 60; suffering of, 69; tracing steps of, 20; traditional roles of, 2
Anderson, Marian, 64
Assimilation, 5, 24, 28, 29, 63; replacing, 73; temporary, 55
Association of Barbadian Homeowners and Businessmen, 9, 11, 13, 18, 19
Awakenings: political, 2; sexual, 2

163

Baker, Josephine, 96, 99
Baldwin, James, 96
Barbados: colonial exploitation of blacks in, 7; Franchise Act in, 8; as launching pad for colonization of Caribbean, 7; migration from, 6; system of poor relief in, 8
"Barbados" *(Soul Clap Hands and Sing)*, 2, 3, 23–26; intersections with *Brown Girl, Brownstones*, 24; signifiers of whiteness in, 24
Bats, 43
Beaufils, Justin *(Daughters)*, 75, 81, 89; advocates peoples' rights, 84; runs for election, 76; wins election, 90
Bechet, Sidney, 96
Bellegarde, Celestine Marie-Claire *(Daughters)*, 76, 90; contempt for Estelle, 82; related to Congo Jane, 90
Berman, Max *(Soul Clap Hands and Sings)*, 26–28, 100; avoidance of struggle out of fear and futility by, 28; considers self as outcast, 26; decides he shares "collective suffering" with Miss Williams, 27, 28; disdainful connection to black women by, 27, 28; effort to reclaim life by, 2, 3; uses Miss Williams to regain own life, 26, 27, 28
Big Drum dance, 69
Black Arts Movement, 9
Boyce, Deighton *(Brown Girls, Brownstones)*, 2, 100; death of, 17, 18; dissolution of union with Silla, 16, 17; dreams of return to Barbados, 2, 9, 10; inheritance in Barbados, 10, 16; leaves colonial exploitation of blacks in Barbados, 7; pleased with deportation to Barbados, 17; preference for old ways, 10; visions and daydreams of, 16; yearning for peace and pleasure by, 14
Boyce, Selina *(Brown Girls, Brownstones)*, 100; attempts to navigate through past and future, 18; bonding with Rachel, 19; caught in parental battle, 10; collapses Deighton's dream into her own, 19, 20; confides in Miss Thompson, 11; creation of idealized female-based life with friend Beryl, 11, 12; denounces Silla for turning against Deighton, 17; determination to protect Deighton, 15, 16; determination to survive racist society, 10; difficulty fitting in with community, 7, 17; grows apart from Beryl, 13; leaves Brooklyn for Barbados, 19, 20; longing for outside world, 7; pieces past, present, future together, 4; questions community need for empowerment amid bigotry, 10; realizes mother's duplicity in handling father's inheritance, 11; rejection of white values, 12, 13; sees Silla as bird of prey, 16; traveling between identities, 2; understanding of Silla's craving for property, 15; voluntary migration to Barbados, 2
Boyce, Silla *(Brown Girl, Brownstones)*, 2, 100; anesthetization of human feelings by, 15; as collective voice of Bajan women, 13, 14; destruction of relationship with Deighton, 16, 17; determination to own brownstone, 8, 9, 11, 12;

driven by economic desperation, 16; duplicitious behavior toward Deighton, 15, 16; escapes from colonial exploitation of blacks in Barbados, 7; expropriates Deighton's inheritance, 10, 15, 16; refusal to be deprived again, 10; representation in Ulysses, 18; work in defense factory, 14, 15

Brathwaite, Leon *(Brown Girl, Brownstones)*, 16

"Brazil" *(Soul Clap Hands and Sing)*, 23, 33–35; exhibition of degradation in, 34; intersection with "Brooklyn" and "British Guiana," 34, 35; recapture of self in, 3

"British Guiana" *(Soul Clap Hands and Sing)*, 3, 23, 28–32

"Brooklyn" *(Soul Clap Hands and Sing)*, 2, 3, 23; white academic setting, 26

Brown Girl, Brownstones (Marshall), 1, 7–21, 46, 93; assumptions about Jews in, 13; community need for empowerment amid bigotry, 10; "ladder of success" in, 8, 9; metaphoric wartime in, 13; power of property ownership and, 8, 9; struggles with traditional values in, 2

Brownstones, 96; correlative of peoples' bonding, 8, 9; destruction of, 8, 9; European-style architecture and, 9; offering form of identity to community, 8, 9; ownership, 20; representation of community icons, 9; as site of resistance, 8, 9

Burke, Sam, 104

Burnham, Forbes, 32

Caliban *(Soul Clap Hands and Sing)*: as creation of others, 33; eluding of past life, 34; embraces new identity, 33; feels connection to others, 34; insecurity of, 33; lack of own identity, 33; at odds with self, 34; scapegoat for colonial voyeurism, 3

Caribbean: anti-colonial history of, 3; conflicted elite in, 3. *See also* individual stories

Carruthers, Lowell *(Daughters)*, 4; civil rights activism, 86; counteracting bigotry, 77; enters orbit of marginality, 86; as site of resistance, 84

Challenor, Beryl *(Brown Girl, Brownstones)*, 2, 12, 13; considers law career, 12, 13; creation of idealized female-based life with friend Selina, 11, 12

The Chosen Place, the Timeless People (Marshall), 1, 3, 4, 37–54, 93; collective community actions in, 53; coping with colonial intervention, 37–54; cultural regeneration in, 38; dangers of monoculture economy in, 39; economic pragmatism by community, 41; interactions and intersections between people, 38; need to recover community history of resistance, 38; perpetuation of imperial profiteering in, 43; pro-imperial development plan in, 41; reenaction of slave rebellion in, 47; representation of colonialism through bogus philanthropy, 44; seeking viable selves in, 38; self-sufficiency in, 40; smoke, sea, stones, and cassia foreshadowing community resistance, 49–52; sugar and slavery in, 37–54

INDEX

Class: issues of, 4
Clement, Adriana, 104
Clement, Alberta Jane, 104
Clyde *(Brown Girl, Brownstones)*, 2
Colonial: behavior, 40; efforts to "whiten" black people, 31; exploitation, 7, 70; expropriation, 29, 85; interventions, 37; logic, 75; mystification, 4; omnipresence, 72; philanthropy, 87; power, 29; practices, 29; propaganda, 30; values, 30; violence, 85; voyeurism, 33
Colonialism, 2, 28, 29, 39; corrupt, 75; dehumanisation of, 2; forcing chronic conditions on communities, 39; as historical contamination, 73; paternalistic, 75; represented through bogus philanthropy, 44
Communities: benefit of labor of to capitalist world markets, 48; collective actions by, 53; diasporic, 4, 37, 50; displaced, 1; experiencing sense of, 68; of female workers, 8; fitting in with, 7; historical memories of, 30; imaginative saga of, 2; island networks of, 7; participation in Black Arts Movement by, 9; relocation of, 8, 9; resistance by, 49–53; subject to invasive visitors from U.S., 44; transformations for, 39
Congo Jane *(Daughters)*, 77, 79, 84, 85, 86, 87, 88, 89; as ancestor-slave, 5; model of resistance, 77
"Constellation" (Marshall), 76
Corruption: diverse, 76; historical, 53; imminence of, 41; imperial, 52; institutionalized, 4; perpetuating, 52; political, 76
Cotton, 60

Countermemory, 30
Cudjoe, Will, 77, 79, 88; as ancestor-slave, 5
Cuffee, Ned *(The Chosen Place, the Timeless People)*, 46, 47, 48, 53
Cultural: abandonment, 69; alterity, 64; awareness, 5; beliefs, 27; history, 65; icons, 3; identity, 21; memory, 100; nationalism, 9; practices, 29; practices surviving Middle Passage, 4; regeneration, 38; retreat, 30; rights, 89
Culture(s): ancestral, 16; embrace of, 1
Cuney *(Praisesong for the Widow)*, 4, 56, 58, 59–73; in Avey's dream, 61–64; chastises Avey for living like a rich white person, 65; keeping history in play, 62; ritualistic walk with Avey, 60; wants Avey to join opposition, 63; as wedge between Avey and white world, 62

Daniels, Viney *(Daughters)*, 4, 85, 86; as site of resistance, 84
Daughters (Marshall), 1, 4, 5, 75–92, 93; "Constellation," 76; double exposures in, 75, 76, 77, 79; flashbacks and reminiscences in, 76; intercontinental journey of, 4, 5; "Little Girls of All the Daughters," 76; the Monument in, 77, 80; "Polestar," 76; "Tin Cans and Graveyard Bones," 76; war of independence staged in, 75
Davies, Carole Boyce, 2
Dawson, Shad *(Praisesong for the Widow)*, 62
Dembo, Millicent *(Soul Clap Hands and Sing)*, 31
Diaspora: African, 1, 2, 5, 19; Caribbean, 2; finding restoration

of soul in, 98; history of, 5; natal links to, 94; reality of life in, 19; satisfaction of need for personal and historical authenticity in, 100; United States, 2, 3; warnings of life in, 27
Discrimination: against migrants, 8. *See also* Racism
Dislocation, 5

Eggs, 43
Elders: traditional roles of, 2
Emanuel C. (ship), 67, 68
Employment, 7, 80; issues of genocide and, 14; opportunities, 5; in society flooded with G.I.s, 17, 18
Experience(s): diasporic, 1, 25; memories of, 4; sensory, 94; sharing similar, 19

Feminist issues, 35
Fine, Rachel *(Brown Girl, Brownstones)*, 19, 21
The Fisher King (Marshall), 1, 5, 93–99; glamour and racism in, 98; issues of desire and loss in, 97; recapitulation of themes of earlier works, 93; redrawing feminist angle of vision by featuring male protagonist, 93; vindication of people's struggle through exilic suffering in, 98; youth and community healing wounds in, 98
Fitzroy, James, 104
Forde, Astral Dolores *(Daughters)*, 76, 81, 90; becomes Primus' mistress, 80; discovered to be Primus' mistress by Estelle, 87, 88; double exposure and, 79, 80; imperial hegemony in life of, 87, 88; manages Mile Trees Colony Hotel, 80
Freedom: within self, 33

Fusso, Allen *(The Chosen Place, the Timeless People)*, 42, 50

Garvey, Marcus, 6
Garvey Day, 6
Gender: agency and, 2; narratives on, 6; power relations of, 8; relationships between old men and younger women, 23–35; role in transformation, 23
Gide, André, 28
Goodman, Mr. *(Soul Clap Hands and Sing)*, 25
Grady *(Daughters)*: in Black Power movement, 80; civil rights activism, 83
Guimares, Heitor Baptista, 33
Guittirez, Hector, 33
Gullah, 60, 70, 73

Harbin, Susan *(The Chosen Place, the Timeless People)*, 42, 44, 50
Harriet *(The Chosen Place, the Timeless People)*, 3
Hattie *(The Fisher King)*, 6; fears loss of identity as surrogate mother to Sonny, 97, 98; reminisces about Sonny Rett at memorial, 97, 98
Hetty *(The Fisher King)*, 5
Hitler, Adolf, 14, 17
Homosexuality, 12, 13, 28, 31, 32, 46
House Un-American Activities Committee, 103
Hutson, Lyle *(The Chosen Place, a Timeless People)*: complicity with establishment, 42; co-optation by, 40; gives up activism for less radical pursuits, 40–41; opts for expedience over principle, 42; pragmatic standpoint of, 37, 41; pro-capital position on island

Hutson, Lyle (*continued*)
  economy, 41; pro-corporate commentary, 40

Ibo people, 60, 61, 73
Identity: collective, 5; complex, 4; confronting, 38; cultural, 7, 21; embracing, 33; erasure of, 33; ethnic, 28, 29; lack of, 33; loss of, 97; neon, 34; personal, 5; preservation of, 99, 100; quests for, 2; understanding, 73
Immigration. *See* Migration
Insurgencies: slave, 5

Jagan, Cheddi, 32
Jazz: evolution of, 6; relationship to race relations, 6. *See also The Fisher King*
Jewelry, 20; African, 64–65; gold *vs.* silver, 13; historical meanings of, 21; representative of slavery, 10, 13, 47; symbolism of, 3, 46
Jews: assumptions about, 13, 14; atrocities against, 14; black relations with, 17; genocide and, 14; persecution of, 44; respect for in black community, 14
Johnson, Avey (*Praisesong for the Widow*), 100; ability to feel rooted, 4; affected deeply by ruins of earthquake/volcano, 58; affirms black motherhood as response to racist constructs, 73; alienation from community, 56; becomes participant in post-slavery life honoring tradition, 69; becomes restless with cruises when suppressed feelings arise, 57.65; connects with politically aware daughter, 68; Cuney's chastisements about living as a rich white person, 65; denial of Afro-Caribbean roots, 55; disenchantment with frivolity of cruise, 57, 58; dreams of Cuney, 61–64; exertion of pull on by the sea, 55; feels entrusted (through Cuney) with future mission, 62; in Grenada, 66–69; inability to remember ancestry, 67; leaves luxury cruise, 56, 59, 65, 66; liberating self-cleansing for, 68; living in white community, 55; loses sight of self, 56, 67; memories of great-aunt Cuney and importance of tradition, 59–73; pieces past, present, future together, 4; recognizes pointlessness of possessions, 58, 59; refuses to travel to ancestral home, 55; rejection of "home" by, 4; repulsion at imperial-referenced dinner item, 58, 65, 72; revisits nausea of Middle Passage, 68; ritualistic walk with Cuney, 60; sees fragility of so-called civilizatioin, 59; temporary embrace of assimilation and Anglocentric values, 55; voyage detaching her from diasporic home emotionally and spiritually, 56
Johnson, Jerome (*Praisesong for the Widow*), 56, 62, 73; death of, 57; transforms himself to hard-working accountant, 57
Johnson, Marion (*Praisesong for the Widow*), 55; Avey's political altercations with, 64; criticizes Avey for going on meaningless cruise with white folks, 64; draws politico-historical issues out, 73; fond memories of trip to Ghana, 68; participation in Black Power movement, 64; in Poor People's March on Washington, 64

Joseph, Lebert *(Praisesong for the Widow)*, 4, 70; emblematic role in healing of Avey Johnson, 67
Journey(s): diasporic, 23; emotional, 23; spiritual, 23

Al Kazwini, 78
Ke'ram, 79, 92
Kimbona, Merle *(The Chosen Place, the Timeless People)*, 38; adopts isolationist stance, 41; attempts to reconcile conflicting elements of self, 38; bonding with Saul, 45; confronts African identity, 38; denounces white, male ruling class, 40; departure for Africa, 54; former activism with Lyle, 40; insurgent representative, 39; labels Lyle "Judas," 41; longing to know and accept self, 46; opposes status quo, 38; pieces past, present, future together, 4; rejects idea of foreign investment in island, 41; returns to Africa, 50; revolutionary spirit of, 38; sheds shroud of colonialism, 47; tells Saul of bigotry suffered at the hands of Jews, 44; as warrion ancestor, 39; works to make community self-sufficient, 40
Ku Klux Klan, 63

Lawson, Sandy *(Daughters)*, 76, 77, 81, 85; capitulates to white power structure, 83; enables white elite economic success, 84; reactionary activities of, 83
"Little Girls of All the Daughters" (Marshall), 76

Mack, Miss *(Daughters)*, 76, 81
Mackenzie, Estelle *(Daughters)*, 76, 77, 78; anti-imperial resistance of, 83; discovers Astral is Primus' mistress, 87; miscarriages, 80, 81, 87; as site of resistance, 84, 86; takes on Congo Jane's fight against colonialism, 86
Mackenzie, Primus *(Daughters)*, 75; assumes role of oral historian of island, 77; becomes invested in post-colonial apparatus, 83; capitulation to gunboat diplomacy, 82, 83; derives from Ursa Major, 81; double exposure and, 81, 84; embattled political principles of, 4, 88; enables white elite economic success, 84; exposure of secret life, 90; fixation on external signs of empire, 82; idealistic dreams of, 81, 82; mimics U.S. values, 89; opportunism of, 85; political downfall, 89; political transformation to conservatist mode, 82, 88; runs for reelection, 76; "sells-out," 84, 88; takes Astral as mistress, 80
Mackenzie, Ursa *(Daughters)*, 75, 81, 100; anti-imperial resistance of, 83; childhood memories, 79; as chronicler of slave insurgencies, 5; civil rights ancestors, 4; cultural awareness of, 5; double exposure and, 83; exposes corrupt paternalistic colonialism, 75; female mentors for, 5; finds direction, 90; hallucinations, 79; rejection of thesis topic by Professor Crowder, 79; returns to Caribbean to support father in election, 76, 78; store of memories, 79; symbolically named for constellation/ African roots, 78; takes up mantle of Congo Jane, 88, 89; as Ursa Minor to Primus' Ursa Major, 81

"The Making of a Writer: From the Poets in the Kitchen" (Marshall), 5

Malvern *(Daughters)*, 76, 80, 82; fears rocking status quo, 80

Marshall, Paule: "Barbados" *(Soul Clap Hands and Sing)*, 23–26; "British Guiana" *(Soul Clap Hands and Sing)*, 28–32; "Brooklyn" *(Soul Clap Hands and Sing)*, 26–28; *Brown Girl, Brownstones*, 1, 2, 7–21; *The Chosen Place, the Timeless People*, 37–54; chronicles of post-slavery sagas, 5; *Daughters*, 75–92; *The Fisher King*, 93–99; Pan African strands in works of, 99, 100; *Praisesong for the Widow*, 55–73; problematic encounters with gay men and lesbians in fiction of, 28; *Soul Clap Hands and Sing*, 23–35; *Triangular Road: A Memoir*, 103–106

Mary and Martizke *(Brown Girl, Brownstones)*, 11–12

Masons, 57, 63

Medford *(Soul Clap Hands and Sing)*: as ancient female warrior, 30, 31

Men: protagonists, 23–35; reaching out to women, 24

Mentors, 2

Middle Passage, 6, 60, 104; holding boxes in, 8, 9; opthalmia and, 78; represented in Carnival floats, 47; sites of, 50; tortuous journey of, 69

Migration: from Caribbean, 95; discrimination and, 8; forced, 1; historical continuum of, 7, 8; laws to prevent, 7–8; movements of, 7; to Panama Canal building, 8; seasonal, 8; South-North, 95, 96, 104; voluntary, 2

Miranda *(Soul Clap Hands and Sing)*, 33, 34

Moore, Thomasina *(Praisesong for the Widow)*, 57, 66, 70, 71, 72

Motley, Gerald *(Soul Clap Hands and Sings)*, 100; becomes "puppet director" of British Guiana Broadcasting, 29; colonial symbolism by, 29; complacency is challenged, 32; complicitous with status quo, 32; death of, 32; declination of resistance by, 29; effect of colonial past on, 3; emotional attachment to Sidney, 3, 31, 32; extends self in altruistic gesture, 3, 31, 32; fails to understand capitalist colonial power, 29; fear of homosexual feelings for Sydney, 31, 32; marginalization of, 30; as non-confrontational conformist, 29; opts for assimilation, 28, 29; opts out of political struggle, 32; relations with Sybil, 29, 30; spurns ethnic identity, 28, 29; symbolic confrontation with black nationalism, 30

Narratives: of ancestors, 6; eurocentric, 38; European settings, 6; of evolution of jazz, 6; on gender, 6; of injustice, 38; Landing, 60, 65; slave, 72

Nationalism: black, 30

North Star, 78, 79

Obeah, 16

Panama Money, 104

Parrish, Sydney *(Soul Clap Hands and Sing)*, 29; coexistence of resistance and assimilation in, 30

Payne, Edgar *(The Fisher King)*: trans-

forms diasporic community with employment opportunities, 5
Payne, Sonny Carmichael *(The Fisher King)*, 6; historical position as son of transcontinental slavery, 99; ploy by Uncle Edgar to keep in Brooklyn, 97; return to Brooklyn for memorial for grandfather, 5, 93, 94
Payne, Sonny Rhett *(The Fisher King)*, 5, 93, 94; appearance of in person of grandson, 94; contextualizes exile through presentation of slavery by Hattie, 98; exodus to Paris, 94; returns international legacy to natal community, 98; unable to return to Brooklyn, 96
Payne, Ulene *(The Fisher King)*, 94
Peace, Father *(Brown Girl, Brownstones)*, 2, 17
PIg sticking, 48, 49
Pinckney, Darryl, 8
Polaris, 78
"Polestar" (Marshall), 76
Pollard, Daphne *(The Chosen Place, the Timeless People)*, 44
Praisesong for the Widow (Marshall), 1, 4, 55–73, 93
Protagonists: facing complex histories of home and exile, 1; gender and, 1; geographical/spiritual travel by, 1; male, 23–35

Rachel *(Brown Girl, Brownstones)*, 2
Racism: enduring, 76; issues of, 4; repressed, 44
Reality: gaining ascendance over, 23; ontological, 34, 35; quotidian, 30; securing oneself from, 24
Reena and Other Stories (Marshall), 35–36
Resistance: to colonial expropriation, 85; indigenous, 70; models of, 77
Resistance, elements foreshadowing: boulders, 51–52; cassia, 52; pig sticking, 48, 49; sea, 50–51; smoke, 49, 50
Ring Shout circle dance, 60, 65, 68
Robert Fulton (ship), 20, 56, 68, 70
Rylands, Mae *(Daughters)*, 4, 77; agitates for justice, 83; confronts Ursa with her apathy, 85; inherits Congo Jane's orbit, 84; opposition to colonial violence, 85; as site of resistance, 84

Saul *(The Chosen Place, the Timeless People)*, 3
Seifert, Yearwood *(Brown Girl, Brownstones)*, 14
Self: confrontation, 20; denial, 31; freedom within, 33; help, 8, 9; indulgence, 27; knowledge, 25; loss, 18; reclamation of, 33
Sexual: awakenings, 2; love, 31
Sidney *(Soul Clap Hands and Sing)*, 3
Skeete, Suggie *(Brown Girl, Brownstones):* referred to as "black, foreign scum," 12; tries to forget slavery, 12
Slavery, 42; Barbados' connection to, 104; community knowledge about historical situation of people in, 14; destruction of selves through, 47; emancipation in 1838, 7; historical continuum of, 31; institutionalized, 78; as "Peculiar Institution," 6; privations of, 7; reenactments of, 47; sites of, 94; tumultuous history of, 39; U.S. denial of complicity in, 47, 48
Slaves: insurgents, 75; longing of to return to Africa, 55; runaway, 7; transported to Caribbean, 60

Social: justice, 35; relations, 36
Soul Clap Hands and Sing (Marshall), 1, 23–35, 93, 100; "Barbados," 23–26; "British Guiana," 28–32; "Brooklyn," 26–28; of hollow men with dried voices, 35; interrogation of old men facing unattainability of contentment, 34, 35; intersection of novellas, 34, 35; men striking out at female counterparts, 35; searching for love to replace loss, 2, 3; women returning fire on men, 35
Springer, Clive *(Brown Girl, Brownstones)*, 18, 19
Stokes, Sir John *(The Chosen Place, the Timeless People)*, 37; aura of imperial mastery about, 40
Sugar industry, 37–54; closing of sugar factory before people can harvest private plots, 39–40, 46, 48; community organizes against, 48; community role in, 42; enables community to earn a living but still enslaves, 39; in-crop/out-of-crop, 39; indeterminacy of, 39; talk of nationalization of, 40; total dependence on, 42; transhistorical role of, 39
Sweet, Suggie *(Brown Girl, Brownstones)*, 2
Sybil *(Soul Clap Hands and Sing)*, 29, 30; challenges Gerald's complacency, 32; as textual insurgent, 30; urges Gerald to stand up and fight, 30

Thompson, Miss *(Brown Girl, Brownstones)*, 2; enables Selina to situater herself transculturally, 10, 11; mentors Selina, 10, 11; representation of ancestral time, 11; returns to The South, 11
"Tin Cans and Graveyard Bones" (Marshall), 76
"To Da-Duh, In Memoriam" (Marshall), 35, 98
Tradition: honoring, 59, 69; importance of, 59; values of, 2
Triangular Road: A Memoir (Marshall), 103–106; "Homage to Mr. (Langston) Hughes," 103; "I've Know Rivers; The James River," 103, 104; "I've Knows Seas: The Caribbean Sea," 104
Trotman, Florrie *(Brown Girl, Brownstones)*, 14

Ursa Major, 81
Ursa Minor, 78

"The Valley Between" (Marshall), 36
Values: Anglocentric, 55; capitalist, 40; colonial, 30; internalization of, 29; traditional, 2; white, 4, 11, 12, 13
Viney *(Daughters)*: counteracting bigotry, 77
Violence: racist, 10

Walkes, Leesey *(The Chosen Place, the Timeless People)*, 49, 52; waits for a brighter world, 38
Walkes, Vereson *(The Chosen Place, the Timeless People)*, 52, 53
Watford, Mr. *(Soul Clap Hands and Sings)*, 40, 100; asceticism of, 24, 25; attempts to communicate with young woman fail, 25, 26; avoidance of struggle out of fear and futility by, 28; detached from community, 2, 3; diasporic experience of, 24; distances self from Barbadian community, 24; inabil-

ity to change, 26; lonliness and apprehension of, 24; looks back on waste and pretense in his life, 26; pervasive whiteness of surroundings of, 24; return to Barbados from US diaspora, 2, 3; suppressed rage at racism in youth, 25; thwarted in efforts to connect, 2; tropes of imperial incursion by, 24

Williams, Miss *(Soul Clap Hands and Sing)*, 26–28; becomes political activist, 28; claims right to agency and resistance, 27; in continuum of ancestral female warriors in diasporas, 27; exposure of protagonist by, 2, 3; recoils from Berman, 27, 28; refuses masculinist self-indulgence, 27; reminds Berman of Gauguin character, 26, 27; sees through Berman's callowness and scorns him, 28; transformed thinking of, 27

Women: as bringers of truth, 24; disdainful connections by men, 27, 28; as insurgent force, 28; realization of strength as result of encounters with men, 24; treated as private property, 36; triumphing over oppressive males, 28

Wright, Richard, 96

Yeats, William Butler, 23, 35

www.ingramcontent.com/pod-product-compliance
Ingram Content Group UK Ltd.
Pitfield, Milton Keynes, MK11 3LW, UK
UKHW042015140426
5217IPUK00015B/1189